Children and Controversial Issues

Children and Controversial Issues:

Strategies for the Early and Middle Years of Schooling

Edited by
Bruce Carrington and Barry Troyna

The Falmer Press
(A member of the Taylor & Francis Group)
London · New York · Philadelphia

UK   The Falmer Press, Falmer House, Barcombe, Lewes, East Sussex, BN8 5DL

USA   The Falmer Press, Taylor & Francis Inc., 242 Cherry Street, Philadelphia, PA 19106-1906

First published 1988

British Library Cataloguing in Publication Data

Children and controversial issues: strategies
  for the early and middle years.
  1. Social controversies – For teaching
  I. Carrington, Bruce II. Troyna, Barry
  300
  ISBN 1-85000-416-1
  ISBN 1-85000-417-X (pbk.)

Library of Congress Cataloguing in Publication Data is available on request

Jacket design by Caroline Archer and Bruce Carrington

Typeset in 11/13 Bembo by
David John Services Ltd, Slough, Berkshire

Printed in Great Britain by
Taylor & Francis (Printers) Ltd, Basingstoke

Contents

Acknowledgements

We are grateful for the administrative support provided by Lynn Herron, Evelyn Roche, Hazel Taylor (at the University of Newcastle Upon Tyne) and Val Stephenson at Sunderland Polytechnic. We would also like to thank the contributors for meeting the deadlines and responding with good humour to our (often nit-picking) suggestions.

Thanks to Liz, Alex and Rebecca for their continuing support (B.C.) and to dad and Jayne for 'being there' even when I'm *brögas* (B.T.).

Bruce Carrington
Barry Troyna

Chapter 1

Children and Controversial Issues

Bruce Carrington and Barry Troyna

In his pithy critique of the Great Educational Reform Bill (GERBIL) now, of course, the Education Reform Act (ERA), Robin Richardson has argued that the legislation will ensure that teachers are less able to broach controversial issues in the classroom because, 'most of the time the new national curriculum will prevent controversy arising' (1988, p. 21). From this vantage point, ERA can be construed as the logical enactment of a campaign waged by the New Right against educational reform in Britain since the late 1960s. From the publication of the first of the 'Black Papers' in 1969, allegations about indoctrination and bias in schools, and the apparent growth of indiscipline alongside an attendant decline in academic attainment levels have featured prominently in this assault on contemporary education. As Paul Gordon has pointed out, this campaign is not so much for change as against it: '... against the moves towards a system of comprehensive education ... and for the retention of formal learning styles, traditional disciplines, academic streaming within the schools, public (fee paying) schools and the traditional examination structure' (1988, p. 96). The move from 'Black Paper' to 'White Paper' status of the New Right's educational campaign has, of course, been expedited through the supportive role of the press and other media. Here, the policies of some Labour-controlled local education authorities such as Brent, Haringey and the Inner London Education Authority (ILEAs) have been subjected to sustained criticism. As many of the contributors to this volume acknowledge, curricular initiatives in peace studies, sex education, multicultural/anti-racist education, anti-sexist education, political education and non-competitive games have been parodied and dismissed as 'biased', even subversive, and as anathema to 'good' education.

Against this background, the legitimation of the teaching of controversial issues in the early and middle years of pupils' schooling seems a long way off. In sanctioning the educational project of the 'Black Paperites', ERA and related legislation provide the state's endorsement for views such as those expressed by John Marks in his critique of 'peace studies' (see Hicks' chapter in this volume for a response to these and other criticisms of 'peace studies'). For Marks, 'politically contentious subjects should normally form no part of the curriculum for pupils below the age of 16 and should be rigorously excluded from primary schools' (1984, p. 1). Thus, despite the absence of sustained or logical argument in support of this contention, this principle found its way onto the statute book as part of the 1986 Education Act. There it was declared that the teaching of such subjects should be proscribed:

> The local education authority by whom any county, voluntary or special school is maintained, and the governing body and head-teacher of the school shall forbid
>
> (a) the pursuit of partisan political activities by any of those registered pupils at the school who are junior pupils... (1986, para. 44).

Needless to say, neither Marks nor the legislation engage in the debate about what constitutes 'partisan political activities' or 'politically contentious subjects' or the criteria by which these might be identified. Quite clearly, there can be no universalistic criteria to determine what may be regarded as a taboo topic for children of, say, primary school age. After all, perceptions of what is appropriate tend to vary and such variations generally reflect contextual and temporal differences as well as contrasting educational ideologies. As the Inner London Education Authority's (ILEA) Inspectors' report, *The Teaching of Controversial Issues in Schools*, has put it:

> A controversial issue is a matter which different individuals and groups interpret and understand in differing ways and about which there are conflicting courses of action. It is an issue for which society has not found a solution that can be universally accepted. It is an issue of sufficient significance that each of the proposed ways of dealing with it is objectionable to some sections of the community and arouses dissent, opposition or protest. When a course of action is formulated that virtually all sectors of society accept, the issue is no longer controversial. There is much more to a controversial issue than the content of what is studied. The ways in which pupils study a subject, which in itself may have general approval, can also create discord (1986, p. 5).

In common with the 1986 Education Act (para. 45b) the ILEA report stresses the need for schools to present pupils with a 'balanced presentation of opposing views'. But, of course, 'balance', like 'controversial' or 'partisan', is a contested concept and amenable to a variety of (conflicting) interpretations. In relation to *pedagogy*, one might ask: How is such balance to be achieved?

In his recent appraisal of the literature on the roles available to teachers on handling controversial political issues in the primary school, Doug Harwood (1986, p. 52) has identified the following approaches:

1.	The 'Committed' role	teacher is free to propagate her own views on controversial political issues
2.	The 'Objective' or 'Academic' role	teacher transmits an explanation of all the available viewpoints without stating her own position.
3.	The 'Devil's Advocate' role	teacher deliberately confronts individuals and groups by adopting provocative and oppositional stances, irrespective of her own viewpoint.
4.	The 'Advocate' role	teacher presents all of the available viewpoints and then concludes by stating her own position, with reasons.
5.	The 'Impartial Chairperson' role	teacher ensures that all viewpoints are represented, either through pupil-statements or published sources. Teacher organises and facilitates pupil contributions by observing procedural rules, but refrains from stating her own position.
6.	The 'Declared-Interest' role	teacher begins by declaring her own viewpoint, so that pupils can better judge bias later. Teacher then presents all available positions as objectively as possible.

Together with the ILEA inspectorate, Ruddock and Plaskow (1985) and many others, Harwood argues strongly in favour of the 'Impartial Chairperson' or, as it is more commonly known, the 'Neutral-Chair approach'. This was developed by Lawrence Stenhouse and his colleagues on the Humanities Curriculum Project (1970) and centralized neutrality as a principle of procedure. The ILEA inspectorate, amongst others, has contended that teachers' strict observance of procedural neutrality in the classroom is likely to work well in settings where pupils are willing and able to voice a wide range of beliefs and opinions and where the ethos is such that they are actively encouraged to listen to the views of others, show tolerance and a respect for evidence. But there are also profound objections to the neutral–chair stance amongst which two are of particular concern here (see the chapters by Singh and Gammage for an elaboration of this critique).

To begin with, it can result in a weak relativistic ethic being espoused in the classroom; an ethic informed by the conviction that all opinions are equally valid and that 'anything and everything goes'. On some issues, however, it may be morally reprehensible for teachers not to take sides, according to some critics. For instance, in the field of multicultural/anti-racist education, Robert Jeffcoate (1984) has been especially prominent in his support for procedural neutrality in the teaching of, and about, race relations. His critics have objected to the fact that this approach had the following effect: the racist views expressed by some pupils were legitimated (and thereby condoned by default) because they were treated as having the same validity as other views expressed during classroom debate (Harrison, 1986; Milner, 1983; Troyna and Carrington, 1987). Another objection to the neutral–chair approach is its self-contradictory nature, a property, according to Orlando Patterson, which is inherent in all relativist dogma; for Patterson, relativism

> is self-contradictory both in a general categorical sense and in a substantive, specific way. It postulates on the most general level, a basic negative statement (there is no universal value) that is the implication of its own contradiction (there is at least one universal value, relativism). In more specific, substantive terms, it is also self-contradictory, since it asserts a general value (the values of all peoples are of equal worth) then contradicts it by implying the superiority of the values of the group consisting of relativists (it is good to see other peoples in their own terms) (1973–4, pp. 125–26).

Such fundamental criticisms of the relativist ethic enshrined in the neutral–chair stance suggest that it is necessary for teachers to indicate their own position (and give reasons for it) if they are to avoid the problems associated with this form of non-partisanship. In other words, it may be more appropriate to give primacy to truth and justice rather than neutrality. At the same time, care must be taken when adopting what Harwood (1986) has typified as the 'Declared-Interest' or 'Advocate' roles.

Leaving aside the practical problem of how and when in a lesson a teacher might confront a class with his or her own views (an issue dealt with in the chapters by Singh and Gammage), it is our contention that the emphasis often given to such procedural matters in the debate about teaching controversial issues is probably misplaced. Arguably, more attention needs to be given to the 'hidden curriculum' which both contextualizes and underpins this teaching. The chapters by Skelton, Gammage, and Carrington and Troyna stress that the structure of social relationships within the school, especially between staff and pupils, and the quality of the relationship between the home and the school may be of more crucial importance. Echoing the work of writers such as Gordon Allport (1954) and Pat White (1983) these contributions lend support to Bob Dunn's assertion that: '...the internal organisation of schools can have a strong influence in shaping the political attitudes of their pupils' (1985, p. 295).

The Case for Political Education in Primary Schools

Despite the oppositional context alluded to earlier, there are signs that secondary schools are giving more attention to the development of their pupils' political knowledge and skills through programmes arranged under the auspices of, say, TVEI and personal and social education (PSE), (see Jeffs' contribution in this volume; Harber, 1987; Stradling *et al.* 1984). In stark contrast, there have been few formal, or explicit, attempts to introduce political education in the primary sector. We have already seen how exponents of the New Right and those responsible for drafting current government policy are vehemently opposed to political education for younger children. Clive Harber also points out that in the late 1960s respected commentators on political education in schools, such as Bernard Crick and Harold Entwhistle, also considered this an unsuitable area for the primary school curriculum (1987, p. 3) Contributors to this volume, however, are united in their conviction that politically contentious issues should be addressed during the primary and middle phases of pupils' educational careers. What is more, they are concerned to demonstrate that primary school teachers' reluctance to consider socio-political controversies with their pupils is predicated on largely untenable grounds.

Geoffrey Short's chapter gives particular consideration to the enduring influence of Piaget's theory of sequential developmentalism and idealist conceptions of childhood innocence. According to Short, the confluence of these ideas has prompted teachers to argue that controversial subjects such as racism, sexism, the nuclear issue, unemployment and international conflict should not be dealt with in the primary curriculum. The reason: because they are largely beyond the comprehension of those who have yet to reach the 'stage of formal operations'. Short appraises critically this conception of development and, in the process, attempts to 'dethrone' Piagetian theories of child development which, he argues, constitute a major barrier to engagement with controversial political issues in the primary school. By looking at the research of Olive Stevens (1982), who studied the political consciousness of 800 7- to 11-year-olds, evidence about young children's understanding of 'race' and gender-related concepts and themes, and the work of cognitive psychologists such as Bruner and Vygotsky, Short concludes that teachers' protective attitudes towards younger children are indefensible. His chapter, along with the work of Connell (1971), Cohen (1981) and, in this volume, Ross, Jeffs, and Carrington and Troyna, demonstrates that teachers of younger children often underestimate their pupils' degree of political awareness and understanding.

Andrew Pollard draws on the influential theory of 'moral panics' (Cohen, 1972) in his attempt to interpret why certain topics and themes exist outside the 'normal' and 'routine' curriculum. In recent years, 'moral panics' have emerged over issues such as anti-racist education, sex education and non-competitive games and those teachers who broach such subjects run the risk of being 'isolated, marginalised or forced into conformity', according to Pollard. In this context, then, it is clearly tempting to limit one's professional activities to those issues around which there exists a groundswell of acceptability: '"the Seasons", "pets" and other variants of "all things bright and beautiful" (King, 1978)'. But Pollard insists that although 'not getting involved' is one (common) way that primary school teachers deal with controversial issues it is not the preferred manner, especially within a liberal–democratic society. For him 'reflective teaching' (Pollard and Tann, 1987) constitutes the appropriate conceptual framework within which strategies for the teaching of controversial issues might be operationalized. His case study of a student primary school teacher is included to illustrate this argument.

In her appraisal of primary and middle school curriculum practice, Hilary Burgess develops some of the themes examined by Short and Pollard. She focuses on teachers' professional ideologies and explores their continuing influence on the characteristics of the 'routine' or 'normal' curriculum. The prevailing 'common-sense' definition of the 'routine' curriculum in which areas such as language, mathematics and, increasingly, science are accorded high status (and regarded as 'the basics') coupled with teachers' perceptions of children's 'innocence' does not augur well for political education in this sector. Furthermore, ERA and associated documents, exemplifying what Burgess describes as 'the ideology of achievement', are likely to stultify any nascent projects in political education for younger children. This is extremely disconcerting, not least because of the crucial role in political socialization of informal agencies such as the media, family and peer group. This is an issue which Tony Jeffs and Basil Singh elaborate on in their respective chapters. Jeffs premises his arguments on the basis of children's rights and specifies political education in primary schools as necessary preparation for participatory democracy. Together with other contributors, he stresses the crucial role of the school in equipping young people with the necessary skills to appreciate how power is exercised (and by whom) in a variety of formal and everyday settings. Both Jeffs and Singh point out that, in contrast to the arbitrary nature of other socializing institutions, schools can provide a systematic and structured opportunity for young people to explore fundamental questions relating to social justice and equality. Unlike other more parochial, partisan and particularistic influences, schools offer young people a context in which they might rehearse their roles as politically responsible citizens. Unless this teaching begins in the primary school, pupils' attitudes, values and beliefs on a range of political matters are likely to be well entrenched and difficult to change by the secondary school, according to Singh and others (White, 1983; Lane and Lane, 1987).

The chapters by Short, Pollard, Burgess and Jeffs provide a raison d'être for teaching controversial issues in the early and middle years of schooling. Singh's contribution, which follows, focuses on the controversies surrounding the neutral-chair approach and offers some important salutary remarks on a strategy which, in the words of Ruddock and Plaskow, is the 'only tenable one' in classroom settings (1985, p. 4). As we have already seen, the wider social, political and cultural context can have a significant bearing upon the teaching of controversial issues in schools. This is especially true in a subject area such as Religious Education where feelings often run high. In ethnically mixed schools, Muslim or Sikh parents, for example, may express disquiet, even hostility towards aspects of religious education in their child's school (Taylor and Hegarty, 1985). A World Religions approach may well be dismissed as incompatible with their own religious values and convictions. In Northern Ireland, where the division between the Protestant and Catholic communities remains entrenched, this presents a particular cause for concern. In her chapter, Una McNicholl outlines some of the dilemmas which schools committed to a pluralist ethic in the Province face when dealing with this controversial matter. She discusses contemporary initiatives at the secondary level to promote mutual understanding and reconciliation. The case is then made for extending these to the primary sector where, according to McNicholl, children are both segregated and prejudiced. In her view, primary as well as secondary schools in Northern Ireland should be 'up front' in combating sectarianism.

If primary teachers are to make meaningful interventions to encourage the development of children's political and moral under-standing, account must be taken of the values, beliefs and assumptions which underpin their reading materials. Following the work of Dixon (1977a; 1977b), Klein (1985) and Kamenetsky (1984), Steve Whitley examines some of the ways in which gender, 'race' and political bias suffuse children's books. As well as specifying some approaches for dealing with such bias in the classroom, he provides teachers with a useful, 'alternative' reading list for primary school pupils.

The following chapters deal with specific, substantive issues often, though not always, deemed controversial: industry education (Alistair Ross), gender relations (Christine Skelton), peace and conflict (Dave Hicks), sex education (Sarah Gammage) and racism and political education (Bruce Carrington and Barry Troyna). These chapters adumbrate the dilemmas for teachers handling these particu-lar controversial issues with younger children. They also provide examples of appropriate curricular and organisational strategies for use in the early and middle years of schooling.

We have argued, then, that there is no consensus about what constitutes a controversial issue in the curriculum. In the present political climate, opinions about the role of the school in economic socialization, for example, vary considerably. One feature of this debate crystallizes around this distinction: education for work/ education about work. At secondary level disputes over this distinction have surfaced in the way vocational education has been introduced and interpreted (Gleeson, 1987). This debate also has implications for the primary school, as Ross's chapter shows. In line with the other contributors, Ross emphasises that schools should engage critically with various perceptions of reality. It remains to be seen, however, the extent to which legislation such as ERA or Clause 28 of the Local Government Act will inhibit the realization of this goal.

References

ALLPORT, G. (1954) *The Nature of Prejudice*, Reading, Mass: Addison Wesley.

COHEN, L. (1981) 'Political literacy and the primary school: a Dutch experiment', *Teaching Politics*, 10, 3, pp. 259–67.

COHEN, S. (1972) *Folk Devils and Moral Panics*, London, MacGibbon and Kee.

CONNELL, R.W. (1971) *The Child's Construction of Politics*, Melbourne, Melbourne University Press.

DEPARTMENT OF EDUCATION AND SCIENCE (1986) *Education Act (No. 2)*, London, HMSO.

DIXON, B. (1977a) *Catching Them Young 1: Sex, Race and Class in Children's Fiction*, London, Pluto Press.

DIXON, B. (1977b) *Catching Them Young 2: Political Ideas in Children's Fiction*, London, Pluto Press.

DUNN, R. (1985) 'Political education in schools', *Teaching Politics*, 14 February, p. 295.

GLEESON. D. (Ed.) (1987) *TVEI and Secondary Education: A Critical Appraisal*, Milton Keynes, Open University Press.

GORDON, P. (1988) 'The New Right, race and education – or how the Black Papers became a White Paper', *Race and Class*, 29, 3, pp. 95–103.

HARBER, C. (Ed.) (1987) *Political Education in Britain*, Lewes, Falmer Press.

HARRISON, S. (1986) 'Swann: the implications for schools', *Journal of Education Policy*, 1, 2, pp. 183–95.

HARWOOD, D. (1986) 'To advocate or educate', *Education 3–13*, 14, 1, pp. 51–7.

INNER LONDON EDUCATION AUTHORITY (1986) *The Teaching of Controversial Issues in Schools: Advice for the Inspectorate*, London, ILEA.

JEFFCOATE, R. (1984) *Ethnic Minorities and Education*, London, Harper and Row.

KAMENETSKY, C. (1984) *Children's Literature in Hitler's Germany*, Athens, Ohio, Ohio University Press.

KING, R. (1978) *All Things Bright and Beautiful: A Sociological Study of Infants' Classrooms*, Chichester, Wiley.

KLEIN, G. (1985) *Reading into Racism: Bias in Children's Literature and Learning Materials*, London, Routledge and Kegan Paul.

LANE, N.R. and LANE, S.R. (1986) 'Rationality, self-esteem and autonomy through collaborative enquiry', *Oxford Review of Education*, 12, 3, pp. 263–75.

MARKS, J. (1984) *'Peace Studies' in Our Schools: Propaganda for Defencelessness*, London, Women and Families for Defence.

MILNER, D. (1983) *Children and Race: Ten Years On*, London, Ward Lock.

PATTERSON, O. (1973–4) 'On guilt, relativism and Black-White relations', *American Scholar*, 43, pp. 122–32.

POLLARD, A. AND TANN, S. (1987) *Reflective Teaching in the Primary School*, London, Cassell.

RICHARDSON, R. (1988) 'The right approach', *New Internationalist*, February, p. 11.

RUDDOCK, J. and PLASKOW, M. (1985) 'Bring back the neutral-chairman', *Times Educational Supplement*, 21 June, p. 4.

STENHOUSE, L. (1970) *The Humanities Project: An Introduction*, London, Heinemann.

STEVENS, O. (1982) *Children Talking Politics*, Oxford, Martin Robertson.

STRADLING, R., NOCTOR, M. and BAINS, B. (1984) *Teaching Controversial Issues*, London, Edward Arnold.

TAYLOR, M. and HEGARTY, S. (1987) *The Best of Both Worlds?* Slough, NFER-Nelson.

TROYNA, B. and CARRINGTON, B. (1987) 'Antisexist/antiracist education – a false dilemma: a reply to Walkling and Brannigan', *Journal of Moral Education*, 16, 1, pp. 60–5.

WHITE, P. (1983) *Beyond Domination: An Essay in the Political Philosophy of Education*, London, Routledge and Kegan Paul.

Chapter 2

Children's Grasp of Controversial Issues

Geoffrey Short

'Primary Ideology' and the Curriculum

Various commentators in recent years have drawn attention to the neglect of controversial issues in the primary curriculum. Ross (1984, p. 131), for instance, believes: 'it would be fair to say that most primary teachers have never considered politically educating their children' and adds that 'politics is something that teachers (of young children) wish to avoid.' Harwood (1985, p. 12) apparently concurs with this view, for when reflecting on his experience of in-service courses he also noted 'a fairly general resistance to the idea of political education amongst primary (and) middle school teachers'.

There are, no doubt, a number of reasons for staff in the primary sector steering clear of contentious material. According to Harwood (ibid.), the resistance stems partly from 'teachers' (lack of) confidence in their ability to handle political education and (their uncertainty) about the nature of its objectives'. Explanations have also been sought in the *alleged* prevalence among teachers in infant and junior schools of what Robin Alexander (1984) has dubbed 'the primary ideology'. This is a form of pedagogic folklore which, *inter alia*, views childhood as an age of innocence and recognizes that infants in particular, whilst capable of unacceptable behaviour, remain free from malicious intent. In marked contrast to the doctrine of original sin, evil is assumed to reside in a world beyond childhood and thus teachers (together presumably with other adults), have a responsibility to protect the young from a harsh and corrupt reality. The acceptance by infant teachers of children's moral purity was commented upon by King (1978) in his observational study of three schools. Among the incidents he reported was that of a class teacher who had reinforced a 6-year-old's faith in fairies offering financial compensation for lost teeth. The teacher later remarked to King (p. 13): 'it's not up to me to destroy his innocence'. On another occasion staff were found removing infirm guinea pigs from the classroom, partly (p. 14) 'to prevent their deaths being witnessed by the children'. Now if observations such as these are typical of infant teachers it is hardly surprising that they eschew any form of political education in which conflict and controversy are the principal elements. Junior school teachers might be expected to show rather less concern with protecting the naive innocence of their pupils, but they too appear to draw the line at controversial issues (Ross, op. cit.).

Despite the paucity of empirical evidence (Desforges, 1986), Alexander may well be corrected in pointing to a second facet of primary ideology as a major constraint on the teaching of contentious subject matter to young children. I refer to the notion of 'sequential developmentalism' defined by Alexander (op. cit. p. 22) as:

> the idea that the child passes through a naturally ordered sequence of physiological, psychological and social develop-ment where... the rate of development will vary from child to child (but) the sequence and stages will be the same. Linked with developmentalism (is) the notion of "readiness" particu-larly in relation to reading – the idea that children's capacity to cope with specific sorts of learning is determined by the developmental stage they have reached.

The theoretical roots of both developmentalism and readiness are, of course, linked most often with the name of Jean Piaget. It is he who has provided the best known, (though certainly not the only), description of cognitive development as a series of discrete stages, each defined in terms of a specific cognitive structure, (or unique way of understanding the world), and associated with an approximate age range. According to his account, most children under the age of 7 or so are incapable of logical thought, for they tend to be seduced by appearances and thus cannot conserve; nor can they regard experience from any point of view except their own – clearly an obstacle to the reversibility of thought required for logical reasoning. During the junior school years, however, Piaget believes that the average child develops an ability to reverse actions mentally, though only in so far as they refer to 'concrete' situations. At this juncture too, most children manage to focus their thought on more than one aspect of a situation simultaneously and are thus in a position to relate ideas to one another. Finally, Piaget claimed that it is not until the secondary stage of schooling that children can normally think in the abstract and so discuss political and other concepts without having recourse to their own experience.

Whilst our understanding of children's progression towards logical thought has obvious relevance for the teaching of mathematics and the natural sciences, our understanding of how children of different ages think about morality has particular relevance for the teaching of controversial issues. Here too Piaget has been active and in 1932 published a monograph mapping the developmental milestones *en route* to adult conceptions of morality. He claimed that children below the age of 6 or 7 tend to subscribe to a heteronomous way of thinking in which rules are regarded as sacrosanct and punishment is thought to follow inevitably upon their contravention. In addition, ethical judgements are generally based on consequences rather than intentions. Children at junior school, in contrast, are more likely to adhere to an autonomous morality where rules are seen as arbitrary, the acceptance of immanent justice is less in evidence and intention assumes a more prominent role in moral judgement.

If primary teachers accept Piaget's views on children's cognitive limitations, it follows, *ceteres paribus*, that they will oppose all exhortations to stretch, or test the limits of, their pupils' intellectual competence. Circumstantial evidence in support of this speculation focuses on the extent of under-expectation alleged to exist in primary schools (e.g., Nash, 1976; Sharp and Green, 1975); a charge which has prompted Alexander (op. cit. p. 24) to link under-expectation with an exaggerated commitment to sequential developmentalism. By way of illustration, he cites the following extract from the NUT's (1979, p. 25) response to HMI's (1978) Primary Survey:

> The Union would not agree with (HMI's) analysis of what is suitable in the teaching of history to young children; the passage of time is a very difficult concept for children of this age to grasp.

Insofar as political education is thought to demand a high level of abstract thought, teachers influenced by Piaget are unlikely to consider it a suitable subject for the primary curriculum. Probing the young child's grasp of controversial issues might be expected to prove particularly unremunerative since the skills required to appreciate a range of arguments and to evaluate conflicting evidence are normally assumed within Piagetian theory to be unavailable prior to adolescence.

Learning about Society: The Case for Sequential Development

Regardless of whether primary ideology is as widespread as Alexander believes, it would appear that until comparatively recently, developmental psychologists and educationists have offered primary teachers little encouragement to challenge the fundamental validity of Piaget's conclusions. On the contrary, the stress that Piaget placed on the young child's limited intellectual grasp has been extended, (in the form of various stage analyses), to areas that Piaget himself never considered. Selman (1980), for instance, has proposed five stages, or levels, in children's social-perspective taking, an intellectual function with obvious implications for political education. He maintains that children below the age of approximately 6 adopt an egocentric viewpoint in that they fail to distinguish their own interpretation of an event from what they consider to be true. Between the ages of 6 and 8 they become aware that others may have a different perspective and over the next two years learn that individuals can know about other people's thoughts and feelings. These early stages are then followed by a period of 'mutual role taking' when children, usually aged between 10 and 12, develop the ability to view an interaction from the standpoint of a third person such as a parent or mutual friend. It is only when children are at secondary school that they finally come to terms with the full complexity of human behaviour and acknowledge, for example, the impact of genetics, social class and other forces over which the individual has no control.

Other theorists whose work reflects Piaget's ideas on the growth of understanding include Damon (1977), who studied children's changing notions of authority, and Livesley and Bromley (1973) who did likewise in respect of person perception. The best known extension of Piaget's own work has been provided by Kohlberg (1958, *et seq.*). He charted the course of moral development well beyond childhood but retained Piaget's emphasis on the core concepts of stage and sequence.

Researchers with a more direct interest in children's political literacy have sometimes nailed their theoretical colours to Piaget's mast (in the sense of prospecting for stages) and, in the process, may unwittingly have reinforced conventional beliefs concerning the 'right' age to teach politics. Leahy's (1983) study of how children understand social class is a case in point. In anticipating the nature of his data, he wrote:

Cognitive-developmental theory suggests that the ordering of societal conceptions will be similar to the ordering of other kinds of social cognition, such as moral judgment, person descriptions and attributions for achievement. This is based on the idea that intelligence is *organised* – that is, common structures will be applied to a variety of contents.

Essentially the same point is made by Furth (1979, p. 233). He asserts that:

Piagetian research and theory has been severely limited by an almost exclusive emphasis on strictly logical-mathematical thinking. If the theory is to be maximally useful, it is necessary to apply it to other areas.

In a manner fully consonant with Piagetian theory, Furth examined the way that children aged between 5 and 11 understand money, societal roles and the concepts of community and government. In reviewing the cognate literature, he highlighted studies of national and ethnic identity (Jahoda, 1963; Hartley *et al.* 1948) which, *prima facie*, confirm the young child's lack of political sophistication. Jahoda's subjects were aged between 6 and 11 and came from both working- and middle-class schools in Glasgow. They were initially asked questions such as: Where is Glasgow? Where is Scotland? What is Scotland? and What is Britain? Jahoda analysed and classified the children's responses in terms of a four stage sequence. The first (and least mature) is characterised by a notion of Glasgow as 'some kind of vague entity' close to the children's actual geographical location. According to one 6-year-old: 'It's up by the park there – you go round the corner'. At this stage, the children's concept of Scotland is also somewhat nebulous. A 7-year-old said it was a street and when asked if there was a place called Scotland, added: 'Yes, Scotland the Brave, it's up in the Highlands'. Another 7-year-old claimed that 'Scotland is the capital of Edinburgh. It's in Glasgow'.

The majority of children at this point could say nothing at all about Britain, and although Jahoda's second stage is distinguished principally by the realization that Glasgow refers in some way to the immediate vicinity, the idea of a country remains ill-defined. One 7-year-old said of Britain: 'It's a city in England' and a 9-year-old thought it 'a city in Scotland'. Superficially, children begin to understand the concept of a country during stage three. They possess the appropriate vocabulary but Jahoda believes it amounts to little more than empty rhetoric. He cites an 11-year-old as saying: 'Britain is a lot of different countries... Glasgow, London, France'. The most advanced level of comprehension (stage four) is marked by an awareness of Britain as a composite unity. In the words of a 6-year-old: 'Glasgow is in Scotland. Scotland is a country in Great Britain. Britain is some countries joined together'. (This final stage was reached by the vast majority of children from middle-class schools but by less than half of those from working-class schools). When asked if it was possible to be both Scottish and British, a number of children who replied affirmatively could not provide an adequate justification. Those who denied the possibility often confused language with nationality; a 9-year-old saying: 'You can't talk Scottish and British at the same time'.

The struggle that many primary children apparently face in grasping the concept of nationality has also been observed in respect of ethnicity. In one of the earliest studies in the area, Hartley *et al.* (op. cit.) examined children's perceptions of ethnic group membership and were particularly interested in 'the role of being Jewish in America'. Once the children (aged between 3½ and 10½) had identified themselves as either Jewish or American in response to the question 'What are you?' they were asked, 'What does Jewish mean?' and 'What does American mean?' Responses to the definition of Jewishness included the following: 'It means Jewish people. God makes them. The whole world is Jewish' (age 6:6). 'Jewish is people who don't go to church' (7:11). 'Jewish is a religion just like Christian. You go to Hebrew (school)... It means to believe in these things, to respect your parents. You shouldn't steal' (10:5). With reference to their understanding of the term 'American': 'I was an American when I had my gun, but when they took my gun away, I wasn't any more' (4:0). 'God makes us Jewish or American which is both the same, just that some people talk American instead of Jewish' (7:1). 'A nationality. A nation you come from. If you are a citizen born in America, you are American' (9:10). Hartley *et al.* (op. cit., p. 389) summarise their data by suggesting that:

> Younger children, who characteristically define their life-space concretely in terms of activities, describe ethnic terms comparably. Older children are mentally mature enough to attempt the use of abstractions.

Thus far, I have tried to show how Piaget and some of his apostles have *indirectly* bolstered, or at least done nothing to undermine, primary teachers' reluctance to broach controversial issues with their pupils. Other researchers, in contrast, have quite openly related their findings to the classroom and, in particular, to the teaching of social studies. Hallam (1969), for example, has discussed the secondary school history syllabus from the standpoint of Piaget's theory. He seems chiefly concerned to demonstrate that if (p. 6) 'material is too advanced for the children they will either assimilate it without understanding, or will reject it with possible damage to their whole attitude to the subject'. To obviate this possibility, he recommends that:

> history taught in the early years of secondary school should not be over-abstract in form, nor should it contain too many variables... Used wisely, topics... can be arranged so that the younger children learn the less detailed history of early times, while the history of recent years, which contains important yet complex topics, can then be taught when the pupils are able to reason at a more mature level (p. 4).

Whilst the research of Jahoda and Hartley *et al.* and the evidence adduced by Hallam in support of his prescriptions may be perfectly valid, the inferences drawn from these and related studies have been both misleading and damaging. For, if children are unable to cope with a given task administered under specific conditions, it cannot, *a priori*, be assumed that they will encounter similar difficulties in an experimental or pedagogic setting that departs, however slightly, from the original. It is the failure to appreciate the extent to which data generated in one context *cannot* generalize to others that has been responsible, at least to some degree, for the persistent belief in children's limited grasp of controversial issues. I turn now to consider the legitimacy of this belief in the light of recent critiques of Piaget's work.

Dethroning Piaget

Although criticism of Piaget's ideas stretch back more than half a century (e.g. Isaacs, 1930), it is only during the last couple of decades or so that his continued pre-eminence as an authority on cognitive development has been seriously threatened. Essentially, he stands indicted for reading too much into his own experiments and hence failing to realize that alternative procedures could yield very different results. Donaldson (1978) points out that some of Piaget's studies made no human sense to the children involved, for they dealt with subject matter which was unfamiliar and largely meaningless. In relation to egocentricity, her own work has indicated that, contrary to Piaget's conclusions, young children, *under certain circumstances*, can envisage situations from a point of view other than their own. Thus, as Gelman (1978, p. 319) states: 'It no longer seems appropriate to characterise the thought of pre-schoolers as egocentric'. Some researchers such as Bryant (1974) have also claimed that particular intellectual skills may be present at an earlier age than Piaget suggested. They reached this decision having shown that Piaget devised experiments which either tested memory rather than logic or led the child to assume that logical reasoning was not required.

Although other major criticisms can be levelled at Piaget's work (such as whether or not stages of development actually exist), it is his underestimation of children's cognitive abilities that is critical as far as the introduction of controversial issues to the primary classroom is concerned. As a result of recent research focusing on a range of issues previously unexplored, or treated very differently, the reigning orthodoxy now recognizes young children as less naive politically than has traditionally been assumed. An example of this recent research is provided by Stevens (1982) who studied the political consciousness of eight hundred 7- to 11-year-olds in the South of England. She interviewed some of the children directly and administered a questionnaire to the rest. Of her discussion with a couple of 7-year-olds she wrote:

> the little girls found no difficulty in joining in a political discussion. At ease and interested, they were able to show some awareness of highly complex issues, for example, of the limitations of power, of government by consent of the governed and the...notion of accountability (p. 32).

She concluded that:

> Seven year olds can be seen to have some cognitive contact with the political world (encompassing) political information, awareness and not least, interest. What comes across most strongly is the sense the children seemed to have of political power being limited, consented to and conditional upon results (p. 38).

Stevens found that concepts of democracy, leadership and accountability of government were accessible to 9-year-olds. She also found that some children of this age were able to consider alternative social and political arrangements and to justify them in terms of principles. As this ability is usually associated with the stage of formal operations, Stevens asks whether, in relation to social or political understanding, the stages either contract to some degree or overlap more than in other areas. Piaget, of course, attached far greater importance to the invariant sequence of development than to the average age of children at particular stages within the sequence and, to this extent, Stevens' findings cannot be seen as contradictory. Her work does, however, add further weight to the view that children may generally be more *au fait* with their socio-political environment than has traditionally been acknowledged. To emphasize the point, she noted that by the age of 11 children were able to:

> (link) politics not only with roles, structures and policies, but with topics such as conservation, women's rights and an economic re-organisation of the country (p. 150).

When one considers the content of popular children's fiction, the evidence of political consciousness amongst 7- to 11-year-olds becomes all the more convincing. Juvenile comics, for example, not only deal regularly with questions of authority, hierarchy, social class and wealth, but as Dixon (1977) and others (e.g., Carrington and Short, 1984) have revealed, they promote racism, sexism and xenophobia as both natural and acceptable. Dixon (*op. cit.* p. 50) asserts that 'name-calling...national stereotyping (and) hatred of foreigners...is found nowhere so much as in comics published in the United States and Britain'. Whilst not suggesting that this form of literature is the sole, or even the most potent source of aggressive nationalism in children, it is worth noting that Johnson (1966) has uncovered a positive correlation between the reading of certain comics and feelings of antagonism towards some of Britain's erstwhile enemies.

The socio-economic attitudes that comics purvey have also come in for critical scrutiny. Referring to stories where 'myths and illusions...blur the real issues', Dixon notes the prevalence of:

> charity, which oils the wheels of the system and...alleviates ...the distress of the poor and the guilt of the rich; the 'ladder' concept of society, which holds out the hope that...anyone can succeed (and) moral virtue which the unfortunate and the unsuccessful usually have...(p. 32).

Although Stevens has shown clearly that children at primary schools are politically informed, the full significance of her study will not be appreciated unless it is considered in conjunction with recent criticisms of Piaget's research. In this respect, the likely impact of

McNaughton's (1982) contribution to the debate surrounding the place of controversial issues in the primary curriculum is to be regretted. For whilst recognizing the constraints implicit in the notion of stage, he seems either to be unfamiliar with the findings that now contradict much of Piaget's work, or has chosen to ignore them. He argues that:

> If the teacher... believe(s) that no student should be involved in formal political studies until s/he is able to cope with abstract ideas and with arguments that cohere on principles then they would be well advised... to put formal political studies off until the fourth year [of secondary education]. Whereas if they are prepared to be satisfied with sensible discussions about political... matters that concern and involve students in... institutions to which they belong... then they could probably start them on political studies during primary schooling (p. 273).

Whilst McNaughton should be commended for stressing the young child's political awareness, and for advising teachers to capitalize on it, his recommendation surely has negative implications for the teaching of controversial issues. For the latter may well *not* be categorized as 'political and social matters that concern and involve students in the groups and institutions to which they belong'. Racism and sexism are cases in point. Would McNaughton argue that children who attend an 'all-white' or single sex primary school are incapable of benefiting from teaching about race and gender respectively? The evidence, in the form of children's knowledge of these issues, suggests otherwise.

Children and Race

That very young children are racially aware in the sense of being able to distinguish black people from white will clearly surprise no one (Laishley, 1971; Marsh, 1970). However, the fact that 3- and 4-year-olds can express genuinely hostile racial attitudes is, perhaps, rather less obvious, certainly as far as infant teachers committed to childhood innocence are concerned. The earliest reported indications of racism in pre-schoolers were noted by Horowitz. He found (1936, pp. 117–18):

> The development of prejudice against Negroes begins very, very early in the life of the ordinary child... boys, barely over five years of age, demonstrated a preference for whites

...Some few attempts at testing special cases at three and four years of age elicited such comments as (from a three year old) 'I don't like black boys' and (from a four year old) 'I don't like coloured boys'.

The British study that arguably offers the closest parallel to Horowitz's findings was conducted by Jeffcoate (1977) in a Bradford nursery school. It was undertaken in order to draw teachers' attention to the specious nature of the widespread and 'commonsensical' view that, during their time at primary school, children are incapable of displaying animosity towards individuals *qua* members of a racial or ethnic group. Jeffcoate exploded the myth by showing that 4-year-olds can not only discriminate racial differences but can also express racially abusive remarks. When the children were initially asked by their teacher to discuss pictures portraying black people in a 'variety of situations and in a respectful and unstereotyped way', the children's responses could not possibly be construed as racially offensive. However, when the same set of pictures were left 'casually' around the room (but in locations close to concealed tape recorders), the comments made by the children, in the assumed absence of an adult audience, were undeniably racist in tenor. Although this study confirmed the results of previous research into the early onset of anti-black sentiment in white children, it is, perhaps, more important in showing that, even at the nursery stage, children are cognisant of the socially unacceptable nature of these feelings and of the need to conceal them in the presence of adult authority.

At this very young age, children's knowledge of race is probably restricted to a vague intuition that some racial groups should be disparaged. As Allport puts it (1954, p. 307): the child 'is stumbling at the threshold of some abstraction, aware that a particular group is somehow hateworthy but unable to associate the emotion with the referent'. Children of junior school age have no such problem. In Trager and Yarrow's (1952) research with 7- to 9-year-olds, it was found that:

> concepts and feelings about race frequently include adult distinctions of status, ability, character, occupation and economic circumstances... Among the older children stereotyping and expressions of hostility are more frequent... (Quoted in Milner, 1983, p. 111).

In the doll and picture tests used by Trager and Yarrow, the children allocated poor housing and menial employment to black people and generally superior environments to whites.

Not only do children at the upper end of the primary age range possess a sophisticated understanding of individual and structural racism but, as Bruce Carrington and I have recently demonstrated (Short and Carrington, 1987), this understanding is available to children living in an 'all-white' environment who, under normal circumstances, may not construe the world in racial terms. Our case study of anti-racist teaching with a class of top juniors was partly concerned with the children's untutored knowledge of racism. Among the tasks we set the class was to imagine that they had recently entered Britain from either the West Indies or the Indian sub-continent and were writing a letter home to a close relative or good friend who was planning to join them. The class discussion that preceded the writing was intended to excavate the ideas which the children already possessed; no attempt at this stage being made either to refine them or to suggest more plausible alternatives. In their 'letters' the children referred to manifestations of racial violence, racist name-calling and discriminatory practices in housing and work. The following extracts are typical of the children's response (p. 227):

John:....us Black people get beat up as soon as we get off the ship. Would you fancy having to take your luggage every-where by yourself while people just look and laugh at you as you go from house to house trying to get a place to spend the night? Just guess what their reply was after me begging for a bed. It was 'sorry, it's been took' or just a simple 'no, get lost. We don't give rooms to niggers like you'. In the end, when you get a house, they throw you out just because you were not used to their terrible food that they call pasties. And what about the jobs you said were very good for someone like me? Oh, I got a job alright. It was a dishwasher in a rotten old fish and chip shop where the dishes must have been at least twenty years old. Then I got kicked out for dropping an old chipped plate by accident.

Clare:....I never thought it would be like this as we all get on so well back in India. I advise you to stay at home and forget about Britain. The other day I decided to start looking for a job. As you know, I have plenty of skills. I thought even if nobody likes me I'll be sure to get a good decent job but I was wrong. Instead, I got an awful job cleaning toilets. Over here, that's all they seem to think we're good for. Anyway, I started this job today. It was horrible, people pushing you around. One person even flushed my head down the toilet. I wish I never brought Julian, our son, to school. All he ever does is get picked on. He came home the other day covered with bruises and cuts. I am having second thoughts about staying here. Most people are prejudiced.

Despite occasional strains on the credulity ('... get beat up as soon as we get off the ship'), these imaginative accounts provide unequivocal evidence of the children's awareness of racism in its various guises. John's allusion to food is of particular interest in that it shows how some children of this age are able to grasp the relationship of racism to ethnocentrism. Clare's 'letter' is noteworthy in that it demonstrates some cognisance of stereotyping ('that's all they seem to think we're good for'), a concept which had not been mentioned in the previous class discussion. It is also of interest because it refers directly to the gulf between the expectation and the reality of immigrant life in Britain.

Children's Understanding of Gender and Sex Role Stereotypes

Among the many similarities in the development of children's understanding of race and gender is the age at which identification of self and others is made in terms of the two categories (i.e., male or female, black or white). For the majority of children this milestone is reached by the age of 3 although the foundations of racial awareness and concepts probably develop somewhat later and are more variable (Katz, 1983).

A further similarity concerns the acquisition of stereotypes. Those relating to sex roles have been studied in a variety of ways including direct questioning. Khun *et al.* (1978), for instance, read statements such as, 'I'm strong' and 'When I grow up I'll fly an airplane', to a group of 2- to 3-year olds. The children were then required to select the doll (Lisa or Michael) most likely to have made the statement. The results not only revealed a high level of agreement with adult stereotypes, but showed that the children thought positively about their own sex and negatively about the other.

There seems to be little doubt that by the age of 5 most children make few 'errors' in assigning sex stereotyped labels to activities, occupations and playthings (Katz, op. cit.) The learning of sex-typed traits, however, appears to develop rather later. Best and his colleagues (1977) illustrated this developmental progression by asking 5, 8, and 11-year-olds whether particular attributes were more often associated with a male or female silhouette. They found that less than a quarter of their 5-year-olds responded above a chance level as compared with nearly three-quarters of the 8-year-olds and virtually all the 11-year-olds. The traits that children found easiest to differentiate by sex (such as aggression) were those having a relatively familiar concrete referent.

Studies which permit a 'both' or 'neither' response to stereotyped statements (e.g. Marantz and Mansfield, 1977), generally show an increase in flexibility with age. Damon's (op. cit.) research, though, suggests that the relationship may, in fact, be curvilinear. His sample comprised children aged between 4 and 9. After reading them a story about a little boy (George) who wished to play with dolls despite his parents' protestations, he asked the children a number of questions. These included: 'Why do people tell George not to play with dolls? Are they right? Is there a rule that boys shouldn't play with dolls?' The 4-year-olds in this study thought it quite legitimate for George to play with dolls if he wanted. In contrast, the 6-year-olds thought it quite wrong. At this stage, what boys and girls *tend* to do is synonymous with what they *ought* to do. The oldest children were able to recognise sex roles as a social convention and could distinguish the latter from both laws and social values. One of the 9-year-olds said: 'Breaking windows you're not supposed to do. And if you (boys) play with dolls, well you can, but boys usually don't' (p. 263).

This brief and selective review of the literature on children's understanding of race and gender lends powerful support to the Swann Committee's (1985) recommendations on political education (pp. 336–7):

> Some educationists have argued that school pupils are insufficiently mature and responsible to be able to comprehend politically sensitive issues...and to cope with them in a balanced and rational manner. Even primary-aged pupils however have views and opinions on various 'political' issues...We believe that schools have a clear responsibility to provide accurate factual information and opportunities for balanced and sensitive consideration of political issues in order to enable pupils to reflect upon and sometimes reconsider their political opinions within a broader context.

Piaget, the Teacher and Controversial Issues

It seems to be generally agreed that Piaget had relatively little interest in formal education. Bryant (1984, p. 252), for instance, contends that 'Piaget...thought teachers played an insignificant role in children's cognitive development'. In particular, he seemed to lack interest in what he disparagingly referred to as 'the American question', that is, the extent to which a child's progression through the stages can be accelerated. Piaget thought that the rate of progress could be hastened but only within narrow limits and some research findings support this conclusion. Evaluating the literature on the stage of concrete operations, Gardner (1982, p. 403) has written:

> In Piaget's view, concrete operations must develop naturally, over time, as a consequence of direct actions on objects. Attempts to train a child in an operation cannot succeed until the child is just about ready to develop that capacity and by that time training is hardly necessary.

The same point has been made rather more pithily by Phillips (1975) in the form of the following syllogism: 'If a child is not ready to change, no teacher can help him; if he is ready, the change will occur without intervention; therefore intervention is superfluous'.

If primary teachers accept Piaget's explicit reservations regarding the value of formal instruction, the likelihood of them exploring their pupils' capacity to understand controversial issues is bound to diminish. However, other psychologists, most notably Vygotsky (1956) and Bruner (1960), have argued forcefully, and contrary to Piaget, that the teacher's role in fostering cognitive development is crucial. Vygotsky views intellectual potential, not as some innate physiological property, but rather as a quality created in the process of upbringing and education. He distinguishes between children's existing and potential levels of development, the former defined by what they can do without adult assistance, the latter by what they can do with it. Vygotsky refers to the gap between these two levels as the zone of next development. In Sutton's words (1983, p. 196): '(It) indicates what the child is ready to master next on the basis of present achievements, given the best possible adult attention'.

The optimistic implications of Vygotsky's work reinforce Bruner's (1960, p. 33) well-known dictum that 'any subject can be taught to any child of any age in an honest way'. He explains (ibid.):

> Research on the intellectual development of the child high-lights the fact that at each stage of development the child has a characteristic way of viewing the world and explaining it to himself. The task of teaching a subject to a child at any particular age is one of representing the structure of that subject in terms of the child's way of viewing things.

Exactly the same argument had, in fact, been advanced some years earlier by Allport (1954). In advocating what we would describe as an anti-racist initiative, he stated:

> The age at which these lessons should be taught need not worry us. If taught in a simple fashion all the points can be made intelligible to younger children and, in a more fully developed way, they can be presented to older students...In fact...through 'graded lessons' the same content can, and should, be offered year after year (p. 511).

Although Bruner has argued convincingly for this sort of spiral curriculum, the proof of his theoretical pudding, so far as teaching controversial issues is concerned, will, of course, lie in the eating. From the standpoint of anti-racist education, the prospects are encouraging (e.g., Short and Carrington, op. cit.; Burgess, 1986), for children at opposite ends of the primary age range seem able to cope, in their own way, with its demands. However, the full extent to which young children at school can understand and benefit from a study of controversial issues will only be known when their teachers acquire an immunity to ideological and other constraints and begin to find out for themselves.

References

ALEXANDER, R.J. (1984) *Primary Teaching*, London, Holt, Rinehart and Winston.

ALLPORT, G.W. (1954) *The Nature of Prejudice*, Reading, MA, Addison-Wesley.

BEST, D.L., WILLIAMS, J.E., CLOUD, J.M., DAVIS, S.W., ROBERTSON, L.S., EDWARDS, J.R., GILES, H. and FOWLES, J. (1977) 'Development of sex-trait stereotypes among young children in the United States, England and Ireland', *Child Development*, 48, pp. 1375–84.

BRUNER, J. (1960) *The Process of Education*, New York, Vintage Books.

BRYANT, P. (1974) *Perception and Understanding in Young Children*, London, Methuen.

BRYANT, P. (1984) 'Piaget, teachers and psychologists', *Oxford Review of Education*, 10, 3, pp. 251–9.

CARRINGTON, B. and SHORT, G. (1984) 'Comics – a medium for racism', *English in Education*, 18, 2, pp. 10–14.

DAMON, W. (1977) *The Social World of the Child*, San Francisco, Jossey-Bass Publishers.

DESFORGES, C. (1986) 'Developmental psychology applied to teacher training', in *Child Psychology In Action*, London, Croom Helm.

DIXON, B. (1977) *Catching Them Young 2: Political ideas in children's fiction*, London, Pluto Press.

DONALDSON, M. (1978) *Children's Minds*, Glasgow, Fontana/Collins.

FURTH, H.G. (1979) 'Young children's understanding of society', in McGURK, H. (Ed.) *Issues in Childhood Social Development*, London, Methuen pp. 228–56.

GARDNER, H. (1982) *Developmental Psychology*, Boston, Little, Brown and Co.

GELMAN, R. (1978) 'Cognitive Development', *Annual Review of Psychology*, 29, pp. 297–332.

HALLAM, R. (1969) 'Piaget and the teaching of history', *Educational Research*, 12, pp. 3–12.

HARTLEY, E.L., ROSENBAUM, M. and SCHWARTZ, S. (1948) 'Children's perception of ethnic group membership', *Journal of Psychology*, 26, pp. 387–97.

HARWOOD, D. (1985) 'We need political not Political education for 5–13 year olds', *Education 3–13*, 13, 1, pp. 12–17.

HMI (DEPARTMENT OF EDUCATION AND SCIENCE) (1978) *Primary Education in England: a Survey by HM Inspectors of Schools*, London, HMSO.

HOROWITZ, E.L. (1936) 'Development of attitudes towards negroes', in PROSCHANSKY, H. and SEIDENBERG, B. (Eds.) (1965) *Basic Studies in Social Psychology*, New York, Holt, Rinehart and Winston, pp. 111–21.

ISAACS, S. (1930) *Intellectual Growth in Young Children*, London, Routledge and Kegan Paul.

JAHODA, G. (1963) 'The development of children's ideas about country and nationality. Part 1: The conceptual framework', *British Journal of Educational Psychology*, 33, 47–60.

JEFFCOATE, R. (1977) 'Children's racial ideas and feelings', *English in Education*, 11, 1, pp. 32–46.

JOHNSON, N. (1966) 'What do children learn from war comics?' *New Society*, 7 July pp. 7–12.

KATZ, P.A. (1983) 'Developmental foundations of gender and racial attitudes', in LEAHY, R.L. (Ed.) *The Child's Construction of Social Inequality*, New York, Academic Press, pp. 41–78.

KING, R. (1978) *All Things Bright and Beautiful? A Sociological Study of Infants' Classrooms*, Chichester, Wiley.

KOHLBERG, L. (1958) *The development of modes of moral thinking and choice in the years ten to sixteen*, unpublished Ph.D. thesis, University of Chicago.

KUHN, D., NASH, S.C. and BRUCKEN, L. (1978) 'Sex role concepts of two- and three-year-olds', *Child Development*, 49, pp. 445–51.

LAISHLEY, J. (1971) 'Skin colour awareness and preference in London nursery-school children', *Race* 13, 1, pp. 47–64.

LEAHY, R.L. (1983) 'The development of the conception of social class', in LEAHY, R.L. (Ed.) *The Child's Construction of Social Inequality*, New York, Academic Press, pp. 79–108.

LIVESLEY, W. and BROMLEY, D. (1973) *Person Perception in Childhood and Adolescence*, London, Wiley.

McNAUGHTON, A.H. (1982) 'Cognitive development, political understanding and political literacy', *British Journal of Educational Studies*, 30, 3, pp. 264–79.

MARANTZ, S.A. and MANSFIELD, A.F. (1977) 'Maternal employment and the development of sex-role stereotyping in five- to eleven-year-old girls', *Child Development*, 48, pp. 668–73.

MARSH, A. (1970) 'Awareness of Racial Differences in West African and British children', *Race* 11, pp. 289–302.

MILNER, D. (1983) *Children and Race: Ten Years On*, London, Ward Lock.

NASH, R. (1976) *Teacher Expectations and Pupil Learning*, London, Routledge and Kegan Paul.

NATIONAL UNION OF TEACHERS (1979) *Primary Questions: The NUT Response to the Primary Survey*, London, NUT.

PHILLIPS, J. (1975) *The Origins of Intellect: Piaget's Theory*, W.H. Freeman, New York.

PIAGET (1932) *The Moral Judgement of the Child*, London, Routledge and Kegan Paul.

ROSS, A. (1984) 'Developing political concepts and skills in the primary school', *Educational Review*, 36, 2, pp. 131–9.

SELMAN, R.L. (1980) *The Growth of Interpersonal Understanding*, New York, Academic Press.

SHARP, R. and GREEN, A. (1975) *Education and Social Control: a Study in Progressive Primary Education*, London, Routledge and Kegan Paul.

SHORT, G. and CARRINGTON, B. (1987) 'Towards an anti-racist initiative in the all white primary school', in POLLARD, A. (Ed.) *Children and their Primary Schools: A New Perspective*, Lewes, Falmer Press, pp. 220–35.

STEVENS, O. (1982) *Children Talking Politics: political learning in childhood*, Oxford, Martin Robertson.

SUTTON, A. (1983) 'An introduction to Soviet developmental psychology', in MEADOWS, S. (Ed.) *Developing Thinking*, London, Methuen, pp. 188–205.

SWANN, M. (1985) *Education for All*, Cmnd 9453 London, HMSO.

TRAGER, H. and YARROW, M. (1952) *They Learn What They Live*, New York, Harper and Row.

VYGOTSKY, L. (1956) *Selected Psychological Research*, Moscow, Academy of Pedagogic Sciences of USSR.

Chapter 3

Preparing Young People for Participatory Democracy
Tony Jeffs

Introduction

One survey of secondary schools shows that 80 per cent claim to provide political education (Stradling and Noctor, 1981). Politicians from across the political spectrum can be quoted endorsing the view that 'the case for political education ought to be self-evident' (Haselhurst, 1981). So the reader may ask: why should we consider the presence of political education within the curriculum to be at all controversial? In a sense such scepticism is well founded, for significant evidence does exist that, despite much early opposition to 'civics' and political education within the secondary curriculum (Whitmarsh, 1981), it has now become overwhelmingly accepted as an essential ingredient within a well-rounded and balanced secondary curriculum. When closely interrogated this apparent consensus can be seen as nothing but a mirage. Controversy still surrounds the presence of political education within the classroom. In particular, the content and ideology of such courses remains a matter of fierce debate, and the suitability of introducing such material to young people below secondary age is extensively questioned. This chapter will concentrate especially on these two areas of debate.

Initial opposition to political education in the classroom began to evaporate in the immediate post-war period. The principal reason for this was the widespread belief, typically expressed in an influential teachers' handbook of the period, that 'an increased social and political awareness is necessary if the unique virtues of the British way of life are to be preserved and developed' (Dray and Jordan, 1950, p. 17; see also McNair Report, 1944). Political education, civics and the teaching of liberal values within the setting of social studies would help construct, it was widely believed, a bulwark against the internal and external threat posed by totalitarian ideologies and parties. Naively, this belief assumed that such ideologies were most successful in securing converts amongst those who lacked 'political literacy'; the gullibile and ignorant. Advocates and emissaries of political education also exhibited great faith, not only in the inherent worth of their message, but also in the ability of teachers and their powers of persuasion. Such optimism is much less frequently encountered today amongst advocates of curriculum reform or new 'subjects' such as Peace Studies. Possibly, in the light of experience, aims now seem far more modest and horizons limited. Yet it should not be overlooked that new subjects need to draw upon such a well of optimism if they are to gain a toe-hold within an already overcrowded curriculum. Political education was thus well served by the early enthusiasts.

Opposition to the inclusion of political education in the curriculum was encountered from the onset and still exists within sections of the teaching profession, amongst parents and from politicians. The strength of this opposition is difficult to gauge, but many teachers certainly believe it to be a dangerous and slumbering beast best left unroused. Real or imaginary, this belief still impedes the willingness of many teachers and schools to address those topics and issues which might be construed as 'political'. Therefore, the arguments which justify this opposition need to be examined and assessed.

The Case against Political Education

The case against political education within the school setting has always had an important charateristic – age-relatedness. Consistently it has been articulated according to a 'sliding-scale', whereby the justification for inclusion has been assumed to diminish the younger the student. Certainly its presence in Further Education in the guise of Liberal Studies has long been accepted, although it cannot be overlooked that the growing influence of the MSC within this sector has posed a serious threat to the survival of all the less vocational elements within the curriculum. The narrow and Philistine conception of education promulgated by the MSC has exhibited a strong antagonism to liberal education in general, and political education in particular. Since 1983 the declared policy of the MSC, that matters relating 'to the organisation and functioning of society in general' should be excluded from YTS schemes and related teaching programmes, has spelt out a determination to curtail political debate amongst trainees and constrain the autonomy of FE teaching staff. As the 1986 Education Act subsequently laid down skeletal guidelines for the teaching of politics, the actions of the MSC should not be seen as an aberration. Despite these signs of disapproval, political education continues, at least for the time being, to be countenanced as a legitimate area of study within the secondary school; although, in many instances, one sanctioned only for the senior students either as an examination subject or disguised under various brand-names such as civics, social studies, social and life skills, general studies and personal and social education. To an extent, respectability might even be measured according to the official approval it secured when the category 'social and political' was included as one of eight 'areas of experience' listed in a key HMI publication setting out the components for a common curriculum (DES, 1977). Subsequent legislation to construct a national curriculum has, to a marked degree, ignored that structure and displayed little enthusiasm for the inclusion of political education within the mainstream foundation curriculum (DES, 1987; DES, 1988). Consequently, a number of influential figures in the field of political education are now less optimistic concerning the potential for growth and innovation in the near future. For example Brennan predicts that 'future growth will be slow', whilst Robins argues that political education flourishes only in liberal times, consequently, in the present conservative climate 'it is in a trough...The time is not right yet for advances' (all quoted in Reid, 1985, p. 4). Yet the substantive point remains that the teaching of aspects of political education is now accepted by a majority of secondary schools as being of value.

Irrespective of wider objections to the teaching of political education, the strength of the resistance to its intrusion into primary and, to a lesser extent, middle schools has ensured that it is still rarely encountered within them. A Schools Council survey of political education in infant and junior schools found it to be almost totally absent (Lawton, *et al.* 1971). Little evidence exists to indicate that the situation has changed in the intervening years. Why political education continues to be seen, within the overwhelming majority of these schools, as either dangerous, inappropriate, unacceptably controversial or all three, is an issue that needs to be discussed.

A grave danger exists in outlining the case, either for or against, of constructing a 'straw man'. Accusations of that sort can, of course, never be totally countered. Therefore, the reader must be trusted to fill in gaps and correct the glaring omissions. Conscious of that proviso, let us examine the case against, remembering always that those who adopt a particular stance on this issue may well recoil from aligning themselves with others figuring in the lexicon of opposition. With those caveats in mind, the principal objections can be summarised as follows:

political education and civics must primarily be considered with values rather than facts. As a consequence the content will be inherently indoctrinatory and therefore best avoided by teachers and left to other agencies principally the family, the media and the political parties themselves who can offer their wares in the 'open market place'.

allowing 'politics into the classroom' involves giving teachers the opportunity to indoctrinate their students. The temptation will be great and the ability of headteachers, parents and governors to monitor this will be severely constrained. Therefore it is in the interests of all parties to exclude politics from the curriculum. Thus protecting students from the danger of indoctrination, teachers from the temptation and schools from accusations of complicity.

those currently employed within the schools have not been trained for the task of teaching this delicate and specialist subject. Therefore much more in the way of resources needs to be provided before any expansion of politics teaching can be contemplated.

politics in the real world arouses strong passions and is by its very nature divisive. Consequently the importation of politics into the school 'cannot help the cause of education' (Dunlop, 1980, p. 75).

All the above can, to varying degrees, be considered valid irrespective of pupil age. Therefore, special attention must be paid to an objection raised concerning the wisdom of teaching politics in junior and middle schools encapsulated in the following quotation: it is that the early teens 'mark the point before which neither the theory nor practice of politics can meaningfully be introduced into the curriculum of the school' (Entwhistle, 1969, p.199). This view applies not only to the teaching of politics but also to other disciplines and elements within subject areas. Closely aligned to notions of learning readiness it has, on occasions, been crudely linked to the work of Piaget and others who advocate recognisable stages of development (see the chapter by Short in this volume).

Having sought to list objections it is unavoidable that they are addressed. It would be futile to deny that political education is primarily, although never exclusively, about values. However, this in no way sets it apart from the bulk of the curriculum, both overt and hidden. Schools have always been concerned with much more than the narrow presentation of 'facts'. Central to a great deal of their activity is the awareness that they are required to inculcate certain behavioural patterns. Debate may legitimately take place regarding the form and content of this intervention, but not regarding the entitlement of the school to intervene in matters as diverse as influencing diet, personal cleanliness or the treatment of vulnerable citizens of groups within school and wider society. Moral training as well as a moral curriculum is accepted by all parties as a legitimate pursuit. It is expected, for instance, that bullying by pupils be contained or suppressed, respect for the property of others encouraged, good manners promoted and boorish behaviour deprecated. Indeed, schools can draw upon a great deal of public support for the notion that they have a central function as the purveyors of 'values'. Certainly, according to one survey, over 80 per cent of adults thought 'schools should teach children to obey authority' (BSA, 1987).

Without doubt, subject areas such as history, religious education and PE are centrally concerned with questions of values and rightly have an unquestioned role within the moral curriculum, a presence which must weaken the case against political education. With regard to history and RE especially, the content is as open to debate and morally contentious as any within the political arena. Regarding the latter, within many primary schools, although it is indisputable that the truth concerning all religious 'doctrines is seriously doubted and on excellent grounds, ... it must be regarded as an objectionable form of indoctrination to propagate these doctrines in the schools as if they were unquestionably true' (Dearden, 1969 p. 59). Comparable treatment of political ideas and ideologies is not only unimaginable it is also illegal. Therefore, to argue that dealing with political issues in a school setting, and introducing young people to an understanding of the mechanisms and structures of the administrative and electoral system, fractures a consensual agreement to minimize the intrusion of values into the school simply does not stand up to close examination.

Thompson argues that the prime reason for the omission of political education from the curriculum flows from a widespread belief that 'an adequate level of political education can be acquired by indirect means' (1969, p. 90). If this is the case then the majority of young people, at least during the early years of their lives, will continue to derive what political knowledge they have in a haphazard fashion, leaving a great deal to chance. It also ensures that young people born into more privileged surroundings will continue to be politically advantaged. Allowing the present system to remain unreformed will mean that the 'differences in the political participation of adults of different social class background and of men and women (which) are clearly presaged by similar differences among pre-adolescent children' (Greenstein, 1973 p. 155) will be nourished. To continue the exclusion of political education from the educational experiences of those below secondary school age clearly sanctions the continuation of the current overarching dominance of national and local politics by individuals drawn from middle- and upper-class backgrounds. To leave political education to the family is to consign it to the realms of chance, especially for those who emmanate from homes in which 'politics' plays no overt part, as it further helps to ensure that they are denied the opportunity to gain, during their formative years, an informed understanding of the discourse of politics. If entrusting political education to the family is risky, leaving it to the 'media' amounts to dereliction of duty, for the media, as constituted, are overwhelmingly part of the problem and can, therefore, hardly be conceived of as capable of contributing to the solution. Trivialisation of politics by the 'popular press' and tele-vision, the absence of even the most cursory attempts to secure balance in reporting and comment in all but a handful of papers, both lend weight to the case of those who argue for the earliest possible exposure of young people to a political education: to convey to them that beneath the media 'hype', politics comprises more than 'a sort of gladiatorial combat between the major parties...irrelevant to their own lives' (Afshar, 1978, p. 40); a view widely held amongst secondary school students. Further, it would help young people acquire, as soon as they are capable of reading the 'popular press', an ability to interrogate critically its contents. Given the widespread use of pornography to sell papers and the obsessive dwelling upon violence and violent crime within the press, many parents rightly seek to protect their children rather than expose them to substantial sections of the media. It is enough to say that no teacher would feel confident of escaping criticism if they left in a classroom any of those newspapers that the average 8-year-old could either read or is most likely to have encountered in his/her homes. Alternatively, the papers that a teacher might with confidence leave unattended on the desk are the very publications that younger pupils would require encourage-ment and support to read, with respect to language, style and layout.

Although television may, in part, escape some of the harsher critisisms that educationalists must direct towards the press, the same fundamental problem does arise. Television presents political issues in a way that assumes both an adult and, to a degree, an informed audience. This means that if young people are obliged to shop in the market place of political ideas unprepared, 'with completely open minds', then, as Strike argues, they will be unable to 'make rational choices, for they will lack the means. Ideas are the means of rational choice' (Strike, 1982, p. 34). Teachers and schools cannot morally escape the responsibility of preparing young people for this encounter with the maelstrom of politics; neither can it be left to the political parties, which is the equivalent of giving MacDonalds responsibility for instructing young people on nutrition. Firstly, the parties do not have equal access to the means of communication nor commensurate funds to propagate their message, so would, consequently, further advantage the prosperous parties at the expense of the others. Secondly, it would also run the very real risk of giving an edge to those parties, such as the National Front, that are the least scrupulous in the methods they adopt to secure the allegiance of young people, whilst disadvantaging parties with superior ethics. As with the media, the key to choosing between the conflicting and often misleading, if not downright dishonest, messages emanating from political parties resides in the capacity of young people to assess critically the content of those messages; a capacity that must be learnt not merely by chance but also in a guided and structured fashion within the setting of a classroom.

Bias, Indoctrination and Appropriateness

To argue the case for political education in the school setting invariably raises the spectre of bias. This is perhaps understandable, given that the handling of political issues by the parties is overwhelmingly enacted according to a confrontational model that seeks to accentuate differences, and, except where advantageous to one party or another, obscure common areas of agreement. This is of course reflected, if not encouraged, by the media presentation of politics, wherein the most popular metaphors are those of conflict – 'fighting speech', 'smash the opposition', 'hard-hitting performance', 'take on the government', 'defeat the amendment' and so on. Whilst the most anxiously sought after visual image is of the eyeball-to-eyeball conflict between politicians so frequently stage-managed by TV interviewers and presenters, thoughtful politicians and measured debate make for poor television and spiked copy, and are, therefore, rarely encountered by the public. Given the dominant model, it is inevitable that some individuals believe politics cannot be discussed without arousing dangerous passions and in anything but a conflictual manner, and that all who teach it must, consciously or otherwise, be seeking to influence or convert their pupils. So the argument goes, as politics enters the classroom balance, like truth in war-time, becomes the first casualty. Understandable this viewpoint may be, but it is wrong.

Bias is not a problem somehow unique to the teaching of politics and allied topics. All teachers must continuously seek to refrain from the abuse of their power and influence over young people. As Scheffler posits, what sets teaching apart from such interventions as the transference of propaganda, brainwashing or indoctrination is that it alone:

> engages the mind, no matter what the subject matter. The teacher is prepared to *explain*, that is, to acknowledge the student's right to ask for reasons and his concomitant right to exercise his judgement on the merits of the case. Teaching is, in this standard sense, an initiation into open rational discussion (1973, p. 62, emphasis in original)

In the same way, the teaching of all controversial issues and all subject areas must seek to be an honest attempt to encourage the pupil to enter into a discourse and the engagement of their judgment with the underlying issues, so should the teaching of political and social issues. The same ground rules must apply across the curriculum. Preferential to seeking vainly some will-o'-the wisp 'value-free' methodology, it should candidly be acknowledged that neither teachers nor schools can eliminate bias or achieve balance in the presentation of ideas or material. Far better is to set them the task of teaching the pupils themselves the means 'to perceive bias and resist indoctrination' (Porter, 1980, p. 203).

Scant evidence exists of overt political indoctrination by teachers. Gaspar (1985) reports that he encountered nothing that could be termed 'gross bias', a view endorsed by an HMI who found 'the vast majority of teachers who are attempting to teach controversial issues...are trying desperately hard to do it with a degree of professional integrity' (Slater, 1984, p. 28). Perhaps not surprisingly Reid unearthed little community concern over the teaching of politics and, in all of the schools visited, 'an absence of parental antipathy' (1985, p. 7). All this should not be interpreted as proof that the 'gross bias' that Crick (1977) describes in his discussion of the issue is unknown, but it does imply the problem is on a scale schools, parents and employers can handle. Available evidence certainly indicates that Clause 45 of the 1986 Education Act, which makes it mandatory 'where political issues are brought to the attention of pupils...they are offered a balanced presentation of opposing views', is unwarranted and gratuitous. Worse, rather than guaranteeing open and balanced debate it may simply stifle creative discussion in the classroom; for, if the legal responsibility to ensure 'balance' obliges teachers to include in their presentation the views and material of such groups as the NF, which could not but be offensive to certain pupils, then from the highest motives many teachers will eschew discussion of certain 'controversial' issues. The evidence simply fails to justify Clause 45 or warrant any curtailment or prohibition being placed in the way of schools who correctly choose to address what Stenhouse terms 'matters of widespread and enduring significance' (1970, p. 4). With regard to political education at least, all the research indicates it is safe to trust our teachers and that the onus of proof must reside with those who would question the wisdom of that trust. If concern needs to be articulated regarding this issue, it ought to be directed towards the historic conservatism of the teaching profession and the general reluctance to tackle 'controversial issues' rather than supposed bias. In conclusion, it is perhaps best to remind ourselves of the perceptive comment of Crick that if teachers cannot be trusted to teach politics 'they ultimately should not be trusted to teach geometry' (1977, p. 45).

The concerns expressed respecting the ability of the current teaching force to handle the delicate material subsumed within political education embody two distinct issues. The first relates to technical competence and the familiarity of teachers with the material and content of the subject. The second asks if they possess the pedagogic skills required if the examination of political issues is not to damage the 'cause of education'. Given the long and vibrant tradition within education of seeking to keep controversial issues beyond the school gates and 'politics out of the classroom', it is almost inevitable that a paucity of good teaching material exists in a number of areas, and that specialist teachers of politics are in short supply, especially in the primary and middle schools. Politics graduates and specialists entering teaching tend to be attracted to those schools which offer the opportunity for examination level teaching. Initial teacher education programmes have, in the main, neither been encouraged nor sought to prepare their students for teaching political issues (Heater, 1969). Despite the recommendations of the McNair Report on Teacher Training that all colleges should have on their staff teachers who had made a special study of the machinery of government, central and local, and that 'in each training area there should be one or more training institutions which include these matters in their curricula' (1944, p. 68; also Brennan, 1981) little has been achieved. According to one study the handful that do 'have had little impact on the number of probationer teachers adequately prepared to teach programmes of political education' (Porter and Noctor, 1981, p. 256). Therefore, as the authors conclude: 'If political education is ever to get beyond mere rhetoric, to become other than a set of interesting issues for abstract articles and cosy seminars, the example must be set in the impressionable years of initial training' (*ibid*). Yet, if the case is accepted that political education should be included in the curriculum for non-secondary pupils, it is unrealistic for implementation to be held in abeyance until a new generation of graduates with the requisite skills are trained, especially when such a policy option, set alongside the decline in pupil numbers and the more restricted movement of teachers between schools, is tantamount to maintaining the *status quo* for the foreseeable future. All curricular reform and development is inextricably linked to the provision and expansion of in-service training opportunities. Absence of such provision and the paucity of specialists may impede progress but it is hardly an insurmountable problem. Furnishing an excuse for inaction for some, others, convinced of the value of political education in the primary sector, will perceive it as merely a hindrance.

The second element should not delay us overlong. Although theoretically a possibility, the notion that inviting politics and other controversial issues into the classroom risks inflaming passions and sowing the seeds of dissension is rarely, if ever, the case in practice. All competent educationalists learn the subtle art of handling contentious ideas and delicate situations with sensitivity. Teachers continually respond to questions and occurrences which elsewhere might be considered inflammatory; they learn how to diffuse them and, more importantly, how to exploit them as a learning opportunity. Just as sports teachers provide instruction in tennis without reproducing in every lesson the pathetic histrionics of some Wimbledon 'stars', so all but the most incompetent classroom teacher is capable of setting the agenda for rational and harmonious debate amongst pupils. Indeed, one of the most powerful arguments for the presence of politics in the classroom and games in the playground is that, by encountering these activities in the context of the school, young people learn to respect and understand their importance and function, their language and symbolism, their history and values, without automatically adopting negative behaviour patterns traditionally associated with them. As a consequence, the earlier this process begins the better; otherwise 'the greater the probability that such prejudices will have become more deeply ingrained' (Cohen, 1981, p. 260).

Concern has always been voiced regarding the age at which it is advisable to commence teaching particular subjects. In relation to the subject area under discussion, 'political education is generally thought of as something only for the secondary school child' (White and White, 1976, p. 260). Why this is so is not easy to ascertain. To begin with, substantial evidence exists which highlights the extent to which school students of below secondary age grasp the significance of political issues. Research offers convincing evidence of their capacity to discuss complex and sophisticated political questions (Stevens, 1979; 1982: Connell, 1971: Dawson and Prewitt, 1971), contradicting many 'of our present assumptions about what nine year olds and even eleven year olds can do' (Stevens, 1982, p. 29). This lends support to the maxim of Bruner (1966) that any subject can be taught in an intellectually honest way at any stage of cognitive development. On balance, research clearly indicates that 'people learn political identifica-tions, knowledge, awareness of political problems, the capacity to discuss them, assess them and make decisions about them, at a much earlier age than popular opinion imagines' (Franklin, 1986, p. 42). Writers such as Franklin (1986) and Holt (1975) have, as a result, persuasively argued for a substantial lowering of the voting age. Without wishing to enter into the rights and wrongs of that case here, it does appear difficult on grounds of equity and political competence to justify voting being restricted to those over 18. This is not to argue that many young people do not display serious gaps in their knowledge of the political system and issues. Abundant evidence exists which spotlights 'serious political ignorance amongst students' (Lister, 1987, p. 3). Unambiguous correlation between this and chronological age cannot, however, be simplistically assumed.

Leaving aside the arguments over when it is appropriate for young people to be enfranchised, what research strongly indicates is that educationalists tend to leave their intervention in this area until too late; that they under-estimate the capacity of younger pupils to engage with controversial and political questions (Harwood, 1985). Freezing political education out of the pre-secondary sector flies in the face of the rationale used both to underwrite the inclusion of almost every other subject in the curriculum and justify the moral education role of the school: namely that people will behave in socially acceptable ways and abstain from anti-social behaviour 'if they are initially discouraged from so doing than if they are not' (Barrow, 1976, p. 113). This may not be especially profound but if we seriously wish to prepare young people for a future role as a 'moral citizen' (White, 1977), or as a politically aware elector, then it is essential that the social and educational groundwork needs to commence in the primary school.

Certainly, it should not be ignored in the hope that a crash course thrown together for consumption in the final years of schooling will suffice, partly because, as Ridley (1981) argues, by that stage many young people are so alienated from, and resistant to, the school experience. In addition, there exists the possibility that however good or committed the teacher an intervention will produce the opposite result to that intended. Further, although voting may be some distance hence, this in no way obviates on the part of young people the necessity for making political judgments and decisions. It is as ridiculous to delay the teaching of politics until late in the school career on grounds of irrelevance as it would be to refrain from discussing the dangers of cigarettes until just before the age at which they can legally be purchased. Young people are, by the primary stage, already obliged to make political judgments which cannot be shelved until the law deems they are fit and ready. The racist graffiti on the playground wall; the political broadcast slipped in before the popular programme; the newspaper headline on the sweetshop counter; the increasing use of children as the fund-raising shock troops of charities and appeals; all confront young people with the need to make assessments and evaluations of a highly political nature. Politics resolutely refuses to vacate the classroom and the daily lives of young people. When the NF announce their intention to leaflet schools to recruit members (Hugill, 1988), calling the police to disperse them can at best be only a partial and even counter-productive solution. In the end, you can only protect young people from the attentions of such groups in the same way as you would seek to protect them from the blandishments of cigarette manufacturers, purveyors of pornography or dangerous games on railway lines– that is, by educating them. Ignorance serves the interests of no party, and if teachers don't believe in the intrinsic value of education as a force for good it is difficult to know what justification they have for their existence.

Schools in Democratic Societies

It needs to be asked: who better than the school to teach political education? Certainly within the present context no superior alternative is waiting to undertake the responsibility. Once the necessity of taking on that responsibility is accepted, there appears to be no purpose served by delaying the process of education and initiation. Not least because in regard to the teaching of politics as in most matters educational, procrastination merely diminishes the probability of ultimate success.

A wide range of models and theories of democracy exist and, to a degree, coexist (see Held, 1987; Wringe, 1984; Macpherson, 1977; Benn and Peters, 1959). All have in common a belief that democracy entails the involvement and interaction of individuals within a collective decision-making process. In contrast, these models can be differentiated by the extent to which they emphasise the range and intensity of that involvement. Political education within the school setting has historically reflected an allegiance to an identifiable model: liberal–representative democracy. No criticism should be implied from this statement, but account needs to be taken of what this means in relation to the curriculum offered and the age at which tuition commences. Allegiance to this model may be inevitable for, according to Dearlove and Saunders, 'since Dicey, most constitutional authorities...have seen liberal–democratic constitutional theory and British political practice as of one' (1984, p. 28). This link has produced within political education practice and curricula an 'emphasis supporting a subject rather than citizen role', with stress being laid upon 'the development of an obedient, deferential individual' (Gardner, quoted in Lister, 1987, p. 3). Teaching, even at the upper age range, concentrates on the transference of knowledge about politics. As Stradling confirms, the teachers he interviewed 'simply have not thought of political education in any other terms, than the transmission of knowledge about national or local government, and, if they had considered alternative approaches, they had not known how to set about developing appropriate courses and modules' (1984, p. 38).

The importance of teaching political literacy should not be underestimated, but evidence tends to indicate that of itself it is not overwhelmingly successful. In the United States, where civics teaching has a much longer history and established presence, research indicates that any evidence that it has any impact on political beliefs and behaviour 'is scarce and generally inconclusive' (Jennings and Langton, 1974, p. 205). In the UK context it is similarly possible to point to an absence of impact with over 70 per cent of young people declaring 'no interest in politics' (DES, 1983). To see this indifference in solely a negative light, reflecting personal stupidity and ignorance, is overly simplistic. The ignorance of young people and adults regarding political issues can with equal force be interpreted, as Harris points out, as a rational response to powerlessness. For, after all, it is reasonable that 'opinions become inconsistent about things that do not matter or cannot be affected. The role of citizenship is, for the majority, one of the least important' (1968,p. 57). We have a political system that structurally reduces all but a tiny minority to spectator status. Given the increasing concentration of power in the hands of the executive, the ability of infrequently selected representatives to check the actions of government shifts into the hands of a non-elected judiciary and largely hereditary House of Lords. A government which enjoys such freedom of action by keeping the electorate at a distance is, therefore, unlikely to invest much in the way of resources and energy in political education. Politicians of all parties, especially those in power, will tend to favour a curriculum that stresses the importance of 'trusting' institutions and 'elected representatives'; displaying a paranoia towards mass participation and an active inquisitive electorate similar to the loathing and fear barrack-room lawyers generate amongst army officers. If schools adopt a minimalist approach to political education, with a pattern of little and late being the norm, it is important before apportioning blame to recall this; not least because it helps to clarify why schools have received so little encouragement from those with the power and resources to provide it and why teachers seem so hesitant to tackle political education and controversial topics. All but the most naive teachers must be aware that beneath the rhetoric of encouragement politicians are quick to criticise and reluctant to sustain their efforts. The pessimism of Tapper and Salter (1978) may not, therefore, be misplaced, and a liberating and effective political education within schools is perhaps not even a remote possibility within the context of our present structures and climate? Maybe it must be accepted that the thin gruel of political literacy and civics is the best we can hope for under a liberal–democratic system?

The limitations of liberal–democratic models and practice have been highlighted by numerous writers such as Held (1987), Macpherson (1977), Pateman (1970) and Green (1985). All argue for an extension of democracy into those areas of politics, the economy, education, industry and commerce from which, at present, it is partially or totally excluded. Amongst the competing models used to delineate alternative theories of democracy this is frequently, but not exclusively, accorded the epithet of participatory democracy. The radical extension of democracy which it embodies is justified on a number of grounds; for example that:

> an extension of democracy would help to overcome the problems generated by its absence of 'apathy and low feelings of political efficacy' (Pateman, 1970, p. 104);

> the widening of democratic control would contribute to a higher degree of commitment, creativity, efficiency and productivity. This is in particular, although, not exclusively, an argument offered in support of an extension of workers' control and industrial democracy;

participation prevents waste by enabling consumers to influence the pattern of production and/or service delivery;

participatory democracy is morally superior to both totalitarian systems and what Green (1985) terms the 'pseudo-democracy' we at present enjoy, wherein a representative government may be periodically held accountable to an electorate but is in no way controlled by the people. The superiority of participatory democracy partially resides in the degree to which it has the potential to reflect 'the active expression of our faith in the dignity and worth of the individual' (Cahn and Cahn, 1971, p. 31);

without the active participation of immediate involvement the sense of responsibility on the part of the individual will remain underdeveloped and ignorance persist. As a consequence, the typical citizen will argue and analyze politics in 'an infantile way' (Schumpeter, 1976, p. 262). A real risk emerges that they will become prey to prejudice and the cats-paw of self-seeking, careerist politicians and axe-grinders;

it raises the quality of life of the population by enhancing 'the choices and benefits which flow from living in a society that does not leave large categories of citizens in a permanently subordinate position, at the mercy of forces entirely outside their control' (Held, 1987, p. 296);

a more participatory approach would encourage the removal of many of the more gross inequalities in our society for 'low participation and social inequity are so bound up with each other that a more equitable and humane society requires a more participatory political system' (Macpherson, 1977, p. 94).

Significant support for this latter model is to be found amongst educationalists. Importantly, it has provided a theoretical under-pinning for a number of key reforms and innovations (Richardson, 1983, pp. 36–7). A desire to extend participatory democracy can be recognized as offering a justification for such elements of policies as comprehensivisation, community schools, non-streaming, open schools, heightened parental involvement, the delegation of powers to parents, anti-racist initiatives, positive discrimination policies and progressivism in general. It would be mistaken to overestimate the extent to which any commitment at the macro level to the precepts of participatory democracy has altered practice at school and classroom level.

Irrespective of individual allegiance to the participatory model, a clear relationship can be perceived between the long term health and survival of a democratic system and the ability of schools to prepare young people for their role as citizens. As Popper stresses, the need continuously to prepare young people for this cannot be overlooked, for democratic institutions 'are like fortresses. They must be well-designed and manned' (1957, p. 126). Clearly it is naive to imagine that democratic institutions once established will, of themselves, remain secure. The experience of a number of countries, such as Greece, shows that even within the most apparently well-entrenched democracy forces exist, internally and externally, capable of under-mining it. Democracy, it appears, is far more likely to fall victim to agencies of the state than to the much vaunted dark forces of insurrection and disorder. Within Britain a highly efficient 'secret state' already operates, and with terrifying rapidity has accumulated the resources and techniques to manage and contain a subject population, and 'the apparatuses of coercion and administration have generated considerable capacity to contain opposition' (Held, 1984, p. 351). If nothing else, the virtual destruction of centuries-old traditions of local democracy, first in Northern Ireland and subsequently on the mainland, points to the speed with which the seemingly fixed and immutable can vanish. Similarly, within a decade we have seen in one corner of the United Kingdom: the abolition of jury trials; extension of controls over the right of voters to elect whom they chose; withdrawal of the ability to withold local taxes and rents as a form of protest; the right to travel freely within the United Kingdom; the introduction of internment without trial; the use of torture (McGuffin, 1974); state violence and death squad killings carried out by the police and military (Stalker, 1988). Reflection on that list is perhaps enough to drive home the message that the survival of a democratic system must always depend on the vigilance of the ruled, coupled to a willingness and ability to challenge the excesses of government. The capacity of an individual or collective group to do this will, to a degree, be dependent upon their level of education; a point well made by Perry in a comment worth reproducing at length:

Education is not merely a boon conferred by democracy, but a condition of its survival and of its becoming that which it undertakes to be. Democracy is that form of social organization which most depends on personal character and moral autonomy. The members of a democratic society cannot be the wards of their betters; for there is no class of betters... Democracy demands of every man what in other forms of social organization is demanded only of a segment of society (1954, p. 431).

Quite clearly this applies to an education system operating in a democratic society. If power is devolved within a given society, the more the the system approximates to that of a participatory model of democracy the greater the demands that will be made upon the individual and the education system. As Pateman argues, participation can be 'educative in the very widest sense' and will itself develop and foster 'the very qualities necessary for it; the more individuals participate the better able they are to do so' (1970, pp. 42-3). Be that as it may, the bricks of participation require the straw of education. In its absence, any attempt to short-circuit the painstaking process of familiarisation with the ways and means of participation will, for many, be at best hazardous and at worst debilitating. Certainly, where participation has been extended without serious consideration being given to the need to minimize any disparity in the knowledge bases of the participants the results have not been encouraging. A good illustration of this can be found in attempts to democratize school governing bodies. These have largely operated to strengthen the hand of headteachers and done 'little to reallocate power in favour of either groups of clients, students or workers, or even people in the wider community' (Bacon, 1978, p. 197). The 1988 Education Reform Act may partially alter the balance of power within governing bodies but is unlikely to denude the existing ascendancy of headteachers. Removing school students and non-teaching staff from even the handful of governing bodies on which they previously sat can only be a retrograde step. Whilst weakening the ability of LEAs to intervene it must, to a worrying extent, deprive teachers of the protection, albeit limited, they have enjoyed from the capricious power of headteachers. Clearly the Act must operate to restrain further independence of thought and action amongst teacher representatives. Shifting power to often untrained, ill-prepared parents and to the unread Babbitts of the local 'business community' is hardly likely to generate, within the foreseeable future, any widespread challenge to the entrenched power of headteachers. In fact if it did, one suspects the Government would reassess the Act for, in tune with the overall tenor of so much recent legislation, it is primarily designed to empower management, to set it free to manage, not the reverse. Therefore to question the 1988 Act should not be interpreted as arguing against the extension of citizen participation, quite the opposite. It is to argue for a genuine extension that would encourage the involvement of groups such as pupils, non-teaching staff and the wider community who, quite deliberately, will continue to be denied a meaningful voice. It is also to argue for a sustained programme of political education to accompany the restructuring for without it, participation will, for the majority of parents, comprise little more than a sleight-of-hand which obscures the transference of yet more power to the articulate middle-class, the petty bourgeoisie and upper echelon professionals. Even such a programme can for many be too little too late. Giving participatory democracy a chance of survival means that young people must, from the onset of their educational experience, be inducted into the arts and crafts of decision-making; be given the essential skills to interrogate service providers; and be furnished with, above all else, the confidence to shed the ingrained servility that so successfully sustains the current inequalities in the distribution of power and life chances. Without that early educational experience we need to recognize that much in the way of participation is reduced to a charade and a mockery.

Teaching political literacy I have argued is important and should not be dismissed as irrelevant; no strong grounds exist for delaying the introduction of this subject matter. Pupils of primary and middle school age have not only the capacity to manage the content but they will also benefit from access to this area of knowledge. For although they may not vote they, like all citizens, are obliged to make moral and political judgments. Numerous examples exist of teachers successfully introducing 'politics' into the primary classroom without galvanizing parental hostility. Indeed, the evidence appears to indicate that there is little to fear on this front for, as Riches found, despite initial fears parent reaction 'was entirely favourable' (1974, p. 201).

Political Education and the National Curriculum

The imposition of a national curriculum is of immense significance. It will not exclude the possibility of introducing young people to political debates and issues via the medium of history (Heater, 1974; Hesketh, 1976), geography (Hodgkinson, 1975), English (Clayton, 1978; Ross, 1981) or for that matter any other subject, but it must impede and make far more problematic the construction of a clearly designated entity, political education. Legislation, by designating foundation subjects and in particular core ones, will, in conjunction with the introduction of attainment testing, engender a narrowing of the focus within subject areas. Whatever the intention it cannot but discourage teachers and schools from straying from the core areas where their performance is under scrutiny. Linked to the oppressive treatment of pupils within the 1986 Act (Clause 44a) which expressly forbids 'the pursuit of partisan political activities by any of those registered pupils at the school who are junior pupils', it might be considered that a number of key avenues have been closed off. Thus the political education for primary and middle school pupils advocated by a number of writers (Harwood, 1985; Harries, 1979; Porter, 1975; Riches, 1974, 1974a; Robins and Robins, 1978) is unlikely to achieve prominence. It is impossible to predict what the long term impact of the centralization of decision-making with regard to curriculum content will be. However, it is self-evident, even at the time of writing, that it will become essential that the case for improved levels of political literacy needs to be strenuously argued if political education is to secure a niche in the national curriculum.

Despondancy need not be the order of the day, for, as with the teaching of other controversial areas, it is essential not to overestimate the importance of the curriculum and the timetable, since in relation to matters of belief, attitude and values the wider context of the school organization and the pattern of classroom control are far more influential than the content of the lessons. As Webb concludes: 'what has been established by all the research so far? – classroom climates are crucial to the success of democratic political education in schools' (1979, p. 222). The relative ineffectiveness of civics teaching has already been commented upon but this should in no way be seen as a unique failing. Equally, the vast quantity of hours spent on English teaching despite, one assumes, a contrary intention, produces 11 *Sun* readers for every one teenage *Guardian, Times* or *Independent* reader. Carefully structured lessons and projects can only go so far towards generating amongst young people a respect and commitment to democratic politics and participatory practices. As Stanworth (1983) found, it is the subtle classroom encounters and norms of the school which regenerate sexual hierarchy, marginalize young women and undermine the formal attempts embodied in the curriculum and 'official policy' of schools to prevent the definition of young women as second-class citizens (see the chapter by Skelton in this volume). Thus we encounter a central problem, the structure and organization of the school itself, as well as the attitudes of teachers. Schools are profoundly anti-democratic institutions. Unavoidably one must conclude that in many respects they are amongst the least suitable sites that could be envisaged for teaching a respect for democracy; sadly no alternatives appear to be on hand. Few would argue with the conclusion of Wringe: 'that despite pressure for centralisation and public accountability the headteacher in most schools is unequivocally in charge' (1984, p. 69). The power of the headteacher percolates the school, with most:

> managed and organised like a major but conventional theatrical production. The Head-teacher directs, or is expected to direct, the school as if it were a Shakesperian drama, selecting a cast of players to win a competition of some kind. All authority is vested in the director so that the stage manager, house manager, technicians, cast and even audience depend upon an oracle for their activity and entertainment. Parents choose schools because of the Head and interpret their children's education through a single leader (Barker, 1986, p. 59).

The price paid for this is widespread servility amongst staff, to the extent that when required to act in an autonomous manner on governing bodies teachers commonly appear unable to do so (Sallis, 1988). In addition teachers display a reticence to exercise initiative, in the main accepting as given the existing concentration of authority. Not surprisingly this encourages the conditioning of pupils 'to accept knowledge as if it were faith and to suppress critical impulses' (Barker, 1986, p. 59).

Schools convey myriad messages reinforcing and inculcating the primacy of hierarchical control. Centralisation is unambiguously equated with efficiency; power with age. Schools are places 'in which the division between the weak and the powerful is clearly drawn' (Jackson, 1968, p. 10). Nuances of status between staff, for example the social chasm which separates the mental labourers (teachers) from the manual labourers (cleaners, caretakers), linked to the exclusion of pupils from given facilities and space, the locking of doors and expulsion of pupils into the playground, the speech patterns of many teachers, all combine with countless other aspects of school life to signify a clear rejection of democratic forms of management. Young people learn that age, knowledge and status convey power and that it is legitimate for this to be exercised and distributed without any clear notions of accountability. Linking the intellectual authority of the teacher to administrative autocracy, has, as Green (1985) points out, inevitably corrupted the educational process. In the context of a democratic, rather than totalitarian, society, it is doubly damaging as it serves to erode the value system of the community within which the school is located. We allow, indeed in many instances encourage, teachers and educational administrators to behave in ways 'that express contempt for the values of a free society' (Strike, 1982, p. 147), then wonder why school-leavers show such overwhelming indifference to the political system that sustains that society. The all-pervading air of autocracy within the majority of schools ensures that 'no amount of simulation exercises, games, or mock elections can compensate for the learning that takes place in an environment which is conducive to participation in making decisions' (Robins and Robins, 1978, p. 131). Teaching democratic and participatory practices and values thus enters the realm of the controversial for they challenge the established norms of educational administration and practice, affirming values that may be consistent with those of a free society but which are subversive of the institutional values of the school itself. Yet this need not be the case; schools can teach political education and induct young people into democratic practices without undermining their educational role. Indeed the opposite is the case. It may be risky for it 'entrusts our current conceptions to the judgement of our pupils' (Scheffler, 1973, p. 143), but it does offer the only means of creating a genuinely educational community that matches the ideals of a democratic society.

A small number of schools have successfully shown that it is possible to devolve power and involve young people in the decision-making processes of the school: to organise and administer themselves in ways that affirm the values of a democratic society. Within the British context, a limited number of secondary schools have sought to engage young people in the internal decision-making process (Gordon, 1986; Fletcher, 1983): seeking to convey to their students, via the ethos of the school itself, the feasibility of democratic processes; to use the school as a test-bed wherein young people can learn the skills so essential for effective participation in later life. There is absolutely no reason why such involvement should be restricted to the secondary sector. As Cohen (1981) clearly shows in his fascinating description of a Dutch primary school which devolved key areas of decision-making into the hands of the pupils, not only do we invariably overlook the extent to which young people could share in the running of our schools, but also the maturity and good sense they could potentially inject into the managerial processes. Genuine innovation is feasible within the primary sector and major areas of decision-making currently reserved as the exclusive domain of the headteacher, teachers or governing body can and should be relocated in the interests of efficiency and good educational practice. Increasing centralisation of control over the curriculum may close down one avenue, not only for political education but also for developing programmes designed to tackle racism and sexism. If this is the case then possibly it should be seen in a positive light, for potentially it may lead to the far more fruitful and effective strategy of addressing the organizational and social ethos of the school itself. Rather than tinkering with syllabi and curriculum we may, as a consequence, more single-mindedly focus attention upon the school structures themselves, which have so effectively undermined the impact of curricular reform in the past and proved so resistant to reform.

'Democracy is more than a form of government; it is primarily a mode of associated living, of conjoint communicated experience' (Dewey, 1961, p. 87). If our present democratic system is not only going to survive but more importantly develop then, from the very onset of schooling, modes of behaviour and attitudes must be formed that are fundamentally democratic. Indeed, unless such practices commence in the primary sector the chances of involving young people in participatory decision-making, even in such informal educational settings as the Youth Service, appear to be slight. As Gordon (1987) found, by the time they reach their teens they have neither the skills, confidence nor experience to take power even when it is genuinely offered them. It must be stressed, however, that the value of such reforms will not only accrue to wider society. Excitingly, they offer teachers the only feasible means of escaping from the custodial and disciplinary roles which have so consistently lowered the standing of their profession: to move on from an educational structure that so often rewards the bully and the disciplinarian whilst marginalizing the reflective and intellectual practitioner, which in the classroom prioritizes order rather than content, and in the school seeks passivity at the expense of creativity. Only when educationalists, from the very first days of schooling, come to perceive their role as being initiators of young people into a democratic way of life will they escape the bondage of acting out the role of warden and turnkey. It is doubtful if any group has more to gain from the democratization of our schools than teachers; the tragedy is that no group, perhaps, requires more convincing.

References

AFSHAR, H. (1978) 'Teaching and Learning Politics', *Teaching Politics*, 7, 1, pp. 37–44.

BACON (1978) *Public Accountability and the Schooling System*, London, Harper Row.

BARKER, B. (1986) *Rescuing the Comprehensive Experience*, Milton Keynes, Open University Press.

BARROW, R. (1976) *Common Sense and the Curriculum*, London, Allen and Unwin.

BENN, S.I. and PETERS, R.S. (1959) *Social Principles and the Democratic State*, London, Allen and Unwin.

BRENNAN, T. (1981) *Political Education and Democracy*, Cambridge University Press.

BRUNER, J. (1966) *Towards a Theory of Instruction*, Harvard University Press.

BSA (1987) *British Social Attitudes: the 1987 Report*, Aldershot, Gower.

CAHN, E.S. and CAHN, J.C. (1971) 'Maximum Feasible Participation: a General Overview', in CAHN, E.S. and PASSANT, B. (Eds) *Citizen Participation: Effecting Community Change*, London, Praeger, pp. 28–45.

CLAYTON, A. (1978) 'Teaching Politics Via English', *Teaching Politics*, 7, 2, pp. 273–8.

COHEN, L. (1981) 'Political Literacy and the Primary School: A Dutch Experiment', *Teaching Politics*, 10, 3, pp. 259–67.

CONNELL, R.W. (1971) *The Child's Construction of Politics*, Melbourne University Press.

CRICK, B. (1977) 'On Bias', in CRICK, B. and HEATER, D. (Eds) *Essays on Political Education*, Lewes, Falmer Press, pp. 34–50.

DAWSON, R.E. and PREWITT, K. (1971) *Political Socialisation*, Boston, Little Brown.

DEARDEN, R. (1969) 'The Aims of Primary Education', in PETERS, R.S. (Ed.) *Perspectives on Plowden*, London, RKP.

DEARLOVE, J. and SAUNDERS, P. (1984) *Introduction to British Politics*, Cambridge, Polity Press.

DEPARTMENT OF EDUCATION AND SCIENCE (1977) *Curiculum 11 to 16*, London, HMSO.

DEPARTMENT OF EDUCATION AND SCIENCE (1983) *Young People in the 1980s: a Survey*, London, HMSO.

DEPARTMENT OF EDUCATION AND SCIENCE (1987) *The National Curriculum 5–16: a Consultation Document*, London, HMSO.

DEPARTMENT OF EDUCATION AND SCIENCE (1988) *National Curriculum: Task Group on Assessment and Testing*, London, HMSO.

DEWEY, J. (1961) *Democracy and Education*, New York, Macmillan.

DRAY, J. and JORDAN, D. (1950) *A Handbook of Social Studies*, London, Methuen.

DUNLOP, F. (1980) 'On Separating Moral From Political Education: a Reply to Pat White', in *Journal of Further and Higher Education*, 4, 2, pp. 73–81.

ENTWHISTLE, H. (1969) 'Educational Theory and the Teaching of Politics', in HEATER, D. (Ed.) *The Teaching of Politics*, London, Methuen, pp. 181–201.

FLETCHER, C. (1983) *The Challenges of Community Education*, Dept. of Adult Education, University of Nottingham.

FRANKLIN, B. (1986) 'Children's Political Rights', in FRANKLIN, B. (Ed.) *The Rights of Children*, Oxford, Blackwell.

GASPER, I. (1985) 'Handling Politics in the Classroom', *Teaching Politics*, 14, 1, pp. 41–51.

GORDON, S. (1987) *Balancing Acts: Strategies for the Promotion of Member Participation in Youth Clubs and Youth Groups*, unpublished M.Phil thesis, Cranfield Institute of Technology.

GORDON, T. (1986) *Democracy In One School?*, Lewes, Falmer.

GREEN, P. (1985) *Retrieving Democracy*, London, Methuen.

GREENSTEIN, F. (1974) *Children and Politics*, Yale University Press.

HARRIES, E. (1979) 'The Implications of Politics for Teachers of Children in the 7–16 Age Range', *Teaching Politics*, 8, 3, pp. 249–61.

HARRIS, N. (1968) *Beliefs in Society*, Harmondsworth, Penguin.

HARWOOD, D. (1985) 'We need political not Political education for 5–13 year olds', *Education 3–13*, 13, 1, pp. 12–17.

HASELHURST, A. (1981) 'Political Education: an Independent Tory View', *Teaching Politics*, 8, 2, pp. 191–2.

HEATER, D. (1969) 'Teacher Training', in HEATER, D. (Ed.) *The Teaching of Politics*, London, Methuen, pp. 126–44.

HEATER, D. (1974) *History Teaching and Political Education*, London, The Politics Association.

HELD, D. (1984) 'Power and Legitimacy in Contemporary Britain', in MCLENNAN, G., HELD, D. and HALL, S. (Eds.) *State and Society in Contemporary Britain*, Cambridge University Press, pp. 299–369.

HELD, D. (1987) *Models of Democracy*, Cambridge, Polity Press.

HESKETH, G. (1976) 'Leaders and Followers in History: Teaching Elites in the Primary School', *Teaching Politics*, 5, 1, pp. 55–9.

HODGKINSON, K. (1975) 'The Effects of History and Geography Teaching on Pupils' Political Knowledge in Two Secondary Schools', *Teaching Politics*, 4, 3, pp. 177–82.

HOLT (1975) *Escape From Childhood*, Harmondsworth, Penguin.

HUGILL, B. (1988) 'National Front Renews Action at the School Gate', *Times Educational Supplement*, 29 January 1988, p. 12.

JACKSON, P. (1968) *Life in Classrooms*, New York, Holt, Rinehart and Winston.

JENNINGS, M.K. and LANGTON, K.P. (1974) 'Effects of the High School Civics Curriculum', in JENNINGS, M.K. and NIEMI, R.G. (Eds) *The Political Character of Adolescence: the Influence of Families and Schools*, Princeton University Press, pp. 181–206.

LAWTON, D., CAMPBELL, J. and BURKITT, V. (1971) *Social Studies: Schools Council Working Paper 39*, London, Evans/Methuen.

LISTER, I. (1987) 'Political Education in England, 1974–84', *Teaching Politics*, 16, 1, pp. 3–25.

McGUFFIN, J. (1974) *The Guinea Pigs*, Harmondsworth, Penguin.

McNAIR REPORT (1944) *Teachers and Youth Leaders: Report of the Committee Appointed by the President of the Board of Education to Consider the Supply, Recruitment and Training of Teachers and Youth Leaders (McNair Report)*, London, Board of Education.

MACPHERSON, C.B. (1977) *The Life and Times of Liberal Democracy*, Oxford University Press.

PATEMAN, C. (1970) *Participation and Democratic Theory*, Cambridge University Press.

PERRY, R.B. (1954) *Realms of Value*, Harvard University Press.

PETERS, R.S. (1957) *Authority, Responsibility and Education*, London, Unwin.

POPPER, K.R. (1957) *The Poverty of Historicism*, London, RKP.

PORTER, A. (1975) 'Political Education Below 14', *Teaching Politics*, 4, 3, pp. 172–6.

PORTER, A. (1980) 'Much Ado About Nothing? A Critical Consideration of the Problem of Bias and Indoctrination in Political Education', *Teaching Politics*, 9, 2, pp. 103–14.

PORTER, A. and NOCTOR, M. (1981) 'Political Education in the Initial Training of Teachers', *Teaching Politics*, 10, 3, pp. 243–57.

REID, A. (1985) 'An Outsider's View of Political Education: Past and Present', *Teaching Politics*, 14, 1, pp. 3–18.

REID, A. and WHITTINGHAM, B. (1984) 'The Constitutional Classroom: A Political Education for Democracy', *Teaching Politics*, 13, 3, pp. 307–29.

RICHARDSON, A. (1983) *Participation*, London, RKP.

RICHES, J. (1974) 'Education for Democracy: Description of a Curriculum Unit for Upper Juniors', *Teaching Politics*, 3, 2, pp. 121–125.

RICHES, J. (1974a) 'Education for Democracy: A Curriculum Unit for Upper Juniors in Action', *Teaching Politics*, 3, 3, pp. 197–201.

RIDLEY, F.F. (1981) 'Schools, Youth Programmes, Employment and Political Skills', *International Journal of Political Education*, December.

ROBINS, L. and ROBINS, V. (1978) 'Politics in the First School: This Year, Next Year, Sometime...Never?', *Teaching Politics*, 7, 2, pp. 137–47.

ROSS, A. (1981) 'Short Course Number Three: Using Literature to Develop Political Concepts in the Primary School', *Teaching Politics*, 10, 1, pp. 85–96.

SALLIS, J. (1988) 'Agenda', in *Times Educational Supplement*, 5 February, p. 22.

SHEFFLER, I. (1973) *Reason and Teaching*, London, RKP.

SCHUMPETER, I. (1976) *Capitalism, Socialism and Democracy*, London, Allen and Unwin.

SLATER, J. (1976) 'An HMI Perspective on Peace Education', in *Educating People*, London, The National Council of Women of Great Britain.

STALKER, J. (1988) *Stalker*, London, Harrap.

STANWORTH, M. (1983) *Gender and Schooling*, London, Hutchinson.

STENHOUSE, L. (1970) *The Humanities Curriculum Project: An Introduction*, London, Heinemann.

STEVENS, O. (1979) 'Politics and the Juniors: The Political Thinking of Younger Children', *Teaching Politics*, 8, 3, pp. 263–72.

STEVENS, O. (1982) *Children Talking Politics*, Oxford, Martin Robertson.

STRADLING, R. (1977) *The Political Awareness of the School Leaver*, London, Hansard Society.

STRADLING, R. and NOCTOR, M. (1981) *The Provision of Political Education in Schools: a National Survey*, Political Education Research Unit, University of York.

STRADLING, R. *et al.* (1984) *An Assessment of Innovations in Political Education*, London, Curriculum Review Unit, DES.

STRIKE, K. (1982) *Liberty and Learning*, Oxford, Martin Robertson.

TAPPER, T. and SALTER, B. (1978) *Education and the Political Order*, London, Macmillan.

THOMPSON (1969) 'The Teaching of Politics in Practice', in HEATER, D. (Ed.) *The Teaching of Politics*, London, Methuen.

WEBB, K. (1979) 'Classroom Interaction and Political Education', *Teaching Politics*, 8, 3, pp. 221–31.

WHITE, P. (1973) 'Education, Democracy and the Public Interest', in PETERS, R.S. (Ed.) *The Philosophy of Education*, Oxford University Press, pp. 217–38.

WHITE, P. (1977) 'Political Education in a Democracy: the Implications for Teacher Education', *Journal of Further and Higher Education*, 1, 3, pp. 40–55.

WHITE, P. and WHITE, J. (1976) A Programme for Political Education: A Critique', *Teaching Politics*, 5, 3, pp. 257–71.

WHITEMARSH, G. (1981) 'Change and Tradition in the Teaching of Politics in Schools', *Teaching Politics*, 10, 1, pp. 3–12.

WRINGE, C. (1984) *Democracy, Schooling and Political Education*, London, Allen and Unwin.

Chapter 4

Controversial Issues and Reflective Teaching

Andrew Pollard

Introduction

This paper is, in essence, concerned with trying to identify and discuss a morally and politically tenable professional posture which teachers might adopt – particularly with regard to the teaching of controversial issues, but also with regard to less contentious aspects of school work. At a time when external control of the curriculum and of teachers' practice is tightening, it seems particularly necessary for the profession to try to evolve a position which is grounded in positive self-confidence and in trust in our own collective integrity and commitment. However, such an approach must be forward-looking rather than professionally defensive, and, if this can be achieved, might well provide some tenable counterpoint to legislative forms of centralized control and to crude forms of managerialism.

The paper has three parts. In the first I discuss the significance of values and interests in generating controversy and I distinguish between what I have called the 'controversial' and the 'routine' curriculum. In the second part I consider an 'official' model of 'good-teaching' derived from various recent Government documents and discuss some possible implications of legislation to establish a national curriculum. I also discuss the value of introducing children to ways of discussing controversial issues as a preparation for participation in the democratic process. In the third part of the paper a model of 'reflective teaching' is introduced and some features of this are illustrated through a case study of a student-teacher working with a class of 10-year-olds on a topic on jobs and a local government election.

Values, the 'Controversial' and the 'Routine' Curriculum

The 1986 Education Act (No.2) outlaws 'the promotion of partisan political views' and requires that 'where political issues are brought to the attention of pupils...they are offered a balanced presentation'. That might, at first sight, sound reasonable and straight-forward enough, but we should at once be alerted by Kogan's (1978) insistence that the educational process itself is inevitably 'political' because it is concerned with what 'ought to be rather than with what is' (p. 15). In focusing on 'controversial issues' then, we are dealing with a particular case – a class of topics within the curriculum about which contrasting views and the seeds of controversy can be predicted. But we must not forget the more general point about the involvement of values in educational activity *per se*.

With that in mind, I would suggest that almost all teaching involves teachers in making value judgements. I believe that this is inevitable as practitioners try to resolve the dilemmas which are inherent in the teaching role, to juggle with the conflicting expecta-tions which others make of them and to decide on their educational priorities from the bewildering array of possibilities which confront them. Strangely though, and at the same time, teaching often does not seem quite so problematic in practice. I would suggest that this is so because socially accepted patterns of resolution for the dilemmas (and thus routine forms of behaviour) have often been established (Berlak and Berlak, 1981). These may be influenced by the culture and ideologies of a particular staff-group and/or the community which a school serves, or they may relate to sets of beliefs and opinions which exist more widely in society. In other words, many of the value decisions in teaching are not so much actively 'taken' as passively 'assumed' on the basis of values which are uncontroversially accepted and even taken for granted.

One way to describe the existence of such an array of culturally reinforced beliefs and expectations is in terms of the concept of 'hegemony'. This concept, as developed by Gramsci (1978), en-compasses and describes the interrelationship and mutual reinforce-ment of 'commonsense knowledge' and the interests of powerful social groups. It suggests that the majority of people take on and accept particular ideas about notions like 'normality' and 'human nature' despite the fact that such ideas may have implications which do not favour their socio-economic interests. Ironically though, the ideas themselves are reproduced through the everyday practice of the very people whom they subordinate. Now, of course, such a sociological concept may be seen as being contentious, particularly in its application. For instance, the case has often been made that Mrs Thatcher's greatest achievement since 1979 has been the establishment of a new hegemony to replace the post-war consensus which underpinned the Welfare State.

Without being drawn into such issues and accepting a significant degree of over-simplification, we might say that a dominant bourgeois hegemony influences many aspects of British society and that, among other things, this encompasses expectations about the nature and range of the curriculum which is 'suitable' for young children. Thus, in respect of the curriculum at least, children tend to be seen as being impressionable, innocent and in need of protection from the 'nastier' things in life. For this reason, and to parody a little, issues like 'the Seasons', 'rainbows', 'pets', 'people who help us' and other variants of 'all things bright and beautiful' (King, 1978) take the primary school stage. Meanwhile, however worthwhile such topics may be, it remains the case that dealing with issues such as unemployment, poverty or conflict are often thought of as being inappropriate for young children.

On such arguments we might identify the 'controversial curriculum' as being that which lies on or outside the boundary of the dominant hegemony. It consists of issues about which no core groundswell of 'common-sense' acceptability exists. Thus, with the due prudence of many of our worldly-wise colleagues, we might think ourselves wise to approach such issues with caution – or, more simply, to avoid them altogether.

Returning to the issue of value judgments as a basis for decision-making, we can now, on this argument, characterize as 'normal' those value judgments which are made in ways which go almost unnoticed. They form the large class of educational decisions which are usually taken in the absence of controversy and they inform the 'normal curriculum'. 'Controversial' issues tend to call for value judgments which lack such grounding and thus yield a 'controversial curriculum'. This, like a deviant pupil, may well cause trouble. But why should this be? Is it just the issue of values?

Bridges (1986) followed this argument when he suggested that controversy arises because people are either 'attached to different values, attach different priority to the same values or give different interpretations to the same value' (p. 26). However, he also pointed out that it is in the area of moral, social and political affairs – rather than in areas such as science or history – that controversy is most likely to arise. These areas are, of course, precisely those within which considerations about 'what ought to be' are likely to be prominent – they thus overtly call for value judgments. But Bridges is, in my opinion, somewhat coy about this, for the use of the term 'values' tends to gloss the question of the interests and power which might lie behind such values – an issue to which the concept of hegemony can be applied directly. It is fairly clear, and many of the papers in this collection bear the point out, that controversy is particularly associated with perceived threats to the *status quo* which are taken up by those with significant degrees of power. Thus, whilst a 'normal' value judgment and a 'normal curriculum' in education poses no fundamental social challenge and can be safely left to the professionals, consideration of 'controversial issues' is seen as being potentially de-stabilising. After all, in one sense, such a 'controversial curriculum' represents a direct threat to the hegemony and thus to the legitimation which underpins existing social arrangements.

If such a situation of perceived threat arises it is very common to find that a 'moral panic' (Cohen, 1972) is generated in the media and elsewhere. Such 'moral panics' tend to follow a familiar pattern. The work or activity of a particular group – e.g. of anti-racist teachers or of proponents of peace studies – comes to the attention of some people who are 'shocked' at what they see as a move outside the normal boundaries of the curriculum or of practice. This is followed by public expressions of disquiet and gradually, often with amplification from the media, a sense of 'moral outrage' is generated whilst, at the same time, particular 'true values and traditions' are asserted by concerned interest groups. This puts the 'deviants' under considerable pressure and they are either isolated, marginalized or forced into conformity. This pattern of events has been documented on many occasions (e.g., see Pollard [1988] on the case of non-competitive games in education).

To recognize social phenomena such as 'moral panics', or to draw distinctions between a 'normal' and a 'controversial' curriculum may help a little to place relevant events in some sort of perspective when they occur. If controversy rages it is reassuring to have at least one way of interpreting what may be going on – particularly if it highlights the commonality of people's experience. This though, whilst it highlights some of the issues involved, does not get us around the central question of how teachers should conduct themselves if they wish to deal with issues which might be deemed controversial.

'Good Teachers', Controversy and the Democratic Process

As we have seen, one answer to the question of how teachers should deal with controversial issues is simply to say 'don't get involved in the first place' and it is interesting, in the context of the preceding discussion of 'normal' and 'controversial' aspects of the curriculum, to consider the view on characteristics of the 'good teacher' which has been emerging from the DES in recent years. With this in mind

Broadhead (1987) conducted a review of three important documents, *The New Teacher in School* (NTS), *Education Observed 3 – Good Teachers* (EO), and *Better Schools* (BS). From his study of these documents he distilled a 'blueprint' for a 'good teacher' – a model, the official 'ideal'. The teacher characteristics in this official blueprint are listed below:

The professional behaviour
The good teacher is:

1.	Reliable, punctual, cooperative and willing.	EO5
2.	Committed to further professional training.	EO7/8
3.	In conjunction with colleagues, able to establish long term aims and short term objectives and can set learning objectives.	EO19
4.	Capable of responding to professional teamwork.	BS143
5.	Capable of carrying out professional tasks without bias.	BS144
6.	Involved in after school activities and clubs.	EO29/32 NTS5.5

The personal characteristics
The good teacher is:

1.	Enthusiastic, hard working, common sensical, firm, intelligent, adaptable, tenacious, intuitive, sensitive, friendly, energetic, conscientious, imaginative, resourceful.	NT3.3 NTS5.5
2.	Able to command the respect of pupils and maintain excellent relations.	EO6.NTS3.3
3.	Able to control the class.	EO13
4.	Able to hold the pupils' interest.	BS140
5.	Able to make use of a repertoire of teaching styles.	EO10.BS14
6.	Capable of gaining access to a variety of teaching strategies.	BS136/138 NTS3.3
7.	Able to communicate lesson objectives to the pupils.	EO19
8.	Able to incorporate personal example into classroom life.	EO3.BS19
9.	Able to establish good relationships with parents and the community.	EO34
10.	Able to bring something new into the school and be a source of ideas.	NTS5.5

11. Able to seek and receive advice.	NTS5.5
12. Able to demonstrate a specialist, in depth knowledge in one subject and a wide range of general subject expertise.	NTS5.5

The organisational attributes

The good teacher is:

1. Able to engage in long and short term lesson planning.	EO19. NTS3.3
2. Able to gain access to teaching aids/resources for both self and pupils.	EO20
3. Proficient in class management and the grouping of pupils.	BS138
4. Able to make available a diversity of subject matter within the classroom.	EO13
5. Able to select and present subject matter that will engage the pupils' interest.	BS133
6. Able to encourage pupil exploration by linguistic means by careful and sensitive questioning and the development of small group activities.	EO17
7. Able to encourage the development of pupils' listening skills.	EO17
8. Able to communicate the assessment of performance to individual pupils.	EO21/27

The perceptive qualities

The good teacher is:

1. Able to undertake the role of guide and mentor to pupils when required.	BS135
2. Able to perceive and respond to individual pupil differences.	EO11,NTS3.3
3. Able to determine external factors which are affecting individual pupils.	EO19
4. Able to modify own language and explanation to pupils' needs when so required.	EO11
5. Able to perceive and respond to an external event or sudden upsurge of interest exhibited by the pupils and incorporate this into daily lesson planning.	EO19
6. Able to evaluate the effectiveness of his/her own teaching methods.	BS134

7. Able to evaluate the relevance of the
   subject material.   BS45.
                                                     NTS3.3/5.5

The information gathering skills and evaluative skills
The good teacher is:
1. Proficient at gathering information   EO24
   pertaining to individual pupil's progress.
2. Proficient at identifying reasons for   BS140
   failure.
3. Aware of temporary/permanent factors   BS139.EO7
   which may be affecting pupils'
   behaviour/learning skills.
4. Skilful at drawing on individual pupil's   BS137
   experience.
5. Capable of developing access to   BS139.NTS3.3
   knowledge of which subject matters
   will engage the pupils' interest.
6. Aware of the categories of information   BS133
   that pupils need access to.
7. Thorough in his/her marking.   NTS5.5
8. Aware of the teaching aids and resources   EO24
   that are required in a general classroom
   sense and regarding a specific lesson–based
   need.

It would be foolish to deny the importance of many of these attributes
and forms of behaviour – although if applying the model to specific
instances, one might want to consider the extent to which such
generalizations are really tenable, given the diversity within education.
That being said though, it remains a list which reflects a great deal of
grounded experience and it might well provide a useful checklist for
staff appraisal and/or self-evaluation. However, in another sense the
model strikes me as being rather worrying. In particular, it seems that
the focus of the model is almost exclusively on the effective delivery
of the curriculum. The issue of what that curriculum should consist of
is not systematically or directly faced. Of course, this is perfectly
logical in the context of legislation for a national curriculum
framework. According to the Education Reform Act, we are to have a
core curriculum of science, mathematics and English together with
various 'foundation subjects'. The eventual aim is that children will
work on 'programmes of study' within each subject and teachers will
be specifically guided by 'attainment targets' and provided with
'feedback' by various forms of testing of children's achievements. The

job of specifying the exact nature of these programmes of study is to be carried out by 'working groups' appointed by the Secretary of State.

I do not wish to give the impression that I oppose the general thrust of these measures. I think that we have had ample evidence over the past ten years of considerable variations in provision and practice which, at root, are unacceptable in a democratic society in which all children should have certain educational rights and opportunities in common. To take some action on this issue was thus, in my view, a necessary and responsible action by the Government. However, at the same time, I would also want to argue that the high-profile structuring of the curriculum is masking a failure to address the equally important issue of distribution of resources (particularly between the private and public sectors) and, of course, in many other respects the Education Reform Act is likely to increase social divisions.

For the purpose of this paper though, the point which I want to make is that it may soon be 'controversial' to introduce topics, not just because they lie outside the hegemonic boundary of what 'commonsense' suggests is appropriate for primary school children, but simply because they are not listed in the nationally prescribed programmes of study. In anxious moments one wonders if it will one day be controversial to think divergently! Are 'good' teachers simply to be seen as those who can deliver 'the' curriculum most effectively – as people to be 'trained' in the necessary skills of assessment, equipped with the necessary subject knowledge and inculcated with suitably compliant attitudes?

Many people are concerned about such issues and, at the moment, we know relatively little about the degrees of freedom and scope for local interpretation which will remain for teachers, governors and others who have curricular responsibilities in individual schools. We also know little about how the Secretary of State will, in fact, use the new powers which the Act proposes to give the holder of that office. Provision for updating and revising programmes of study and attainment targets will clearly be important, but it is arguably as essential to monitor what is left out of the nationally prescribed curriculum and to consider what areas of learning and experience might or should be added to it.

For instance, one area which does not appear to be a very high priority in present debates is that of human rights. And yet the seeds have been sown for constructive future development. I have in mind here the Government's acceptance of the 1985 Recommendation from the Council of Europe on the teaching of human rights in schools (Council of Europe 1985). This document asserts that:

The understanding and experience of human rights is an important element of the preparation of all young people for life in a democratic and pluralistic society,

and that:

The study of human rights in schools should lead to an understanding of, and sympathy for, the concepts of justice, equality, freedom, peace, rights and democracy.

Furthermore:

Democracy is best learned in a democratic setting where participation is encouraged, where views can be expressed openly and discussed, where there is freedom of expression for pupils and teachers and where there is freedom and justice.

The interesting thing about this is that, despite the centrality of the issue to our much vaunted national self-image as the cradle of Parliaments, it immediately raises issues which, in a primary school context, are likely to be regarded as being 'controversial'. Despite this, the issue is so important that, in my view, we should have more self-confidence and should look on debating controversial issues in schools in much more positive ways.

It is possible to argue, in fact, that treatment of controversial issues should be seen as an essential part of our national curriculum. I make this case on the basis of a commitment to representative democracy as a peaceful means of decision-making. Of course, I don't always like the decisions which result from such processes but they do provide a relatively ordered and open mechanism for expressing conflicting interests and points of view and for moving forward to provide legitimized legal structures for social behaviour. Whilst fully accepting the danger of complacency, I feel that the value of representative democracy is at its most apparent when one considers the difficulties faced by societies in which such a system does not exist. If this view is accepted then it becomes a reasonable question to ask what school-teachers should be doing to prepare children and young people to understand the system and to participate in it.

I fear that, despite their capacity to develop understanding of such institutions (see the paper by Short in this volume), many young children know of Parliament only because Guy Fawkes tried to blow it up. Others, perhaps a little older, may have the benefit of an explanation of the basic system – for instance, they may have made drawings of the chambers and been involved in discussions as part of social studies or history work. However, a real understanding of the meaning and value of our democratic system can only, in my view, come from active participation in debates in which conflict is expressed and yet both order and respect for one's opponents' right to their point of view are maintained. What better means could there be for this than through debate on controversial issues? In fact, the issue for such a debate has to be controversial if the activity is to have any real meaning.

Controversial issues, therefore, have a place in the school curriculum not only because of the substantive importance of the issues which may be raised (as attested by many of the papers in this volume), but also because they provide an introduction to peaceful processes by which such issues can be fully aired and conflicts resolved. This is a very important educational experience for children and thus, in many ways, a condition of the future health of our democracy.

Given such arguments, let us return to the issue of how teachers might conduct themselves if they wish to address such controversial issues. I approach this through a discussion of the concept of 'reflective teaching'.

Reflective Teaching

The Government has consistently argued that it has been working to introduce more control and structure into the curriculum and management of the education service as a means of improving 'educational standards'. At the same time though, there has been a considerable growth in self-consciously reflective and evaluative activity at both school and classroom levels. The work of Stenhouse (1975, 1983) made a big impact here and 'action research' in schools by teachers enquiring into their own practice is now quite common. The value of this type of activity has been noted by Her Majesty's Inspectors and this is particularly apparent in their report *Quality in Schools: the Initial Training of Teachers* (DES, 1987). There they make very clear their support for 'continuing professional development' and argue for:

A continual personal and collective commitment on the part of teachers themselves to (professional) development, and a readiness to see their career as one of continual growth (p. 30).

They continue:

> The foundations for this view of professional life must be
> established during initial training. Students should become
> accustomed to question, to debate, to analyse, to argue from
> evidence, and to examine their own habitual assumptions (p.
> 30).

In initial and in-service teacher education one product of this interest
has been the growth of courses which derive their rationale from a
conception of a 'reflective teacher'. My own work is no exception to
this and has resulted in the production of a classroom handbook
intended to support teachers and student-teachers who wish to engage
in personal/professional enquiry into their own practice (Pollard and
Tann, 1987).

One influence on our thinking on this topic went back to a
reading of Dewey (1933) who contrasted 'reflective action' with
'routine action'. Routine action exhibits the influence of tradition,
habit and authority together with institutionalized and socially
accepted definitions and expectations. In contrast, reflective action
involves a willingness to engage in a continuous process of self-
appraisal, questioning and development. Sarah Tann and I tried to
apply such ideas and we identified four characteristics of reflective
teaching which we take to be particularly important. I will review
them briefly here.

1. Reflective teaching implies an active concern with aims and
consequences, as well as with means and technical efficiency.

This first point relates directly to my concern, expressed earlier, with
the Government's apparently technicist model of the 'good teacher' –
and yet we can draw some comfort from HMI's (1987) injunction to
question, debate, analyze and argue. We might go further though, and
argue that such activity, and a concern with the consequences and
worthwhileness of educational practices, is both a professional and
personal responsibility and, following White (1978), suggest that
teachers should act (as 'activists') to influence the formation of policies
rather than simply see themselves in an implementation role.

2. Reflective teaching combines enquiry and implementation skills
with attitudes of open-mindedness, responsibility and whole-
heartedness.

This important point asserts the significance of combining technically
competent teaching with active enquiry into one's own practice. It

also suggests that complementary attitudes are needed if the teaching process is to be openly and genuinely reflective. Technical skills, on their own, are not sufficient and the suggested attitudes are certainly demanding.

Open-mindedness implies a genuine willingness to question oneself and one's own ideas and practices. As such, it clearly calls for both self-knowledge and self-confidence and it can be enormously helped by the mutual support of other colleagues. The second attitude, whole-heartedness, refers to the care and commitment which has characterized most primary school teachers for some years – though we must all be aware of, and seek to repair, the damage to morale which has been brought about by the cuts, disputes, impositions and criticism of recent years. Responsibility, the final suggested attitude, is particularly important because it highlights the relationship between the micro-world of the classroom and wider socio-politico contexts and the importance of considering aims and consequences. As Zeichner put it:

> Because of the intimate relationships between the school and the social, political and economic contexts in which it exists, any consideration of the consequences to which classroom action leads must inevitably take one beyond the boundaries of the classroom and even of the school itself and beyond the consideration of educational principles alone. ... An exclusive focus on the level of the classroom and on educational principles alone does not enable the student teacher to contemplate the kinds of basic structural changes that may be necessary for his or her responsibility to be fully exercised. The attention of student teachers remains focused on the amelioration of surface symptoms in individuals and not on an analysis of the social conditions that stand behind, and at least partially explain, the existence of those symptoms (Zeichner 1981/2, pp. 6–7).

3. Reflective teaching is applied in a cyclical or spiralling process, in which teachers continually monitor, evaluate and revise their own practice.

This is a relatively straight-forward point (though a very tough discipline), which essentially describes the action research model of Stenhouse (1975), Elliott (1981) and others.

4. Reflective teaching is based on teacher judgment, informed partly by self-reflection and partly by insights from educational disciplines.

This is the final characteristic in our conceptualization which asserts the primacy of teacher judgment and suggests that it should be supported by both self-evaluation and by whatever research work and analyses may be available.

This model of reflective teaching presents one way of conceptualizing a new type of professional teaching activity. In particular it rests on assumptions about the integrity and commitment of teachers and takes for granted their concern for professional development. However, we also have to recognize that this is a model of a pattern of action, a process, and, save for the suggested attitude of social responsibility, it does not necessarily imply any particular links between the reflective process and the ends to which it is put. Thus, to leave the matter there would be quite inadequate for it would gloss this major issue.

When Sarah Tann and I came to write our book we were rather worried by this point and wanted to find a statement of value commitment which would have some moral authority and would command widespread support. In the end we rested our case on the European Convention of Human Rights and on Recommendation No. R(85)7 of the Council of Europe – parts of which were cited earlier.

Of course, others may feel different allegiances and, as I argued earlier, it is inevitable that value issues have to be faced by teachers who really reflect deeply about their work. Furthermore, if they take the view that education should be concerned with social justice as well as with developing and maximizing the skills and intellectual capacities of individual children, then the pressure to introduce issues which might be deemed controversial into the curriculum may be considerable. And yet it is often done – even on teaching practice, as the case which I discuss below shows.

The case which I draw on here concerns a class of 21 mixed juniors, aged 9 and 10, from a large and very old school in the centre of a major south coast resort. The class was being taught by a young, male post-graduate student on an eight week teaching practice which was the culmination of his teacher education course. I initially visited the school in the role of an external examiner to observe the student at work with the class and to talk with the children, with teachers and with the student. However, since I was impressed by what I saw, I gathered more information about the progress and reception of the topic itself.

Of course, the idea that consideration of the election process by a class of 9-year-olds could be controversial in itself requires comment, particularly in the light of the advice of the Council of Europe. However, the student explained to me that the headteacher had been extremely nervous throughout the project and had feared that there might be parental complaints if it was not handled very carefully. As the head explained to me, it was the first time that anything like this had been done in the school and, whilst he was in favour of it (assuming that no trouble arose), he would not actually have encouraged his staff 'to take such risks'. He need not have worried – for the student was very competent, aware and assured.

The work on elections arose as part of a larger topic on 'work' in which the employment experiences of people were discovered, analyzed and discussed. The topic included a comparison of various people and their work – for instance, when I visited the class a 'debate' took place in which three different groups of children spoke for, respectively, the manager of an optical company, an employee of a large supermarket and a nurse. The focus of the debate was 'which job was the most important'. The children had visited the place of work of each person and had interviewed them about their roles, responsibilities and working conditions. They had worked as a group to research and prepare a case for the person whom they represented and they presented this case to the rest of the class collectively. For this purpose the classroom had been arranged into a horseshoe-shaped debating chamber with the student acting as a kind of 'speaker'. Since it was but one of a series of such debates certain groundrules had been established – signal if you want to speak, don't interrupt, make your point clearly and try to justify it, don't ramble.

The student was self-confident and projected both himself and the activity positively. Thus, in his introductory remarks he provided a crisp review of the topic so far, interested the children in the issues which he thought might come up in the debate and briefly reminded them of the groundrules. He set up the conditions in which controversy could be managed constructively. This had been his practice throughout the period of school experience.

He had linked consideration of the election process to the topic on work by looking at the job of a councillor, of the returning officer and at the role of the candidates and their party workers. This had developed in two ways, legally and politically, so that he had been able to introduce the children to the legal framework which determines the conduct of elections and also to the political activity of the candidates and parties.

A great strength of the election aspect of the topic was that it fed off and monitored a real local government election. Children could thus see a real electoral roll, study real election literature and posters and observe genuine political activity and press reports as the days to polling day slipped away. In the course of this they were able to interview the actual candidates in turn and the returning officer. Before each interview they discussed the issues about which they wanted to enquire and prepared lists of questions. They developed interviewing skills through practising on each other and considered the ways in which they could press their points – politely but firmly. They appointed a secretary for each interview to produce a record. After the interviews the responses were analyzed and discussed and, when the school reopened, having been closed for polling day, the focus of work changed to the mathematical and statistical analysis of the results before further discussion of their political significance.

It is worth drawing out a few things which I think this case illustrates particularly well.

The first is the importance of basing work around real issues – in this case the issues of, by what processes political power and responsibility is allocated and how people feel so strongly about different policies and approaches to life. The genuineness of the events which the children monitored and sought to understand contributed a great deal to the momentum of the topic – and I think the children also responded to the implicit compliment that they were both capable of understanding and had a right to know.

A second point is the crucial importance of teacher competence. The issues which were raised in this class could not have been contained and developed constructively without the thought and skill which went into the structuring and organizing of each session. Combined with this, though, is a third point concerning the breadth, perspective and responsibility which was exhibited by the careful and aware way in which each legitimate shade of opinion was aired. This was done in a way which emphasized respect for the rights of candidates to hold their opinions but also ensured that their policies could be systematically interrogated.

A fourth general point concerns interpersonal relationships between the children and the teacher. I think the case does illustrate the existence of the particular sort of classroom climate which has been called 'incorporative' (Pollard and Tann, 1987). In such a classroom there is a great deal of negotiation with children and their individuality is respected. At the same time though, steps are actively taken to incorporate individual children into the work and purposes of the class as a whole – thus strengthening group-focus and a sense of collectivity. It is interesting, in this respect, to consider findings on group-work which show how resistant and stubborn challenges by individuals can in fact raise the quality of group-learning by forcing deeper reflection (Biott, 1987). Perhaps the discussion of controversial issues can act in a similar way to challenge and extend children's thinking.

Overall, the project revealed the social awareness of the student and stands as an example of how young children's thinking might be guided to an appreciation of how personal concerns, like 'jobs', relate to public issues like pay and employment; how personal troubles, such as 'arguments', relate to public issues like political conflict. Above all, it guided the children into thinking about how they, as individuals, will, one day, as citizens, be able to participate in public decision-making.

The topic which, in the eyes of the headteacher, was seen as being risky and controversial, came to be seen as a great success in the hands of a reflective and conscientious student-teacher.

Conclusion

I began this paper by distinguishing between a 'normal' and a 'controversial' curriculum, and I then argued two main points. First, that the discussion of controversial issues in school can be a valuable preparation, *per se*, for future participation in the democratic process, and second, that teachers need to approach such work in particularly socially aware and reflective ways, in addition to exhibiting the technical competence which is associated with 'good teaching'. I do not know where the national curriculum is leading us at present on these issues but, given that one of the few things in life which seems to be certain is that of change itself, it appears likely that controversial issues cannot really be extinguished from the school curriculum. After all, in one sense, without controversy we would not know what the 'normal' curriculum was and, in addition, is not much controversy simply a symptom of change – a necessary consequence of the disturbance of vested interests produced by 'progress'?

If such arguments do have some merit then there will be plenty of scope for 'good' and 'reflective' teachers to address controversial issues in the future. Furthermore, in my view, such consideration will remain both a valuable and socially responsible activity.

References

BERLAK, H. and BERLAK, A. (1981) *The Dilemmas of Schooling*, London, Methuen.

BIOTT, C. (1987) 'Cooperative group work: pupils' and teachers' membership and participation', *Curriculum*, 8, 2, pp. 5–13.

BRIDGES, D. (1986) 'Dealing with controversy in the school curriculum: a philosophical perspective', in WELLINGTON, J.J. (Ed.) *Controversial Issues in the Curriculum*, Oxford, Blackwell.

BROADHEAD, P. (1987) 'A blueprint for the good teacher? The HMI/DES model of good primary practice', *British Journal of Educational Studies*, 35, 1, pp. 57–70.

COHEN, S. (1972) *Folk Devils and Moral Panics*, Oxford, Martin Robertson.

COUNCIL OF EUROPE, (1985) *Recommendation No. R(85)7 of the Committee of Ministers to Member States on the Teaching and Learning about Human Rights in Schools*, Strasbourg, Council of Europe.

DEPARTMENT OF EDUCATION AND SCIENCE (1985) *Better Schools*, Cmnd 9469, London, HMSO.

DEPARTMENT OF EDUCATION AND SCIENCE (1987) *Quality in Schools: the Initial Training of Teachers*, London, HMSO.

DEWEY, J. (1983) *How We Think: A Restatement of the Relation of Reflective Thinking to the Educative Process*, Chicago, Henry Regnery.

ELLIOTT, J. (1981) 'Action research: a framework for self-evaluation in schools', *Teacher–Pupil Interaction and the Quality of Learning Project, Working Paper No. 1*, Cambridge, Cambridge Institute of Education.

GRAMSCI, A. (1978) *Selections from Political Writings*, London, Lawrence and Wishart.

HER MAJESTY'S INSPECTORATE (1982) *The New Teacher in School*, London, HMSO.

HER MAJESTY'S INSPECTORATE (1985) *Education Observed 3 – Good Teachers*, London, HMSO.

KING, R.A. (1978) *All Things Bright and Beautiful? A Sociological Study of Infant Classrooms*, Chichester, Wiley.

KOGAN, M. (1978) *The Politics of Educational Change*, Manchester, Manchester University Press.

POLLARD, A. (1988) 'Competition and control in primary education', in EVANS, J. (Ed.) *Teachers, Teaching and Control in the P.E. Curriculum*, Lewes, Falmer Press.

POLLARD, A. and TANN, S. (1987) *Reflective Teaching in the Primary School*, London, Cassell.

STENHOUSE, L. (1975) *An Introduction to Curriculum Research and Development*, London, Heinemann.

STENHOUSE, L. (1983) *Authority, Education and Emancipation*, London, Heinemann.

WHITE, J. (1978) 'The primary school teacher as servant of the State', *Education 3–13*, 7, 2, pp. 18–23.

ZEICHNER, K. (1981/2) 'Reflective teaching and field-based experience in pre-service teacher education', *Interchange*, 12, pp. 1–22.

Chapter 5

Perceptions of the Primary and Middle School Curriculum

Hilary Burgess

In recent years there has been much controversy over primary education concerning what is taught, what is learned and what are the purposes of schooling. Some commentators, such as Simon (1981), have examined changes within the primary school from a historical perspective, documenting the major influences since the 1960s. He challenges the widely held belief that the majority of primary schools have adopted a progressive child-centred approach to education. Alexander (1984) examines the question 'what is primary education?' in order to develop an understanding of the process of primary schooling. Through the research of these and other educationalists (Galton, Simon and Croll, 1980; Galton and Simon, 1980), it has become evident that there is a gap between educational theory and classroom practice. Furthermore, as Broadfoot (1987) indicates, there has been a gap between research studies, education policy and practice. Broadfoot examines the sociology of education where she argues:

> The role enjoyed by sociology in the late 50s and 60s as a major informant of various branches of social policy has evolved in more recent decades into one where the very legitimacy of its voice as an independent subject is being challenged. The failure of the policies it helped to inform, along with its inherent radicalism, makes sociology a ready scapegoat for the conservative backlash that the current combination of economic and social problems have combined to produce. In no area of social policy is this more apparent than in education, in which not only research, but even the perceived relevance of the traditional sociological input into initial training, is under attack (Broadfoot, 1987, p. 293).

If, as Broadfoot argues, the contribution of sociology to educational theory is ignored, what is the theoretical foundation of schooling to be based upon? In the past, philosophy has provided the basis for holding discussions on educational values and the forms of knowledge, while psychology has given teachers an insight into child development and theories of learning. Is research within these disciplines reflected in classroom practice? What are the beliefs on which primary school teachers base their teaching? Is there a gap between rhetoric and reality and how do teachers interpret the school curriculum? Are there some topics which may be considered too controversial to teach?

It has been argued by Stradling (1984) that, while all school subjects have their controversies and questions which need resolving, there are some issues which can create serious difficulties for teachers. These controversial issues may be subjects about which society itself is divided, such as racism and the rights of sexual minorities. For example, a book for primary schools, *Jenny lives with Eric and Martin* (Bosche, 1983) caused a major debate. In this case, the rhetoric and concern of some educationalists, parents and politicians about the teaching in primary schools of homosexual relations, far outweighed the reality of classroom practice. Indeed, these and other controversial issues are rarely broached by primary school teachers despite the growing interest in areas such as the development of political education in the primary school. Harwood (1985) has examined teacher attitudes to the teaching of political education in primary and middle schools and has found that many teachers are resistant to the notion of introducing such topics into the school curriculum. Such issues challenge teacher perceptions about the capabilities of young children and their ability to understand political concepts. Including political education in the curriculum may also cause confusion for teachers over the aims and objectives of primary schooling. As the survey by Ashton *et al.* (1985) revealed, the major priority of most primary school teachers was to teach their pupils to communicate with others by being literate and this was closely followed by aims concerning numeracy.

Ross (1984) discusses a range of research studies (Jackson, 1971; Stevens, 1982) which show that children can understand political concepts. He comments:

> Despite this wide-ranging evidence that children can and do
> develop political ideas, the tradition in most primary education is
> to avoid the overtly political in the curriculum. Nevertheless,

at the same time they promote a hidden political message, both within the school in the benign authoritarianism that characterises many teacher-child relationships, and outside the school in the propagation of a consensus view of adults always co-operating, never conflicting (Ross, 1984, pp. 132–3).

Ross argues that political education in the primary school should take place at the level of both the formal and the informal curriculum. The available projects which do examine broad societal issues such as *Place, Time and Society* (Schools Council, 1975), however, are rarely used, and Ross concludes that the responsibility for not tackling controversial issues in the classroom lies with the teachers.

Why primary and middle school teachers avoid tackling political education and other controversial issues in the curriculum is a pertinent question for all those interested in primary and middle schooling. It involves examining the beliefs of teachers concerning the physical, social and cognitive development of their pupils and how this is reflected in the taught curriculum. This chapter, therefore, will focus upon primary school ideology, by examining educational writing and research, reports and policy documents on primary education and the practice of teachers through the example of teaching the primary school mathematics curriculum.

Ideology in the Primary School

How is ideology to be interpreted? The *Oxford English Dictionary* defines it as 'the science of ideas'. An ideology, therefore, is based upon the assumptions, values and beliefs which a group of people may hold and which can be expressed as a coherent view. Golby (1988) identifies two broad traditions within primary education, each supported by its own ideology. They are: the elementary tradition and the progressive tradition. The elementary tradition is based upon the importance of 'drilling' children in the basic subjects of reading, writing and arithmetic, while progressivists focus upon the child as the central feature in all aspects of teaching. Here the content of the curriculum is decided by the needs of the individual child.

During the 1950s, 1960s and early 1970s, the progressive, child-centred view of education emerged as the dominant ideology in education texts, reports and documents. For example, in 1950 Edna Mellor, commenting on infant school education, wrote:

> Education...is concerned with the whole child, and with the
> whole of his experience, whether in the home, the school or
> the neighbourhood, whether at first-hand through sense-
> perception and feeling, or at second-hand through the spoken
> or written word, pictures, diagrams, symbols or sounds
> (Mellor, 1950, p. 3).

Such a view epitomizes the education of the 'whole child' philosophy
espoused by progressivists. Here, schooling is to be a natural part of
children's lives where thy may grow and learn as 'nature intended'.
This line of thought received official support from the Ministry of
Education in 1959 when it claimed:

> Primary education today is deeply concerned with children as
> children, with their great diversity of aptitudes, abilities and
> temperaments, with their many, but inter-dependent and
> changing needs (Ministry of Education, 1959, p. v).

Individualism, described here as 'great diversity of aptitudes, abilities
and temperaments' is a key concept in child-centred education and
developed from the practices of nursery and infant school teachers.
However, the report by the Central Advisory Council for Education
(CACE) in 1967 provided overwhelming support for child-centred
education. First, the committee examined individual differences such
as physical growth, the effects of environment and the development
of behaviour. Indeed, the importance of sequential development, as
expressed by Piaget, is given credence, for the committee state:

> According to Piaget, mental structures appear in a sequence as
> coherent and regular as many aspects of physical growth, and
> all people, whatever their variation in pace and final level, pass
> through the same sequence (CACE, p. 18, para. 49).

Sequential development, another key concept in child-centred education, is based upon the acceptance of psychological theory. This has
come in for considerable criticism alongside other ideas about primary
schooling, such as the non-compartmentalization of knowledge and
the role of the teacher as a helper (Peters, 1969; Wilson, 1974). Further
work by Donaldson (1978) has provided evidence that Piaget's
methodology was not as rigorous as it should have been, which casts
doubt upon his findings. (See also Short's chapter in this volume).

The importance of play and readiness for learning are also key
concepts in progressive education. Once again, Plowden provides full
support for this approach to teaching. For example:

529 The child is the agent in his own learning.
530 Skills of reading and writing or the techniques used in art and craft can best be taught when the need for them is evident to children... It takes much longer than teachers have previously realised for children to master through experience new concepts or new levels of complex concepts (CACE, 1967, pp. 194, 195).

The impression given is that the child will guide the teacher. Specific skills in curricula activities are only to be taught when the child is ready to learn.

How far are these ideologies reflected in recent classroom practice? King (1978), in his sociological study of infants schools identified four elements which expressed the infant teacher's child-centred ideology: developmentalism, individualism, play as learning and childhood innocence. King argued that these ideologies have both a practical application in the classroom and an evaluative purpose, in that they influence what teachers and pupils do and guide what should be done in the future. Burgess (1988a) discusses how teachers' perceptions of the curriculum, particularly mathematics, influenced what teachers did and what was taught. Her case study of a primary school demonstrated that these perceptions involved teacher assumptions about the nature of mathematics; The relevance of mathematics within the school curriculum and the influence of teachers' own mathematical education. Within the infant classes studied 'a whole curriculum' approach was evident and the emphasis was upon individual pupil development through enjoyment and activity, as one teacher stated:

When... you are teaching infants, unless there is a subject which you particularly dislike, which I think you can't allow yourself when you are an infant teacher, you have got to have an interest in everything. There are some things which probably catch on with the children, the children enjoy them and you enjoy them... it can be something in English, something in topic work.

Infant teachers, therefore, did not have 'likes' and 'dislikes' about aspects of the curriculum and it was the view of the curriculum as a whole which influenced the learning situation and classroom activities. Indeed, as Alexander (1984) argues, the organization of the primary school on the class-teacher system required a theory which justified practice and matched the subject-based specialist knowledge of secondary teachers. A child-centred ideology fulfilled this need and Alexander states:

> the language of child-centredness [is] the verbal expression of an ideology which remains in the 1980s as powerful and sometimes vehement as it was in the 1960s (Alexander, 1984, p. 15).

If, as Alexander claims, the 'language' of child-centredness is still espoused by primary school teachers in the 1980s, is it also supported by those who teach in the middle school sector?

Middle school education has a relatively short history, only being introduced in some Local Education Authorities since 1968. This development was also advocated by the Plowden committee under their review of the ages and stages of primary education. It was thought that middle schools would ease the transition from primary to secondary schooling, provide greater academic rigour within the curriculum and yet maintain all the traditions of a good primary school. Indeed, the Plowden committee comment:

> If the middle school is to be a new and progressive force it must develop further the curriculum, methods and attitudes which exist at present in junior schools. It must move forward into what is now regarded as secondary schoolwork, but it must not move so far away that it loses the best of primary education as we now know it (CACE, 1967, p. 146).

Such comments in the Plowden Report imply that middle schools were to adopt a largely child-centred ideology. However, as Hargreaves (1980) argues, two opposing ideologies, the secondary, academic, subject-centred ideology and the primary, child-centred ideology found themselves side by side in the middle school. Hargreaves concludes that it was because of the incompatability of these two views that middle schools developed their own 'invention model' of middle schooling. One head teacher of a middle school for pupils aged 10 to 13, encapsulated most of the features of the invention model when he said:

> Well...um...a middle school should be an entity in itself. Initially it depends, I suppose, what the background of the...uh ...each member of staff as to what...how it functions initially. But it's got to have its own identity. It's not just a transit camp between the primary school on the one hand and the secondary school on the other...uh...but nevertheless it's got to take

account, I think, of the best practices of primary education and also the desirable practices for the lower end of the secondary school which secondary schools were not always to implement, because of all sorts of other factors. And they should be…it should be an amalgam of these two things…but it's got to have its own ethos and it's got to have its own objectives (Hargreaves, 1980, p. 103).

Such rhetoric, as Hargreaves argues, 'refracts rather than reflects' the practice of middle schools. Furthermore, Hargreaves (1986) describes how educational policy differs from middle school practice. Rhetoric versus reality, educational policy versus classroom practice are similar, therefore, in both primary and middle schools. Accordingly, the ideology of primary and middle schools maintains a view of both the child and the curriculum which does not allow for the inclusion of subjects which may affect childhood 'innocence' (King, 1978), and which could be regarded as controversial. How far, then, are the perceptions of primary and middle school teachers evident in the educational documents and reports of the 1980s? What kind of educational concepts are being advanced and are they reflected in classroom practice? These questions will be examined by focusing upon three key primary education documents: the Select Committee Report (1986), the Thomas Report (ILEA, 1985) and the Curriculum 5–16 (DES, 1985).

The Ideology of Achievement

The terms 'achievement' and 'levels of attainment' are becoming the rhetoric of primary education in the 1980s, just as the terms 'needs', 'activity' and 'experience' were part of the ideological vocabulary in the 1960s and early 1970s. These concepts of education are evident in the writings of HMI (DES, 1985) and reports on primary schooling such as the Select Committee Report (1986). Indeed, the Select Committee document represents the most detailed examination of primary education since Plowden and the HMI survey (DES, 1978). The task for the Select Committee was:

…to identify those factors which encourage and those which inhibit a child's achievement at primary school (Select Committee, 1986, xiii, 1.4).

However, it is the committee's interpretation of the word 'achievement' which influences the direction and content of the report and which may also affect the selection of controversial issues for inclusion in the curriculum. Here, the analysis of achievement used by the committee reporting on the curriculum and organization of secondary schools (ILEA, 1984) is adopted:

> Aspect 1: academic attainment as measured by examinations of the traditional kind...The capacity to memorise and organise material...
>
> Aspect 2: the capacity to apply knowledge itself: with the practical rather than the theoretical; with the oral rather than the written. Problem solving and investigational skills are more important than the retention of knowledge.
>
> Aspect 3: is concerned with personal and social skills;...communicate with others...co-operate...initiative... self–reliance...ability to work alone...skills of leadership.
>
> Aspect 4: involves motivation and commitment; the willingness to accept failure; the readiness to persevere; the self-confidence to learn in spite of the difficulty of the task. This aspect may be seen both as a prerequisite to the other three aspects of achievement and as an achievement in its own right (Select Committee, 1986, pp. xviii-xix, para 2. 6).

Achievement, therefore, is considered to be academic attainment, the application of knowledge, the development of personal and social skills and the motivation to persevere when faced with failure. This understanding of achievement may suit the subject-centred and examination-orientated secondary school curriculum for which it was originally intended, but can it be so easily applied to the primary curriculum? Such a view appears incompatible with a child–centred ideology. Here also is the opportunity to emphasize the personal and social skills of pupils and examine how a broadly-based curriculum which includes the teaching of controversial issues may enhance both social and moral development. Galton *et al.* (1980) discuss the way in which societal conflict is reflected in the behaviour of infant school children and examines teacher strategies for handling these situations. The strategies used by teachers formed three major groups: involvement/extension; direction/manipulation; and delay/diversion. Issues which teachers had to deal with included race, sex and religion. This small research study raises questions about the way in which teachers handle controversial issues in the classroom and suggests that earlier research, which has mainly concentrated upon the cognitive development of pupils, provides insufficient knowledge about the ways young children behave and learn. Such research extends our knowledge of the behaviour and learning processes of school pupils. However, what factors influenced the Select Committee and what kind of ideology is being used in their analysis of primary education?

At many points in the discussion, a progressive ideology of primary education is discredited. For example, it is claimed that because since 1976 the major issues in educational debate have been 'standards' and 'accountability', 'the frame of reference within which the Plowden Report assumed primary schools would continue to operate was radically changed' (p. xxiii, 3. 5), and later, 'the broadening of the curriculum had resulted in bad as well as good effects' (p. xxiii, 3.6). Accordingly, there is throughout the document a redefinition of 'official' policy on primary education, with the emphasis upon educating pupils for the future, school effectiveness and high teacher performance.

If the 'official' view of primary school ideology is changing, what is the effect upon middle schools? Within the first section of the report the middle school system is discussed in only one paragraph (4, 24). Middle schooling is seen as an organizational pattern which some local education authorities have introduced and is considered to be a 'minority form of provision' (4, 24). There is, therefore, no recognition from the Select Committee that middle schools are an educational phase in their own right as argued by Hargreaves (1980). Indeed, discussion by the Select Committee on the curriculum reveals that only the two stages of primary and secondary education are included in their comments. Furthermore, the dominance of the 'elementary school' ideology with its emphasis upon basic skills and discipline becomes evident in the report.

The curriculum is discussed alongside teaching method and timetabling. There is an emphasis upon the importance of teaching children 'basic skills' as the first sub-title within the section is 'Primary Education and the "3Rs"'. Here, the Select Committee consider whether primary schools are 'concentrating enough on teaching children how to read, write and calculate'. The use of the term 'calculate' is significant as it implies a move back to arithmetic and ignores the developments in the teaching of primary school mathematics advocated by previous reports such as Cockcroft (1982). Discussion on the content of the curriculum, however, appears to support a less directive style of teaching, as the committee argue that the primary curriculum should not be constrained by the use of subject headings which can be strongly associated with timetabling, thereby limiting the inclusion of new curricular material. Further comment on the curriculum is provided by analyses of curriculum documents produced by HMI and the DES and culminates in what the Select Committee consider to be 'the next step' when they recommend:

> a change in the law so as to require the Secretary of State to issue from time to time general guidance on the curriculum; and to introduce a requirement upon local education authorities, governors of county, controlled and special schools to consider the Secretary of State's curricular policy in the process of determining the curricular policy of the LEA or school (Select Committee, 1986, p. ciii 7.8).

Advice, therefore, on the content of the curriculum is very sparse, consisting largely of condensed versions from other documents (DES, 1980; 1981; 1985), while the remainder of their chapter focuses upon levels of performance, assessment, teachers' judgments and the use of objectives and standardized tests.

The rhetoric of the Select Committee is far removed from the child-centred ideology advanced by the texts and reports discussed earlier in this chapter. The ideology of achievement propounded by the Select Committee is founded upon the teaching of basic skills which it is assumed is lacking in the current primary school curriculum. There is an emphasis upon making judgments and assessing performances, both aspects of teaching which, in a child-centred classroom, may have a different interpretation. In the Select Committee Report teacher judgments are considered to be about what is 'right' or 'wrong' in terms of examples of work. For example, '"they" is not properly spelt as "thay"'. This places the teacher in the role of judge and marker rather than that of helper and provider as advocated by a child-centred approach to education. What kind of ideology is being reflected in other documents? Is the rhetoric of child-centredness evident in *The Curriculum from 5–16* (DES, 1985) and the Thomas Report (ILEA, 1985) or do they also reflect an ideology of achievement?

The HMI document *The Curriculum from 5–16* (DES,1985) examines the years of compulsory schooling for pupils and is based upon the findings of previous reports and surveys (DES, 1978; 1979; 1982; 1983). There is an emphasis upon coherence within the curriculum irrespective of whether the pupil attends a first, primary, middle or secondary school. It is stated that pupils should 'have access to a broad, balanced, relevant and coherent curriculum' (DES, 1985, p. 1). In order to achieve this aim HMI consider aspects of curriculum design in terms of nine areas of learning and experience: aesthetic and creative; human and social; linguistic and literary; mathematical; moral; physical; scientific; spiritual; and technological. Secondly, HMI suggest that teachers examine elements of learning, that is, knowledge, concepts, skills and attitudes which they hope to develop in their pupils. Throughout the discussion the key terms are 'breadth', 'balance' and 'relevance'. Indeed, 'breadth' within the primary curriculum is considered especially important when HMI states:

> The curriculum should be broad. That is to say in the terms of this paper it should bring pupils into contact with the nine areas of learning and experience and with the four elements of learning associated with them: not to involve pupils sufficiently in all these areas and elements is to leave their education lacking in some respects. As *Primary Education in England* demonstrated, there is an association between a broad curriculum and successful performance in aspects of language and mathematics (DES, 1985, p. 42).

Here, the link between a broad curriculum and high achievement in the areas of language and mathematics is restated by HMI. It is perhaps extraordinary that the route to achievement is considered by the Select Committee, writing only a year later, to be entirely different and based upon concentration upon the basic skills. Why is evidence, based upon inspections of practice within primary schools, so lightly ignored?

Within the Thomas report (ILEA, 1985) the primary curriculum is defined in two ways: the practical curriculum and the learning curriculum. It is argued that the learning curriculum consists of the ideas, skills, information and attitudes that teachers intend to teach, while the practical curriculum is what teachers and their pupils actually do. Accordingly, the information presented within the report is based upon the observed practice of teachers and pupils in inner London primary schools. The committee worked with five terms of reference, beginning with identifying whole school strategies which enhance achievement and confidence in primary school pupils, particularly those from working-class backgrounds. Other terms of reference included an examination of the effects of parental aspirations, family stress and the expectations of teachers and pupils on a school educational programme. These issues are discussed in relation to the curriculum and classroom practice, and there is a consideration of primary school work in terms of the whole educational life of a pupil and at the stage of transfer to secondary schooling. It is interesting, however, that the discussion in the Thomas Report, Aspects of Achievement, (ILEA, 1985) is very similar to that used a year later in the Select Committee Report. Indeed, a number of issues, such as the teaching of specialist subjects within the curriculum, share a marked similarity of reporting and both reports conclude that the creation of curriculum posts, as used in ILEA, should be available for all primary schools through the appointment of 15,000 extra teachers. The content of the curriculum, however, is given more detailed consideration in the Thomas Report and key areas, such as mathematics, are discussed in depth. Here, the broadening of the mathematics curriculum endorsed by Cockcroft (DES, 1982) is supported by the Thomas committee, although there were some reservations concerning the amount of time spent on practical and individual work. Observations by the committee of classroom practice showed the majority of pupils to be happy and relaxed in their work, a fact which was thought to be directly attributable to 'the greater use of apparatus as an aid to calculation and through which to investigate mathematical ideas; and to the practice of organizing the work so that children are not continuously competing with each other and with the clock to finish a task set to the whole class' (ILEA, 1985, p. 32 para 2. 110). The committee also expressed concern that there was a marked difference between the number of boys and girls achieving 'O' and 'A' level passes in mathematics. However, the committee do not discuss gender-related issues or the use of sexist materials on girls' performances; factors that others have examined (cf. Burgess, 1986). Indeed, the lack of discussion around controversial issues such as gender is compounded by views about how headteachers might implement the recommendations of the Thomas committee and report upon the school's development plan in a section of the annual report to governors. Such views 'appear to endorse the status quo in primary schools which have a large female teaching force and a male dominated leadership' (Burgess, 1986, p. 95).

The three documents discussed above all argue for coherence and structure within the curriculum and yet there are some noticeable differences among them. HMI emphasize a coherent curriculum but also one that is broad, balanced and relevant and much discussion is devoted to areas of learning and experience in curriculum design. The Thomas Report, while promoting the importance of achievement in the primary school does so alongside other factors, such as the performance of working-class pupils and parental involvement, thereby recommending ways of providing equality of educational experience for primary school children. Only some of these themes can be found in the Select Committee Report, which is dominated by discussion on achievement, assessment and arguments which support a narrowly based curriculum which concentrates upon the basic skills of reading, writing and calculation. There is in none of them the whole-hearted approach to child-centred education advocated by Plowden. The concepts of individualization and learning through activity and experience are overtaken by an examination of common aims and objectives and a concentration upon the teaching of skills. Overall, is the dominance of assessing achievement in the primary school. Accordingly, such an ideology militates against a broadening of the curriculum and therefore does not encourage teachers to include the teaching of controversial issues in the primary curriculum.

These reports represent a view of primary education provided by Members of Parliament, HMI, local education authority inspectors and advisers, and some practising teachers, but they do not provide an analysis of classroom practice. While aspects of the curriculum and methods of teaching are discussed, a portrait of what actually happens inside a primary classroom is not achieved. Can the practice of teachers, therefore, be examined through documents and reports of this nature? In order to examine this issue the final section of this chapter will examine research conducted in the primary school.

The Reality of Classroom Practice

Research on schools and classrooms provides detailed portraits of teachers and the activities of their pupils. Comparisons may then be made between actual classroom practice and the rhetoric of documents, reports and educational texts which are used to shape education policy and inform the professional knowledge of teachers. As Alexander (1984, p.79) argues:

> the teacher's professional knowledge is a key factor not only (as HMI argued) in determining the quality of classroom practice, but also in shaping primary ideology and the actual character of the primary curriculum.

One example of how teachers utilize their professional knowledge in classroom practice is discussed in King's (1978) study of infants' classrooms. In each of the three schools he studied, the child-centred ideology advocated in the Plowden Report was reflected in documents such as letters to parents and guidance notes for teachers written by the headmistresses. Further examples of this ideology were to be found in teacher handbooks and texts written by experts. For example, all three schools used, to differing degrees, the same mathematics scheme, *Mathematics for Schools* often known as 'Fletcher Maths' after the senior author. The teachers' handbook which introduces the series has many inferences to child-centredness through the use of phrases such as 'inspire children', 'lively sense of interest and pleasure' and there are references to discovery activities, mathematical development and readiness for learning. However, as King's observations illustrate, the reality of mathematics teaching in these infant schools did not conform to a child-centred philosophy, partly because of the teachers' reliance upon the use of the mathematics series so that 'no child was allowed to work through Book 2 before completing Book 1, or, for example, to learn how to tell the time before learning how to measure length' (King, 1978, pp. 32–3). Mathematics was also mystified by the use of language such as 'partition the set' or 'complete the number sentence' which many infants were unable to read. As King argues, when pupils were reading or writing they were expected to understand every word but in mathematics words could be left meaningless and, therefore, teachers controlled the activities of infant pupils through the reading of instructions and defined the meaning of mathematics for them.

Research by the ORACLE team (Galton, Simon and Croll, 1980) on primary classrooms examined pupil and teacher activity and identified patterns of classroom behaviour. The main aim was to study different teaching approaches in the major curriculum areas. These researchers examined how far the concepts of child–centredness, individualism, flexibility and learning through activity and experience were reflected in the classroom practice of teachers they saw. However, the team discovered that most of the classrooms they observed were organized to suit managerial purposes rather than for ideological reasons. Indeed, while pupils in many classes were seated in groups, they continued to work individually and both movement and activities were restricted by the teacher. These findings bear out the conclusions of the HMI Survey (1978) that a large proportion of children's time is spent on the learning of basic skills in language and mathematics. The ORACLE team conclude:

> There is little in our data to suggest that teachers have in any sense moved seriously away from what has always been regarded as the main function of the junior (or elementary)

school: the inculcation of basic skills, or the grasp of elementary concepts relating to numeracy and literacy (Galton, Simon and Croll, 1980, p. 78).

Classroom practice, therefore, centres around the teaching of basic skills in mathematics, reading and writing and apparently does not consist of the child-centred approach advocated by Plowden, according to the ORACLE team. Further investigations of primary schools also support this paradox of rhetoric versus reality. Burgess (1988c) reports the views of teachers in a case study of mathematics teaching in one primary school. Here, the aim of the study was to examine the way in which teachers defined and redefined the mathematics curriculum. The school, which I called Elm Park Primary, catered for pupils aged 5–11 years and used the scheme *Mathematics for Schools* (Fletcher Maths) in all classes. There were, however, some differences between the infant teachers and junior teachers in that more use was made of practical work in mathematics in the infant classes. Indeed, one infant teacher was able to identify changes in her style of teaching since using the Fletcher maths scheme. This infant teacher explained that she had adopted a pattern of practical work and discussion in the carpeted corner of her classroom followed by a short period of consolidation, specifically because of the Fletcher mathematics scheme. Previously, her teaching style had been more formal with pupils seated at their desks doing work from the blackboard. However, more formal styles of teaching were observed in some of the junior classes where, similarly to those classes described by Galton, Simon and Croll (1980), pupils were seated in groups but working individually or on a whole class basis. Nevertheless, the aims of the school syllabus emphasized an approach to mathematics teaching which could be regarded as child-centred, as the first three points illustrate:

1) the child shall come to understand and really enjoy mathematics as a creative subject.
2) that he shall become aware of the presence of mathematics all around him in everyday life.
3) that he shall develop an understanding of the various aspects of mathematics, and through much practical experience, shall learn to think for himself both logically and analytically (Burgess, 1988c).

Within these points, there is embodied the notion that children learn mathematics if they 'enjoy' it and if they are able to explore the mathematics all around them. It is also claimed that practical experience will enable pupils to think for themselves. How far, therefore, were these aims represented in the classroom practice at Elm Park?

During my time at Elm Park the teaching of division became an important part of the study, as this topic was being taught in the classrooms I observed. The Fletcher mathematics scheme indicated particular methods for the teaching of division which the staff had rejected as too complicated, and the Headteacher, therefore, had outlined a different method, which is set out below:

$12\overline{)379}$ i) There are 3 hundreds and 12 groups, can they have a hundred each?
ii) How many tens are there altogether?
iii) How many tens can we give to each group?

$$12 \times 1 = 12$$
$$12 \times 2 = 24$$
$$12 \times 3 = 36$$
$$12 \times 4 = 48$$

The answer is between 3 and 4.

$$\begin{array}{r} 3 \\ 12\overline{)379} \\ -36 \\ \hline 19 \end{array}$$

iv) How many tens are left?
v) How many tens and units are left?

$$\begin{array}{r} 31 \\ 12\overline{)379} \\ -36 \\ \hline 19 \\ -12 \\ \hline 7 \end{array}$$

vi) How many units to each group?

$$12 \times 1 = 12$$
$$12 \times 2 = 24$$

vii) How many units are left?
Answer: 31 r 7

However, when I observed a fourth year junior class being taught long division the method was again different; the class were taught as a whole rather than on an individual basis, and no use was made of practical apparatus. The process by which these pupils were taught long division is as follows:

$$\begin{array}{r} 22 \text{ r } 10 \\ 12\overline{)274} \\ -24 \\ \hline 34 \\ 24 \\ \hline 10 \end{array}$$

How many 12s in 27? – 2. Put the answer above the line. 2 12s are 24, take 24 away from 27 and you are left with 3. Move the 4 units next to the 3 tens. How many 12s in 34? – 2. Put the answer above the line. 2 12s are 24, take 24 away from 34 and you are left with 10. How many 12s in 10 – none. Therefore, the answer is 22 r 10.

The aims for mathematics teaching at Elm Park which emphasize enjoyment, activity and awareness of mathematics, the example for teaching division provided by the head teacher and the reality of classroom practice are significantly different. Accordingly, teachers' aims for teaching the mathematics curriculum may be narrowly concerned with basic numeracy skills (Ashton *et al.*, 1985; Burgess, 1988c) or there may be a reliance upon the use of texts (King, 1978). Where classroom practice consists mainly of the teaching of basic skills there is little opportunity for the introduction of controversial issues such as anti-racism, anti-sexism and political education. Indeed, the case of middle schools further highlights the discrepancy between educational rhetoric, educational theory and classroom practice.

Hargreaves (1986) has examined the culture of middle schools in depth. He states:

> When middle schools first emerged in the late 1960s and early 1970s, they were swathed in an optimistic rhetoric of educational justification. While the administrative and economic advantages of middle schools – the fact that they could be conveniently fitted into existing buildings – were commonly acknowledged, a great deal of weight was placed on the *educational* reasons for their development (Hargreaves, 1986, p. 3).

Such educational justification for middle schooling included the desire to extend the best of primary school practice to older pupils. However, the reality of middle school practice may depend, argues Hargreaves, upon whether the teachers regarded themselves as specialists or generalists according to their education and training. The problems and difficulties that this might cause, however, are rarely considered or discussed in educational texts and documents. Hargreaves suggests that the reality of middle schooling as illustrated by his case studies of Riverdale and Moorhead, shows that there may be serious internal imbalances, with the lower years being taught by teachers who are generalists and follow a developmental tradition, while the upper years are taught by secondary trained specialists who emphasize setting by ability, basic skills and firm discipline. The classroom practice, therefore, of primary and middle schools does not appear to reflect the educational rhetoric of official reports, policy papers, HMI discussion documents and school syllabuses.

Conclusion

What has educational research into primary and middle school practice revealed in terms of child-centred education and how might this affect the teaching of controversial issues? The examples from King (1978) and Burgess (1988c) show that while teachers have incorporated into their professional knowledge and educational language the child-centred philosophy, in translation into practice much of the theory is lost. Similarly, Galton, Simon and Croll (1980) suggest that the Plowden ideal of individualization was misinterpreted in practice because of the magnitude of managerial problems, and group teaching, also advocated by Plowden, was, in many classrooms, little more than a seating arrangement. However, both the rhetoric and reality of primary schooling may work against the inclusion of controversial issues in the curriculum. While the ideology of primary school teachers regards young children as being incapable of developing concepts concerning issues such as racial unrest, political education or sexual behaviour, strategies for dealing with these aspects are unlikely to be developed by teachers. And, while the reality of classroom practice for many pupils consists of a concentration upon reading, writing and mathematics, little time will be available for the inclusion of other topics.

Indeed, teachers may be discouraged from changing traditionally held views when educational research by Bennett (1976) and Bennett *et al.* (1984) has examined effective teaching practice and concluded that more formal or traditional teaching styles result in slightly increased pupil achievement in mathematics and language. The overwhelming conclusion appears to be that the child-centred philosophy enshrined in Plowden was never fully implemented in primary and middle schools. Furthermore, research in educational psychology and mathematics (Donaldson, 1978; Hughes, 1986) has shaken the Piagetian based theory of child-centredness. Such educational studies have illuminated the weakness of educational theory since the 1960s. However, more importantly, educational research has shown the direction future classroom studies need to take in examining issues such as effective group-work, classroom management, the use of teacher time and young children's conceptual understanding of a wide range of societal issues. Research in all these areas may begin to provide primary and middle school teachers with a coherent educational theory which they will be able to interpret in practice. This may well depend, however, on the resilience of teachers to survive the 'new rhetoric' of achievement and levels of attainment which is already being perpetrated in official educational policy documents. Indeed, current developments concerning the content of the National Curriculum and proposals for testing primary pupils at the ages of 7 and 11 politically militate against any significant change in teacher attitudes. As Kogan (1987) comments:

> ...the Plowden Committee, as the last of its line, serves as a
> good monument to a healthy tradition, but one already
> moving into social, political and intellectual contexts where its

multiplicity of objectives and of art forms made it inadequate for the more complex challenges of the 1980s. A more detached and expert entity capable of analysing the state of education is needed. And that needs to be placed under the control of a body which is not committed to pursuing the latest policies laid down by Downing Street but instead able to collate the knowledge and feelings of those who use education for good ends (Kogan, 1987, p. 20).

As Kogan argues, a new 'entity' is required to examine the state of education and in particular primary schooling. Such an entity might do well to utilize the expertise of sociologists, psychologists and practising teachers, thereby providing a base for the development of an educational theory which, in the 1990s, can be effectively translated into practice.

References

ALEXANDER, R.J. (1984) *Primary Teaching*, London, Holt, Rinehart and Winston.

ASHTON, P.M.E., KNEEN, P., DAVIES, F. and HOLLEY, B.J. (1975) *The Aims of Primary Education: A Study of Teachers' Opinions*, London, Macmillan.

BENNETT, N. (1976) *Teaching Styles and Pupil Progress*, London, Open Books.

BENNETT, N., DESFORGES, C., COCKBURN, A. and WILKINSON, B. (1984) *The Quality of Pupil Learning Experiences*, London, Lawrence Erlbaum Associates.

BOSCHE, S. (1983) *Mette Bor Hof Morten Og Erik* (English, *Jenny Lives with Eric and Martin*) with photographs by Andreas Hansen, Translated from Danish by Louis Mackay, London, Gay Men's Press.

BROADFOOT, P. (1987) 'Theory and practice in sociology of education', in WALFORD, G. (Ed.) *Doing Sociology of Education*, Lewes, Falmer Press, pp. 293–309.

BURGESS, H. (1986) 'Doubting Thomas: the primary curriculum and classroom practice', *Journal of Education Policy*, 1, 1, pp. 85–99.

BURGESS, H. (1988a) 'Collaborating in curriculum research and evaluation', in WOODS, P. and POLLARD, A. (Eds) *Sociology and Teaching: A New Challenge for the Sociology of Education*, London, Croom Helm, pp. 176–91.

BURGESS, H. (1988b) 'Curriculum practice in the primary school: the case of mathematics', in CULLINGFORD, C. (Ed.) *The Primary Teacher*, London, Cassells.

BURGESS, H. (1988c) *The Primary Curriculum and Classroom Practice*, London, Unwin Hyman.

CACE (1967) *Children and their Primary Schools* (Plowden Report), London, HMSO.

DEPARTMENT OF EDUCATION AND SCIENCE (1978) *Primary Education in England: a Survey by HM Inspectors of Schools*, London, HMSO.

DEPARTMENT OF EDUCATION AND SCIENCE (1979) *Aspects of Secondary Education in England: Survey by HM Inspectors of Schools*, London, HMSO.

DEPARTMENT OF EDUCATION AND SCIENCE (1980) *A View of the Curriculum*, London, HMSO.

DEPARTMENT OF EDUCATION AND SCIENCE (1981) *The School Curriculum*, London, HMSO.

DEPARTMENT OF EDUCATION AND SCIENCE (1982) *Mathematics Counts* (Cockcroft Report), London, HMSO.

DEPARTMENT OF EDUCATION AND SCIENCE (1983) *9–13 Middle Schools: An Illustrative Survey*, London, HMSO.

DEPARTMENT OF EDUCATION AND SCIENCE (1985) *The Curriculum from 5 to 16*, Curriculum Matters 2, An HMI Series, London, HMSO.

DONALDSON, M. (1978) *Children's Minds*, London, Fontana.

GALTON, M. and SIMON, B. (Eds) (1980) *Progress and Performance in the Primary Classroom*, London, Routledge and Kegan Paul.

GALTON, M., SIMON, B. and CROLL, P. (1980) *Inside the Primary Classroom*, London, Routledge and Kegan Paul.

GOLBY, M., (1988) 'Relationships between practice and theory', in Campbell, R.J. (Ed.) *The Routledge Compendium of Primary Education*, London, Routledge and Kegan Paul.

HARGREAVES, A. (1980) 'The ideology of the middle school', in HARGREAVES, A. and TICKLE, L. (Eds) *Middle Schools: Origins, Ideology and Practice*, London, Harper and Row.

HARGREAVES, A. (1986) *Two Cultures of Schooling: The Case of Middle Schools*, Lewes, Falmer Press.

HARWOOD, D. (1985) 'We need political not Political education for 5–13 year olds', *Education 3–13*, 13, 1, pp. 12–17.

HUGHES, M. (1986) *Children and Number: Difficulties in Learning Mathematics*, Oxford, Basil Blackwell.

ILEA (1984) *Improving Secondary Schools* (Hargreaves Report), London, ILEA.

ILEA (1985) *Improving Primary Schools* (Thomas Report), London, ILEA.

JOHNSON, R. (1971) 'The development of political concepts in young children', *Educational Research*, 14, pp. 51–5.

KING, R. (1978) *All Things Bright and Beautiful? A Sociological Study of Infants' Classrooms*, Chichester, Wiley.

KOGAN, M. (1987) 'The Plowden Report twenty years on', *Oxford Review of Education*, 13, 1, pp. 13–21.

MELLOR, E. (1950) *Education Through Experience in the Infant School Years*, Oxford, Blackwell.

MINISTRY OF EDUCATION (1959) *Primary Education (Suggestions for the consideration of teachers and others concerned with the work of Primary Schools)*, London, HMSO.

PETERS, R. (Ed.) (1969) *Perspectives on Plowden*, London, Routledge and Kegan Paul.

ROSS, A. (1984) 'Developing political concepts and skills in the primary school', *Educational Review*, 36, 2, pp. 131–9.

SCHOOLS COUNCIL (1975) *Place, Time and Society 8–13*, London, Schools Council.

SELECT COMMITTEE (1986) *Achievement in Primary Schools* (Third Report from the Education, Science and Arts Committee), London, HMSO.

SIMON, B. (1981) 'The primary school revolution: myth or reality?', in Simon, B. and Willcocks, J. (Eds) *Research and Practice in the Primary Classroom*, London, Routledge and Kegan Paul.

STEVENS, O. (1982) *Children Talking Politics*, Oxford, Martin Robertson.

STRADLING, R. (1984) 'The teaching of Controversial Issues: an evaluation', *Educational Review*, 36, 2, pp. 121–9.

WILSON, P. (1974) 'Plowden aims', *Education 3–13*, 2, 1, pp. 52–5.

Chapter 6

The Teaching of Controversial Issues: The Problems of the Neutral-chair Approach

Basil Singh

If in moments of cool and informed reflection our children decide to become Nazis, should we simply tell them to create the future as they see fit? (Callan, 1985, p. 10).

The fool who yearns for Neutrality indulges a special kind of silliness. There can be no politics without vision, no philosophy without commitment. Neutrality is not just another political slogan. If taken seriously it will destroy the most distinctive feature of politics...(Ackerman, 1983, p. 372).

What is said for politics could well be said for education. Thus, this chapter wishes to emphasize that, if taken seriously, neutrality could destroy some of the most cherished ideals in education, such as the respect for evidence and the respect for others.

Introduction

In every society there are 'absolute prohibitions' against such things as the taking of innocent lives, theft and child abuse, without which the society cannot exist (MacIntyre, 1981, p. 156). Hence in every society the good of the individual is somehow bound up with the well-being of others. It is, therefore, the central task of education to strengthen the individual's desire to promote the good of others as well as, or as a consequence of, promoting their own good. In promoting such a desire one could, of course, try to get pupils to see the reason for doing so. But if such reasons are rejected then we would have to appeal to the individual's feelings. For ultimately, morals cannot be based on reason alone (White *et al.*, 1986, p. 166). Where reasons are rejected, according to White and his colleagues, education must attempt to guide and shape. Where reason is ignored, then education must steer pupils towards altruism: that is, towards a life in which shared moral goods predominate. It is because of this that I wish to argue that an education that is concerned with a life in which shared moral goods ought to predominate cannot be an education that is in essence neutral.

It is the purpose of this chapter to question the basic premise of the neutral-chair approach, especially in relation to the teaching of multicultural or anti-racist education. I will also argue that while the notion of procedural neutrality offers some interesting guides to the practising teacher in terms of the development of pupils' rationality, it is nevertheless only one among many of the existing methods of teaching that could bring about this end. Having said this, it is still not clear whether the use of such a method will result in the development of the qualities of mind or character that is claimed by supporters of the neutral-chair position. More importantly, I see this position as a highly problematic one and quite unacceptable in the teaching of controversial moral issues relating to forms of discrimination.

Cognitive and Affective Development

According to Bridges (1980), an advocate of procedural neutrality, argument based on reason and evidence can take us only so far in ethical argument. It seems to follow then that we cannot rely on reason alone to get racists to change their minds or actions against certain groups of people. There is nothing to stop racists from arguing that their customary practices are morally correct and that their preferred beliefs are true and are based on rational grounds. It may be pointed out by racists that there is no recognisable standard of reasoning by which they can be shown to be absolutely false or incorrect. They could justify their beliefs on cultural grounds, insisting that their argument, as everyone else's, is culturally context bound. In consequence: 'their justification of racism flows deductively with the appearance of rationality'. (Jones, 1985, p. 230)

I want to argue that discrimination based on 'race', for instance, is *not* wholly constituted of reason based on argument, evidence or experiment. Rather, it is constituted of elements of emotions, feelings, attitudes and beliefs. Consequently, mere development of the cognitive faculty, or an appeal to facts or argument, would not be sufficient to remove it. Hence prejudices, according to Phillips-Bell (1982 pp. 169–70), may not be reversible when exposed to new information or further experience: 'There is an emotional resistance to the unseating of a prejudice and a tendency to apprehend new evidence in a manner which distorts the evidence to conform with the prejudice'.

If the resilience of prejudice is true, then it follows that if we want to remove prejudice from the classroom, education directed towards this end must be concerned with right thinking as well as with right feelings and right actions. Rationality must, therefore, be cultivated within a moral, affective framework which provides the pre-condition of the individual attaining his/her own well-being as well as that of others. Education must be seen in terms of the development of the 'whole person'. It must provide the framework within which pupils can appreciate and judge the 'good life of individuals', which could be seen in terms of a quest. As MacIntyre (1981, p. 204) puts it: '...the good life from man is the life spent in seeking for the good life for man'. And, in spite of the problematic nature of what constitutes a good life, I want to agree with the view of White and his colleagues (1986) that the good life cannot be the life of a Nero, a Hitler or a Stalin.

Thus, although teachers should start from the premise that in morals there is no way of proving what system is the best, they must also recognize that there are ways of arguing reasonably and rationally, which at least will exclude some ways or some possibilities. At the end of the day, people may still differ, but it is likely that they may differ less violently the more they know about the lives, motives, beliefs and culture of those they differ from. As Crick observes: 'Prejudice does not vanish with greater knowledge, but it is usually diminished and more containable...' (1972, p.9).

Aims of Neutral Teaching

Neutral teaching is often seen as a means of developing the autonomy of pupils and thereby avoiding indoctrinating them into the values, morals or beliefs of the teacher or of society. Stenhouse (1970), for instance, has argued that neutrality may be seen as the proper business of an education which aims to develop pupils' rationality through a method of discussion rather than by instruction. According to him, in following the stance of procedural neutrality, teachers will be required to facilitate discussion among their pupils by feeding into such discussions evidence and argument drawn from rich and balanced sources. They are not required to take part in such discussions or use their authority to influence the discussion one way or the other. The success of such a procedure, according to its advocates, is judged by the development of open-mindedness in pupils.

It would seem from a reading of the literature that one of the basic assumptions of procedural neutrality is that teachers occupy a position of authority over their students and therefore any views they may express on, say, controversial issues will carry extra weight and influence over the children. However, there is little research evidence to support or invalidate this assumption (Stradling, *et al.*, 1984, p. 7). Even the recent work by Stenhouse and Verma (1981) into the problems and effects of teaching about race relations, does not seem to support this view. In their investigation, teachers were asked to teach about race relations through three differing strategies. Strategy A involved teaching through discussion, in which the teachers acted as neutral-chairs in the tradition of the Humanities Curriculum Project (Stenhouse, 1970). Strategy B was a form of teaching in which the teachers expressed their commitment to fight racism by offering themselves as exemplars of those actively critical of racism in its various forms. Strategy C involved teaching through improvised educational drama. The research by Stenhouse and Verma (1981) adopted the following aims:

> To educate for the elimination of racial tension and ill-feeling within our society – which is and will be multiracial – by undermining prejudice, by developing respect for varied traditions and by encouraging mutual understanding, reason-ableness and justice (p.332).

The results showed that no strategy was superior. What is clear from the study is that in each strategy and in each control group, some pupils moved in each direction, that is, even the strategy where teachers aimed to moderate racism resulted in some pupils becoming more racist. Similar variations occurred from school to school. Hence, the researchers pointed out, however deeply a desired attitude is valued, the teacher cannot expect to win every student in a group towards it (Stenhouse and Verma, 1981, p. 337). If this is the case then one may rightly ask: why so much emphasis on 'neutrality'? And, indeed, this is very much the kind of thing that some critics of the Humanities Curriculum Project have found unacceptable.

One thing seems clear from the study and that is, either attempts to avoid stating one's views or directly taking sides on an issue may fail in its intentions. Nevertheless, there is some evidence carried out by the Schools Council's Moral Education Project which points to the conclusion that:

> The easy identification of teachers' value positions is a good thing from the pupils' point of view and not something to be regretted. Our principal reason for believing this, for favouring commitment, is that 65 per cent of boys and girls between thirteen and sixteen (in a survey referred to elsewhere) ...expected adults to 'come off the fence', to be willing to reveal their views when asked. Adolescents in a survey claimed, and we believed they were right, that to refuse to state what you think about an issue while expecting others to do so is to adopt a superior position in which you treat others as less than persons (McPhail *et al.* 1972, p. 89).

The project described by McPhail and his colleagues favours various 'good reasons for...teacher commitment, rather than attempted neutrality in moral education'. It also raises the salient question: 'If teachers do not reveal their value positions, where do pupils get their value-judgments and suggested behaviour from?'. They recognize the value of discussion and role play as sources of such judgments and suggested behaviour, but add that 'peer group work on occasions requires outside support and stimulation'. They also acknowledge the value of parents as a source of information, judgment and behaviour to their children. However, they warn that sometimes, where parental communication with their children breaks down, this will leave 'the field open to the mass media, books and curriculum material used in schools as sources of value-judgment', if 'the teacher is non-committed' (1972, p. 90).

Thus, without the kind of contribution that teachers can make, children are likely to receive from various sources a selection of views which are in no sense exhaustive. Consequently, children 'badly need criticism and expansion which can only come from individuals, including teachers, who are willing to take the trouble'. They continue by noting that: 'clarification and help over the criteria of judgment are essential', and suggest that by helping pupils to clarify their points of view teachers must not present themselves as the ultimate authority. What is needed is a 'variety of comment from people who care and are willing to speak' (1972, p. 90).

The authors also argue that the teacher should avoid attempting to create too dependent a relationship of pupils on teachers:

> If adolescents are bullied about what is right and wrong, they may either abandon the attempt to find answers for themselves

and remain as inadequate dependent adults devoid of ideas and incapable of change, or retreat into peer groups after severing their relations with the whole parent-teacher generation (McPhail *et al.*, 1972, p. 91).

Bearing this in mind 'a teacher should not inhibit discovery by saying too much, too soon, too often, but this is not equivalent to taking a permanent neutral stand'. After all, it could be argued that for teachers to adopt the role of procedural neutrality is for them to deny the group's opinion, which, in some sense, it is entitled to as part of the reciprocal engagement of discussion. The group might articulate a range of significantly different points of view which may provide a basis for challenging and criticizing the opinions received from the media, peers or family.

Stradling and his colleagues (1984) came to the same conclusion as McPhail *et al.* They found that if this denial is implied in the practice of procedural neutrality, then the practice seems to require something less than what is called open discussion. Their work also shows that teachers seem to view balance, neutrality and commitment not as educational principles but as teaching strategies which may or may not be useful for handling controversial issues. For these teachers, if students have a lot to say, if there is a broad spread of opinion, and if their views are based on knowledge and experience, rather than blind prejudice, then there is a good case for adopting the role of a neutral chair. In other circumstances the balanced or committed approaches might be more appropriate (Stradling *et al.* 1984, p. 11).

Consequently for Stradling and his colleagues, it was simply not possible 'to lay down hard and fast rules about teaching controversial subject matter to be applied at all times'. They argued that teachers have to take account of the knowledge, values and experiences which the pupils bring with them into the classroom, the teaching methods which predominate in other lessons, the climate of the classroom and the age and ability of the students. Teachers must also be responsive to the reactions of pupils, to the content of lessons and the teaching methods being employed. For, according to these investigators, 'any controversial issue can arouse strong emotions leading to a polarization of the class and consequent hostility' (1984, p. 11).

Thus they emphasize that 'different circumstances in the classroom require different methods and strategies and there is no guarantee that a strategy which works with one set of pupils will necessarily work with another group'. Many attitudes and prejudices are formed early in life and are well established before children enter secondary schools. Furthermore, many such prejudices are strongly reinforced at home amongst friends, groups which often have more authority and influence with children than their teachers.

Hence, while the principle of the neutral-chair is correct in advocating that teachers should maintain open enquiry and encourage rationality, it fails to take into account that such ideas may require the teacher to take the opposite view. It may demand that teachers put forward counter-arguments in order to redress the balance. Teachers must not, of course, present themselves as authorities who have the last word. Nonetheless, if the issues are those on which people disagree, then perhaps pupils, too, should be neutral in relation to these views. If this is the case then it will make nonsense of the principle that we should encourage pupils to reason and to make up their own minds. The question is: Why should one make up one's mind on an issue that is controversial? The logical outcome of the neutral-chair stance may lead pupils to become sceptical not only about their own views but about the views, beliefs and values of their parents. Thus, while teachers must not let their pupils believe that the 'professional's' view is the only rational one, they are also under an obligation to stress that parents' and peers' views must also be subjected to the same critical scrutiny. Would it lead to the belief that it does not matter whether one believes in anything? For if one can never claim that certain ideas or views are more rational or acceptable than others, or that one has better reasons than others for entertaining certain views, then one may well ask: Why hold any view at all? Is the teacher then to let sexism, racism, fascism or other kinds of discrimination go unchecked because they are part of the stock of views of some parents, some peer groups or some pupils' culture or religious inheritance (Walkling and Brannigan, 1986, pp. 16–25)? Moreover, what of those views that might promote discrimination based not only on sex, race or class, but also on physical and mental handicap? Might not one ask then: what is the purpose of open enquiry or discussion, if the assumption is that it will not in time lead to justifiable judgments at some point? It is in answer to these questions that I agree with Bailey, who argues that 'protection of divergence of views can only be a temporary tactic in the search for the truth, not an end in itself' (Bailey, 1975, p. 76).

The justification for having a discussion is that it helps us, or should help us, to be clearer about the issues under discussion. The justification, as we are assuming here, must eventually be based either on evidence or argument, even if all evidence 'implies a value position and needs to be critically examined' (Stenhouse, 1970, p. 10).

One is tempted to ask whether some kinds of evidence are not more relevant or more compelling than others and whether teachers shouldn't be in a better position than their pupils to assess the various views and claims made upon evidence in relation to certain topics (Dearden, 1981, p. 42). For as teachers we are concerned not just with giving pupils a shop-window tour of various moral or religious opinions, for example, but with pursuing the question of whether some of them may be correct or mistaken. The procedure whereby we may determine this may require more than a chairperson: we need a teacher and a leader in argument.

Although I do not wish to get into the debate as to what a controversial issue is, I want to draw the reader's attention to the fact that the epithet 'controversial' is not confined to social issues. Furthermore, as Dearden argues, values are by no means a necessary or even a sufficient condition for an issue to be designated controversial. For there are value judgments which are entirely uncontroversial. In justifying this claim, Dearden (1981, p. 42) asks us to:

> Consider the moral value judgement that it is not only wrong but viciously so when someone amuses himself by stubbing out burning cigarettes on a baby entrusted to his care...

That such an act is wrong is uncontroversial. Nevertheless, how we settle this matter is not the same as we would go about settling the issue as to whether the Normans invaded Britain in 1066, or the causes for the disappearance of the Dodo, or of the origin of the universe.

Consequently, in both factual and non-factual cases where teachers think the evidence is genuinely inconclusive, they must say that there is really no definite ground for coming down on one side or the other. What the teachers must not do is to mislead their pupils into believing that either evidence does not matter or there is no such thing as evidence. As Warnock (1975, p. 108) puts it:

> If all evidence were inconclusive, then the concept of evidence itself would be, if not empty, at least radically different.

The principle of neutrality as expressed by Stenhouse (1970) stresses that teachers should protect 'divergence of views', and should seek to improve understanding by feeding into the discussion rich, diverse and balanced evidence. However, such an approach cannot anticipate whether such discussion will be valued. There is also the problem of the selection of topics for debate. Consider, for example, the opinions that the National Front and Commission for Racial Equality might each express on the matter of 'race'. Here there are special difficulties concerning an understanding of the background in which the issues arise and the concepts that characterize them. On the other hand, is there any necessary connection between understanding a viewpoint and gaining an increased respect for persons who hold it? This is an empirical issue which cannot be settled on logical grounds alone. Nonetheless, we cannot be sure that all discrimination on the basis of 'race' (or gender, class, physical and mental handicaps) stems solely from a lack of cognitive understanding. If this were the case then understanding may not only not be enough, but it may not even be necessary for prejudice reduction. It is also questionable that discussion led by a neutral-chair ensures that pupils will consider and understand a divergence of views. And again, it is not self-evidently true that discussion will produce a divergence of views (Stradling *et al.* 1984, p. 8). Thus, whether neutral teaching can claim to be open-minded teaching because it is the most effective method of fostering open-mindedness in students remains an open question (Hare, 1979; 72).

Teachers cannot take an entirely value-free position, either in their professional capacities or as citizens, since their commitment is both towards educational and moral values. Nevertheless, although teachers should reveal their commitments to pupils, especially when invited to do so, the point at which this happens must be a matter for empirical observation and professional judgment. If the authority position of teachers is such that their views will be given undue emphasis and regard (which in turn will seriously limit the readiness of pupils to consider other relevant views), then teachers must refrain from articulating their own positions, especially at the beginning of a discussion. Teachers must not give the impression, however, that they are devoid of any commitment. They must strive to provide or facilitate an understanding of the plausibility (or otherwise) of the differing viewpoints that young people often encounter in their lives. Thus, in the use of materials or resources for discussion, teachers are under an obligation to draw pupils' attention to the nature of the evidence, its differing interpretations and bias (Brown, 1980, p. 210). Equally, they must also try to come to terms with their own value bias. For as Brown (1980) reminds us, many types of bias are possible in the classroom. Some of these may not only be related to issues or principles but may be related to the teachers' reaction to their pupils. Accordingly, some teachers may devalue pupils' views and others may deliberately discredit them. Thus in classroom discussions, especially of controversial social issues, some teachers may exhibit a bias that could prevent an objective consideration of the issues involved in a topic under discussion. For these reasons, Brown advocates a balanced approach which would take into account the bias of teachers and pupils alike, noting: 'The teacher is not faced by innocent, value-free minds' (1980, p. 210).

Both teachers and pupils must be aware of the fact that bias is a feature of human life. The hope is that being aware of such bias, pupils may come to perceive each other more sympathetically. Hence, at the end of the day, after a sense of sympathy has been stimulated for the beliefs, motivations and circumstances of the plurality of social and moral codes that exist in our society, the recognition of bias can be helpful in stimulating a concern for others. By achieving these ends, then, as Crick (1972) rightly points out:

> Biased opinions by themselves do no harm: what matters is *how* we hold our opinions, whether tolerantly, reasonably, with respect for those of others and with some knowledge of the consequences together with regard to contrary evidence.

He goes on to state that:

> Some bias and some confusion of roles cannot be avoided, so to go to drastic extremes to avoid them is usually to create a cure far worse than a mild disease (p. 12).

Teachers, especially in the early years, will have to occupy many roles. Just as they have to show what is evidence, they must also indicate how such evidence can *reasonably* be interpreted differentially. Teachers' views are best offered after a range of alternative opinions have been presented to the class. This is especially the case when the pupils have asked the teacher where he or she stands on an issue. For as Crick argues: 'It would be an evasion not to answer truthfully especially if silence fortified the myth of objectivity of values'. He also warns us that 'it is impertinent...to put the question too soon', for:

> After showing how the same facts get interpreted in typically different ways, then 'my view' as a teacher falls much more in place, can do less direct good than I may rashly hope. But they may be thinking for themselves a little bit more and with a better knowledge of consequences (Crick, 1972, p. 9).

A Plea for a Balanced Approach

My argument is for a balanced approach where teachers put both sides of the argument with equal enthusiasm before their pupils, who in the end will be encouraged to make up their own minds. The making up of one's mind will, however, be based on rational justification.

If truth in certain social or moral issues cannot be established by evidence, argument or experiment, then teachers cannot teach the truth of the matter. But neither would it be sufficient to merely teach the dispute and leave it at that. Teachers may be regarded as being under a moral obligation to teach the rights or wrongs, good or evil of certain moral judgments and in particular their possible harmful consequences on others. Thus the protection of divergence of opinion can only serve as a temporary tactic.

What should teachers do when it becomes evident that the class does not yet possess the concepts and ideas necessary to handle certain topics? Under these circumstances it becomes important for teachers to assume the role of teaching the class new concepts that will help to move the work forward. Moreover, what happens if the discussion flounders because none of the pupils is skilled enough to challenge the dominant ideas offered within the group or through the stimulus material? At such times, as Harwood admits, the teacher may have to adopt 'the devil's advocate' role, in order to act as a model of confronting or of critical-questioning behaviour (1986, p. 55).

The purpose of the balanced approach is not merely to reinforce a particular view or even to change a certain view, for sometimes it is necessary to do both. Whether we attempt to do any one of these will depend on the circumstances, the context of the discussion or on the aims or objectives of the teacher. In the course of most group-work, for example, the teacher will be required to introduce new concepts, ideas and knowledge, or to elucidate the concepts children are using in their work. In this process the teacher may have to call upon a variety of audio-visual aids to assist in the teaching process. A battery of other methods, including simulation exercises, role-play, drama and games could be used to involve children educationally in meaningful interaction with others.

Developing a Sense of Awareness and Respect for Each Other

Although people's ideas of what is right or wrong will differ significantly, one cannot conclude from this that all are equally right or wrong for, according to Cohen (1983), this would itself be another moral judgment and one that is virtually impossible to make with consistency. As Cohen puts it:

The mere making of such a judgement suggests that it is made from outside the human framework, by an external observer who is not himself a part of the world of which he judges that all views are equal. But, of course, no one can possess this detachment, for everyone is involved in the world of human action as participants as well as spectators. In so far as they can make an effort to believe that they can, and that ethical subjectivism entails that they should hold such a position they are committed to, is less one of moral neutrality than of moral inertia and indecision (1983, p. 133).

The good life that education would strive to promote, as White and his colleagues (1986) argue, would not be one in which one is imprisoned within one's own culture but would be one in which one uses one's capacity to reflect on and modify the framework of value assumptions within which one is living. This implies that pupils would be brought up to see their 'good' as consisting predominantly in shared goods but they should not accept this unreflectively. They should be encouraged to test their views against other existing alternatives. Children have to be brought up and cannot be left directionless until they are mature and knowledgeable enough to make autonomous choices. For some may never reach this auto-nomous stage of development, while for others it may be too late to wait until they reach adolescence.

   If our conceptions of the good life are diverse and incommensur-able, and if disputes over controversial issues cannot be settled by reference to facts, argument or experiment, then should not one ask, why include them in class discussion? If such discussion is designed to set pupils on a voyage of discovery, then shouldn't there be some agreement on the reasons for such a journey? Perhaps pupils may more likely go on a voyage of discovery together if they share some conceptions of the good life (Williams 1983, p. 370).

   Human beings are end-oriented, goal-seeking creatures whose actions and patterns of action cannot be understood or assessed apart from their conceptions of the good. Such conceptions of the good and hence the goals of action are irreducibly plural. Hence there is certain to be disagreement and competition in human beings seeking the resources and means necessary to pursue effectively these goods. Consequently, conflict will arise but could be contained within non-destructive limits (Flatham 1983, p. 357). It is the task of the school to arrange and order personal instruction so that each individual has the greatest possible freedom to pursue goals compatible with effective constraints on destructive conflicts. The task of education is to achieve an understanding of human beings and their interactions that will contribute to this objective.

On Basing One's Moral Commitment on Intuition

It is understandable that most people would agree that moral convictions should take precedence over mere preferences. Nevertheless, moral convictions at the intuitive level are not always overriding because intuitions sometimes conflict with each other (Hare 1981, p. 178). Hence, although moral education, for example, lies in the acquisition of moral attitudes, we have to recognize that these could well characterize the moral education and attitudes of those who are racially or religiously intolerant. There are some intuitions which it is good to have, but to which, Hare warns us, '...unthinking subservience...in extreme forms may be an evil'. (1981, p. 172) Thus, for Hare, what is important in the initial stages of a child's development is the inculcation of sound critical thinking, of *prima facie* principles of morality.

Failure to introduce children to critical thinking at an early enough age has, according to Hare, 'produced a generation which contained more than its fair share of fanatics incapable of critical thought'. (Hare, 1981, p. 174) Thus, in trying to force children into rigid principles, on the grounds that we intuitively know them to be correct or right rather than having taught them how to think, we could cause children to rebel against those principles and adopt opposite but equally rigid and uncritical principles. In this sense the young would be logical. For they would be taking some intuitive principle and following out its implications regardless of any other principles which might be equally important, and regardless of the critical thinking which could cope with conflicts between them.

The fanatic, Hare emphasizes, solves the moral problem or the conflict of principles not by critical thought but by elevating one principle, quite irrationally, over all the others. Hence disputes over principles should not be settled or resolved at the intuitive level, for as Hare puts it: 'both sides have perfectly good intuitions to appeal to and will simply go on offering them.' Thus: 'the solution lies in asking which of these principles should override which in a particular case. Only critical thought can answer this question'. (1981, p. 174) Indeed, critical thought can help us to sort out some of our moral dilemmas. But critical thinking could serve the fanatic as it could serve the saint. For a sufficiently determined fanatic could admit all the facts adduced by a critical thinker, and all the logical inferences which he/she used, and still, without offence to logic, reject his/her conclusions.

The implication of Hare's analysis for education is that it is necessary to follow consistent rules for cognitive and moral development. Pupils must come to see the reasons for behaving in certain ways: that is, they must come to do the morally right thing for the morally right reason. The point is not to get pupils merely to memorize the rules of good behaviour, or to behave like machines, but to instil reasonable habits in their earlier stages of development so that earlier growing will provide them with a basis for later development.

Thus, although I recognize the importance of the rational autonomy of individuals who should make up their own minds on moral and social controversial issues, I do not wish to support the idea that the view of the individual should take precedence over the view of others. Moreover, how is the individual, left alone, ever to know that he/she has made the best choice? Perhaps teachers are in a better position to extend the range of options open to the pupil. Among other things teachers must aim to inform their pupils of the major alternatives available. Schools can do much to help the young make rational choices. However, the central purpose of education should not be to entrap the child in a conventional way of life. Rather it should enable children to reflect on the general moral framework within which they live out their lives and also, if possible, to modify those frameworks where they seem to be inadequate (White *et al.* 1986, p. 185). Education, according to these aims, will not predominantly be biased towards the rational or intellectual, nor would it ever exclude them. It would stress the development of the 'whole person' and engage in activities which give an important place to shared moral virtues, aims, objectives and moral activities which predominate in pupils' chosen value systems. The aim of education would be to get pupils to see their own good as inextricably bound up with the good of others. For, as Callan (1985, p.15) warns us:

> A child who has learnt always to advance his own interests at the expense of others will hardly achieve much fulfilment in a world where success depends so much on the goodwill and cooperation of others.

If moral judgment and other modes of thought are rooted in a moral tradition, then education will consist of initiating children into those traditions which constitute our multicultural society (Leicester, 1986, p. 252).

Recognizing that disagreement over conceptions of the good life could be the source of most destructive conflict, teachers could order or organize pupils' interaction on the principle of mutual respect. Although I have already given some indications as to how this end could be achieved, I want to stress that:

> Rather than putting all our faith in one approach to our teaching, we should acknowledge bias as a problem and through evaluation, particularly self-evaluation, discover which strategy is appropriate to our own circumstances (Brown, 1980, p. 214).

In such circumstances we may find that neutrality generates some good results, but then we still need to ask and find out by empirical observation whether some 'un-neutral' stances produce outcomes which are better.

References

ACKERMAN, B.A. (1983) 'What is Neutral about Neutrality?' *Ethics*, 93, 2, pp. 372–90.

BAILEY, C. (1975) 'Neutrality and Rationality in Teaching', in BRIDGES, D. and SCRIMSHAW, P. (Eds) *Values and Authority in Schools*, London, Hodder & Stoughton.

BRIDGES, D. (1980) *Education, Democracy and Discussion*, Windsor, NFER Publishing Co.

BROWN, J.F. (1980) 'Bias Revisited', *Teaching Politics*, 9, 3, pp. 209–15.

CALLAN, E. (1985) 'Moral Education in a Liberal Society', *Journal of Moral Education*, 14, 1, pp. 9–22.

COHEN, B. (1983) 'Ethical Objectivity and Moral Education', *Journal of Moral Education*, 12, 2, pp. 131–6.

CRICK, B.R. (1972) 'On Bias', *Teaching Politics*, 1, 1, pp. 3–12.

DEARDEN, R.F. (1981) 'Controversial Issues in the Curriculum', *Curriculum Studies*, 13, 1, pp. 37–44.

FLATHAM, R.E. (1983) 'Equalitarian Blood and Sceptical Turnip', *Ethics*, 93, 2, pp. 357–66.

HARE, R.M. (1981) *Moral Thinking: Its Levels, Methods and Point*, Oxford Clarendon Press.

HARE, W. (1979) *Open Mindedness and Education*, Montreal, McGill, Queen's University Press.

HARE, W. (1981) 'The Attack on Open-Mindedness', *Oxford Review of Education*, 7, 2, pp. 119–29.

HARWOOD, D. (1986) 'To advocate or to educate? What role should the primary teacher adopt in political education?', *Education 3–13*, 14, 1, pp. 51–7.

JONES, M. (1985) 'Education and Racism', *Journal of Philosophy of Education*, 19, 2, pp. 223–34.

LEICESTER, M. (1986) 'Collective Moral Philosophy and Education for Pluralism: a reply to Graham Haydon', *Journal of Philosophy of Education*, 20, 2, pp. 251–5.

MACINTYRE, J. (1981) *After Virtue. A Study in Moral Theory*, London, Duckworth.

MCPHAIL, P. *et al.* (1972) *Moral Education in Secondary Schools*, Schools Council Project in Moral Education, Longman.

PHILLIPS-BELL, M. (1982) 'Morals, Emotions and Race: Educational Links', *Journal of Moral Education*, 11, 3, pp. 167–80.

STENHOUSE, L. (1970) 'Controversial Value Issues', in CARR, W. (Ed.) *Values in the Curriculum*, Washington DC, NEA, pp. 103–15.

STENHOUSE, L. and VERMA, G.K. (1981) 'Educational Procedures and Attitudinal Objectives: a Paradox', *Journal of Curriculum Studies*, 13, 4, pp. 329–37.

STRADLING, R. *et al.* (1984) *Teaching Controversial Issues*, London, Edward Arnold.

WALKLING, P.H. and BRANNIGAN, C. (1986) 'Anti-Sexist/Anti-Racist Education: a possible dilemma?', *Journal of Moral Education*, 15, pp. 16–25.

WARNOCK, M. (1975) 'The Neutral Teacher', in BROWN, S.C. (Ed.) *Philosophers Discuss Education*, London, Macmillan.

WHITE, J. *et al.* (1986) 'Education, Liberalism and Human Good', in COOPER, D.E. (Ed.) *Education Values and Mind*, London, RKP. pp. 149–72.

WILLIAMS, B. (1983) 'Space Talk: the Conventional Continued', *Ethics*, 93, 2, pp. 367–71.

Chapter 7

Teaching Controversial Issues in a Controversial Society

Una McNicholl

Northern Ireland in 1988 is still a deeply divided society, where communities are polarised by religious and political beliefs and where civil unrest could be considered an accepted norm. In fact, it is often alleged that for most of the people living in Northern Ireland the frequent political and sectarian acts of violence are as distant, in psychological terms, as they would be to anyone living in Britain, to the extent that 'on the surface' there is almost a denial that a conflict actually exists.

But a conflict does exist, and the role of education and the school system in this controversial situation has become a focus for debate. Indeed, since the early 1970s educationalists, supported by the Department of Education for Northern Ireland, which has a statutory responsibility for 'formulating and sponsoring policies for the improvement of community relations' (CRO 1975), have been attempting to direct the school curriculum towards examining these divisions with a view to promoting cultural harmony and understanding.

Consequently, there has been a considerable quantity of material produced for schools that examines the current issues and conflicts. At the same time injections of capital from the Department of Education, Northern Ireland, have made possible the development of projects and exchanges promoting integration that are designed to 'provide shared experiences', 'foster communication', 'encourage mutual understanding' and so on. Unfortunately, more than ten years later the country is still deeply segregated which could lead one to assume that, despite the committed efforts of those involved in these initiatives, they have only had a minimal effect, if any, on reducing divisions and sectarianism in Northern Ireland.

There are many complex, political, economic, social and educational factors responsible for the marginal effect of these initiatives in promoting cultural harmony and understanding. However, it is the concern of this chapter to examine the educational elements which, for further clarity, have been divided into two major categories:

(i)   Nature and structure of the schools
(ii) Content and method of the initiatives themselves

Nature and Structure of the Schools

Northern Ireland schools have been the subject of much research and attention since the outbreak on the 'troubles' . For many, the very process of segregation in Northern Ireland begins with the school, as the school system directly mirrors the overall social and religious divisions of the wider society. A separate but almost identical school system exists for each of the two religious communities, both of which are characterized by their grammar school and 11–plus selection procedure. The legal position of schools is such that 'controlled' or *de facto*, Protestant schools are financed and controlled 100 per cent by the Department of Education in Northern Ireland through local area boards, and that 'voluntary' schools, in which most Catholic schools fall, are Grant Aided by 85 per cent.

The extent of those divisions has been illustrated by Darby *et al.* (1977) in *Schools Apart*. Their research study of four areas enabled them to infer that possibly as many as 70 per cent of Northern Ireland schools were exclusively attended by children from one denomination. In 1962 Barrit and Carter suggested that 98 per cent of Catholic children of primary school age attended Catholic schools. Some fifteen years later the *Schools Apart* study suggested that 95 per cent of state 'controlled' schools have less than 5 per cent of Catholic enrolment and over 98 per cent of Catholic schools have less than 5 per cent Protestant enrolment.

The same research indicated that with teacher employment there was a more obvious segregation in the primary school (the most formative stage in the child's school life). For instance, 90 per cent of Catholic primary schools had no teachers from the Protestant religion and 67 per cent of 'controlled' or Protestant schools had no Catholic teachers. Of the 1521 secondary school teachers interviewed only 29 were employed in a school differing in religion from their own, and 9 out of 480 grammar school teachers interviewed were likewise employed. What is also interesting to note is that, while further and higher education are totally integrated, a separate teacher-training college still exists for the Roman Catholic students and Protestant students respectively. Membership of two of the teachers' unions reflects this religious division.

One could optimistically speculate that, at best, the other professions and skills have not designed their training on a sectarian basis to produce, for example, Catholic dentists. Unfortunately this will probably not be the case for, by the time most young adults have reached higher education, they will, as Boyle and Hadden explain,

> have absorbed one or other of the two communal views of history and legitimacy of Northern Ireland and of British involvement in Ireland as a whole, through formal teaching and through their families and friends (1985, p. 50).

This would suggest that schools offer different curricula and different educational experiences to their pupils, but on the surface, to the observer, there is little evidence to confirm this. Several research projects have indicated the similarities between the two systems. For example, Darby *et al.* (1977) found that the educational qualifications of the teachers were relatively similar, that head teachers had comparable work profiles and that there were no major differences in attitudes towards discipline in the schools concerned. This research also found that both school systems reflected a traditional approach to education, and placed a heavy emphasis on external examinations.

On the other hand the obvious curricula differences could be considered in cultural terms. Catholic schools offer Irish history, Irish language, Gaelic games and Catholic religious instruction as an integral part of their curriculum, while Protestant schools do not. These subjects, however, take up only a small proportion of the school day, competing with the other subjects in the curriculum. Malone (1973) discusses this further and draws attention to the fact that the critical factor is not what is taught but how it is taught. He calls this the 'hidden political agenda', that is, the conscious or unconscious transmission of assumptions and allegiances. The Catholic schools themselves argue that the case for retaining their school system rests firmly on a conviction that they can provide a religio-moral ethos which is integral to Catholic education. The fundamental differences in the two school systems are more implicit than explicit and, therefore, lie mainly in what is known as the 'hidden curriculum'. The situation is also self-perpetuating, for the cumulative effect of an 11-plus selection system, grammar school system and streaming, in association with two separate school systems, (each with its own traditional values, beliefs, images and symbols, selective employment of teaching staff and selective nomination of school governors), is reflected in, and reinforced and legitimized by this 'hidden curriculum'.

In effect then, both educational systems are based on a consensus model of education, where the preservation of culture and tradition predominates. The process of education too, in reflecting the dominant values, assumes that the existing social and political systems are correct, while a denial syndrome predominates in many schools. This is where schools are seen in general as 'havens of peace', free from the violent political world outside and in turn do not challenge or examine current issues and conflicts. Cairns' (1987) research supports this view and informs us that a result of a recent survey by the *Belfast Telegraph* in 1984 revealed that only 23 per cent of respondents believed that teachers should allow their pupils to know their political beliefs, and that this was then 'interpreted as revealing that most Northern Irish parents definitely want to keep politics out of schools'. Jenkins *et al.* (1980) described four ways in which schools might be perceived as coping with the outside world of Northern Ireland troubles. The first of these refers to the denial syndrome, which they define as 'time out' or keeping contemporary cultural and political issues out of the curriculum; in other words denying its existence.

Against such well defined and rigid educational structures and processes outlined above, the controversial educational initiatives designed to reduce sectarian divisions and promote mutual under-standing have had an enormous, if not impossible, task. The next section will attempt to examine the content and method of these initiatives, which have been designed to promote harmony and cultural understanding within the present educational structures and processes.

Content and Method of the Initiatives Themselves

Education is often viewed as a process of change, and schools the agents of social, political and/or cultural change. Where the school system progressively promotes and facilitates cultural change, the process has been referred to as 'reconstructionism' (Skilbeck, 1975).

In Northern Ireland, promoting change effectively and implicitly involves challenging the existing social and political systems which, within the consensus model of education presently adopted by both educational systems, is considered controversial. Even a minimal reconstructionist approach, where the school does not have a primary role in promoting change, would be considered in some schools controversial, as many schools like to promote the 'haven of peace' approach.

The purpose of this section is not to argue the need for change, it assumes that; and the initiatives, approaches/projects concerned with change through promoting mutual understanding, tolerance, harmony and respect among the two cultures in Northern Ireland, whether of minimal or maximum level, are considered here as positive reconstructionist approaches. Generally these initiatives can be placed into three categories:

(a) those concerned with curriculum development and change
(b) those concerned with developing inter-school links and exchange
     programmes
(c) those offering an alternative integrated school system.

(a) Curriculum Development Projects

As stated earlier, there has been a considerable amount of material and projects, produced mainly for secondary schools, that examines the current issues and conflicts and aims to promote tolerance, mutual understanding and education for reconciliation within the curriculum. Of these, the Schools Cultural Studies Project has been of particular significance alongside the Schools Curriculum Project and Religion in Ireland Project, as a curriculum development initiative, and one in which I have had personal teaching experience. Malcolm Skilbeck was responsible for the inception of this project, which was based on a reconstructionist approach. In 1975, the Director of the Project, Alan Robinson, added a further dimension, arguing that the reconstructionist philosophy 'must be held alongside' recognizing and accepting culture in 'all its forms':

> Robinson depicts the school system as one means by which
> the edge of sectarianism might be blunted and the culture of
> Northern Ireland developed. He distinguishes between end
> values and instrumental values. The end values are cultural
> renewal and development, personal awareness and respectful
> mutual understanding and effective citizenship (Jenkins *et al.*
> 1980, p. 23).

In 1980, David Jenkins produced a major evaluation study of the project, *Chocolate, Cream, Soldiers*, wherein he identified four strands in the project's rationale. These included an underlying cultural, social and ideological analysis of the Northern Irish situation, ideas on how schools might contribute to a solution, teachers' own practical actions and specific curriculum input at an appropriate level.

He further outlined the four ways referred to earlier, in which the schools might be perceived as coping with the troubles:

(i)   defining schools as 'time out'
(ii)   putting the school up front in the cause of understanding and eventual reconciliation
(iii)   some compromise, internal conflict or general fuzziness, often without a cross-school policy
(iv)   adopting a local position, i.e. one of 'modified sectarianism'.

Jenkins suggested that the first and third responses may not necessarily be disreputable. In fact the third alternative could be seen as a realistic recipe for survival in some situations. He further added that the project could not reconcile itself with the first and fourth responses. The evaluation also states that the material in the project is organized around:

> themes and issues of human importance rather than subject matter derived from the disciplines of knowledge or those fields of knowledge like geography that pass as school subjects … (it) aims to develop an understanding of social situations and human acts and of the controversial value issues that they raise (1980, p. 127).

The treatment of the Northern Ireland problem in the project is introduced through a gradient approach over five years, concentrating in the fifth year on a direct study of contemporary Ulster.

As with any major curriculum development project there have been problems with this form of project which have been referred to in depth in Jenkins' evaluation. However, the general issues and problems contributing to the marginal effect of such a project are probably fairly representative of all the curriculum initiatives tackling the Northern Ireland situation. The first problem is the school itself, and, despite the fact that Schools Cultural Studies Project material was eventually readily available to any committed teacher, only a minority of schools chose to get involved in this project or any other of the initiatives. The question must be asked if Northern Irish society can any longer afford schools in Jenkins' categories (i) time out, (iii) some compromise, or (iv) modified sectarianism, after twenty years of political and sectarian violence? Has the time not come for (i) and (iv) in particular to become disreputable stands given that the community is as deeply divided and mistrusting as ever? Schools should be 'up front' in the cause of understanding and eventual reconciliation.

This also raises the issue of priority given to such curriculum development projects within the school curriculum. Where the school has decided to get involved it must give priority to such work. My personal experience is of offering such material to the lower streams only and, unfortunately, this was not an isolated example. The lower streams were not necessarily considered more sectarian or more in need of such information, but 'O' level passes were considered, naturally, of a higher priority than teaching tolerance and cultural understanding. In fact, Northern Irish educational standards and 'O' level pass rates are among the highest in the United Kingdom, but at what price are these obtained, given the level of acceptance of 'violence' as normal?

Another crucial issue relating to curriculum development projects is the training of teachers in using these materials and projects. This should become a compulsory part of any Northern Irish teachers' training, regardless of their specialist field. Teachers must be capable of raising controversial issues and dealing with them effectively, and of debating, exposing and challenging sectarianism, the prevailing sub-cultures of the school and the power structures within the schools. Middle-class liberalism, tolerance of sectarianism and prejudice, and avoidance of the issues must be challenged, and teachers and schools should have a clear direct policy on how to promote reconciliation. Finally, projects should be introduced into primary schools, as research and press reports indicated that children at their most formative stages in primary schools are both segregated and prejudiced.

A way forward has been the development of a structure to coordinate and give direction and guidance to schools on these initiatives and projects. The Northern Ireland Council for Educational Development has set up a liaison committee for Mutual Understanding. Education for Mutual Understanding (EMU) is described as standing for:

- a commitment to the promotion of mutual understanding among young people in Northern Ireland;
- a commitment to the school as an agency to facilitate mutual understanding and to the teachers as the professional agents of mutual understanding;
- a commitment to raising and handling controversial issues throughout the education system but particularly in schools; and

— a commitment to the promotion and recognition of affective learning (as well as to the cognitive development) in schools (1987, p. 2).

Its main concern is the whole curriculum of schools and projects, and it is 'committed to encouraging all schools and colleges to analyze their whole curriculum and ethos by applying the concept of cross cultural and mutual understanding'. (1987, p. 2) It has a responsibility for training teachers involved in this form of work, and for distributing the budget allocated by the Department of Education for Northern Ireland for education for reconciliation.

A structure like EMU should be adequately resourced if it is effectively to promote and encourage all schools to participate in education for mutual understanding and reconciliation. It should not only be in the position to give guidelines but have a remit to develop a clear policy on education for mutual understanding to be adopted by all schools, regardless of their religious persuasion or their primary or secondary focus. This might ensure that curriculum development projects and initiatives concerned with promoting understanding and reconciliation have some real effect.

(b) Inter-school Links and Exchanges

There have been a considerable number of small projects and initiatives involving inter-school links and exchanges that have developed over recent years. Whether they take the form of cross cultural exchange (i.e. Catholic/Protestant), north/south exchanges or even international exchanges, their focus has tended to be more of a short-term basis than the curriculum projects mentioned above.

Funding seems to be readily available for such projects, provided an equal number of Catholic and Protestant young people participate. They do provide an opportunity for young people from Northern Ireland, either to visit each others' schools and/or visit another country, which in itself is an educative experience. However, the long-term effects or even mid-term effects seem to be limited. Personal experience of the Cross Cultural Exchange Programme (8–10 schools visiting Denmark annually) and Co-operation North, School Links has shown that it has been very difficult for teachers to support effective ongoing contact after the visits have taken place, and to promote the discussion of controversial issues during the exchanges and visits (because the young people want to get away from it all).

But again this raises the issue of training teachers in how to handle controversial issues. Cairns, (1987), in discussing this form of initiative, believes that if reconciliation is to be achieved 'then contact should take place at an intergroup level and not simply at an interpersonal level' as is normally the case in these initiatives:

> ...the form of interpersonal contact fostered across the sectarian divide by such projects will at best produce a child who can honestly claim 'some of my best friends are Protestants/Catholics but...(1987, p. 160).

He argues that policies addressed directly to changing peoples' social identification and intergroup relations is the most effective way to reduce prejudice and discrimination.

However, no-one can deny the short-term pleasures and educational experiences of these projects, but they should become an integral part of curriculum development projects concerned with education for reconciliation and mutual understanding. They should be phased properly into the curriculum so that every child has an opportunity to participate in a well-planned scheme. They should be extended locally so that more children, and in particular teachers, experience exchanges in schools of a different religion from their own.

(c) Integrated Education

The existing projects dealing with curriculum development and change and the initiatives concerned with developing school links and exchanges are probably a recognition of, and a practical response to, the fact that integrated education for the majority of Northern Irish children will not be provided in the foreseeable future.

Indeed, there has been considerable argument and academic and political debate both verbal and written, on the advantages, disadvantages and the demands for adopting an integrated system of education in Northern Ireland. However, the cumulative effect of the political, religious, social, economic and financial implications make it highly unlikely that integrated education for everyone (that is, the purposeful and planned education of Protestant and Catholic children together), will ever become a reality. Integrated education, as an initiative or approach concerned with change through promoting mutual understanding, tolerance and harmony exists in varying degrees only for a small minority of children in Northern Ireland.

Five purpose-built integrated schools, the most famous of which is Logan College, were developed from the initiatives of the parents' organization 'All Children Together'. In these, the whole ethos of the school is centred around the process of integration. A minimal degree of 'integration' also exists in other primary schools, as referred to earlier in the chapter. But the process of integrated education and the issues involved are not of primary importance in many of these schools. It is also highly unlikely that these schools will have clear policies, guidelines, aims and objectives on integration and its associated issues, or on the teaching of controversial issues in the curriculum. Ironically, 'natural' integrated education, outside of designated integrated schools, primarily exists in Northern Ireland's special schools for the physically and mentally handicapped children. Recently there has also been a move towards providing strictly segregated Protestant schools. These examples further illustrate how complex, and/or polarized, the situation in Northern Ireland has become.

Conclusion

In conclusion, it is very hard as an educationalist (and an idealist), committed to reconciliation and cultural harmony, to accept that the provision of integrated education will not become available for the majority of children in Northern Ireland. The realistic situation, however, is that, while it could be an effective and 'up front' or honest method to tackle the present conflict situation, the practical implications of such a major reorganization of the school system would be horrendous. But then, so is the present unacceptable situation in Northern Ireland.

The question must be asked whether the experience of integration would be any more painful, or even expensive, than the present violent and divided global situation in Northern Ireland? Further, can Northern Ireland afford not to change its present systems of education? Can Northern Ireland afford the massive emigration of young people, especially amongst the educated, that it is now experiencing, or is it even fully aware of the recent escalation in this trend and the implications that this poses?

While there are no solutions to the problems, I would argue that there are only two alternative and yet complementary routes that the system of education in Northern Ireland can take:

(i) Phased, integrated education based on the community school model, where the pupils, teachers, community and the participants are totally involved in the learning process. The school would continually seek to challenge and examine the current religious, social, political and economic issues, conflicts and prejudices and would place emphasis on the teaching of controversial issues in relation to Northern Ireland in the curriculum.

(ii) The implementation of a curriculum development project that places emphasis on putting the school 'up front' in coping with the conflict in Northern Ireland. This should take immediate priority and become a mandatory part of the core curriculum for all schools (both primary and secondary), and all pupils.

Emphasis should be placed on examining and challenging the current issues, conflicts and prejudices and on promoting tolerance, mutual understanding and education for reconciliation. This initiative would also necessitate a structure, possibly like EMU, having the powers and resources to give clear policy and guidelines, to give support and to meet the obvious considerable training requirements for its successful implementation and for effective results.

Finally, the many holidays and exchange visits would still have a valuable role to play within either of these routes, and as an integral part of the wider curriculum: they could ensure effective follow up work with the participants.

References and Further Reading

BARRIT, D. and CARTER, C. (1962) *The Northern Ireland Problem: A Study in Group*, Belfast, Oxford University Press.

BOYLE, K. and HADDEN, T. (1985) *Ireland: A Positive Proposal*, Harmondsworth, Penguin.

CAIRNS, E. (1987) *Caught in Crossfire: Children and the Northern Ireland Conflict*, Belfast, Appletree Press.

CO-OPERATION NORTH (1986) *Annual Report '86: Progress and Plans*, Belfast, Co-Operation North.

CO-OPERATION NORTH (1988) *School Links '88: A North/South School Exchange Scheme*, Belfast, Co-Operation North.

DARBY, A. *et al.* (1977) *Education and Community in Northern Ireland: Schools Apart?* Coleraine, New University of Ulster.

DARBY, A. *et al.* (1983) *Northern Ireland: The Background to the Conflict*, Belfast, Appletree Press.

DUNN, S. (1984) *Schools Together?* Coleraine, New University of Ulster.

DUNN, S. (1986) 'The role of education in the Northern Ireland conflict', *Oxford Review of Education*, 12, 3, pp. 233–42.

HESKIN, K. (1980) *Northern Ireland: A Psychological Analysis*, Dublin, Gill and MacMillan.

HICKLEY, J. (1984) *Religion and the Northern Ireland Problem*, Dublin, Gill and MacMillan.

JENKINS, D. *et al.* (1980) *Chocolate, Cream, Soldiers: A Final Evaluation Report on the 'Schools Cultural Studies Project'*, Coleraine, New University of Ulster Education Centre Occasional Papers.

MALONE, J. (1973) 'Schools and community relations', *The Northern Teacher*, Winter, pp. 19–30.

NORTHERN IRELAND COUNCIL FOR EDUCATIONAL DEVELOPMENT (1987) *Education for Mutual Understanding*, Belfast, NICED.

NORTHERN IRELAND DEPARTMENT OF EDUCATION (1982) *The Improvement of Community Relations: The Contribution of Schools (Circular 1982/21)*, Belfast, Department of Education.

NORTHERN IRELAND DEPARTMENT OF EDUCATION (1987) *Cross Community Contact Scheme (Circular 1987/47: Appendix 1 – Community Relations: Minister's Press Statement, Sept.* Belfast, Department of Education.

SKILBECK, M. (1975) 'Education and cultural change', cited in JENKINS, D., *et al.* (1980) *Chocolate, Cream Soldiers* Coleraine, The New University of Ulster Education Centre Occasional Papers.

Chapter 8

Reading for Bias

Steve Whitley

At the beginning, as you know, is always the most important part, especially in dealing with anything young and tender. That is the time when the character is being moulded and easily takes any impress one may wish to stamp on it. Quite true.
Then shall we simply allow our children to listen to any stories that anyone happens to make up, and so receive into their minds ideas often the very opposite of those we shall think they ought to have when they are grown up?
No, certainly not.
It seems, then, our first business will be to supervise the making of [stories], rejecting all which are unsatisfactory; and we shall induce nurses and mothers to tell their children only those which we have approved... Most of the stories now in use must be discarded (Plato).

This chapter deals with bias in books for young children, especially in the areas of race, gender and politics. That the authors of these books write from a biased standpoint is clear: it is not possible for a person to be neutral in such areas, howsoever vociferously they[1] may claim that they are apolitical and therefore have no view to put forward. As Sutherland writes,

Like other writers, authors of children's books are inescapably influenced by their views and assumptions [when they write their books]; the books thus express their authors' personal ideologies... To publish books which express one's ideology is in essence to promulgate one's values... To promulgate one's values... is a political act (1985, p. 143).

The purpose of this chapter is to examine what kinds of such ideological statements are being made in young children's books today and how the teacher may tackle them.

Two of the ten most popular reading schemes used in Sheffield schools in 1986 continue to reinforce black marginality (Rice, 1987); the representation of girls and women in twentieth-century award-winning picture-books reached a peak in the 1950s, a nadir in the period 1900–1930 and in the 1960s and has been improving only slowly since then (Ford, 1985); and most authors of children's books, unlike, for example, W.E. Johns[2], now prefer to hide their politics within the book rather than making their ideology overt (Sutherland, 1985; Shannon, 1986). It would appear that the reading matter which teachers present to children is not, as right-wing propaganda would have us believe, permeated with anti-racist and anti-sexist sentiment larded with overtly left-wing politics. On the contrary, authors and publishers still have so far to go that a non-racist, non-sexist book-club like Letterbox Library has difficulty in putting together an acceptable quarterly list and is unable to do so from British publishers alone.

Racism

Since Dixon (1977a) reported on some overt racism in children's stories (for example, Enid Blyton's *The Little Black Doll*), there is no doubt that publishers have taken heed of criticism and now are more careful about the content of their books. But some still offend, to such an extent that Lloyd (1984) had to protest that he would not write for The Bodley Head publishing house again unless it withdrew its latest republication of *Little Black Sambo*; and *The Beano Book 1988* contains a 'Ball Boy' story in which a black Brazilian member of the boys' football team had to be made acceptable by being given a blond wig and having his face whitewashed ('That'll hide your tan,' says Ball Boy). The main criticism which is made about publishing policy today, however, is that the racism in children's books is covert: very few books contain strong, positive main characters who are black (Kuya, 1980); some make no acknowledgment at all of the multiracial nature of British society (Klein, 1985); and where acknowledgment is made, it is tokenistic or stereotypical (ibid.).

Nor is this situation, which is created by authors and their publishers, ameliorated by the book selection policy of most teachers in schools. Many ignore questions of race and racism when choosing books to present to their children, appearing to push such factors low down their list of criteria, if indeed they appear in the list at all. One encounters such attitudes even in schools where one might expect the teachers to be more aware than most others of the issues involved. For example, an analysis of books selected by three teachers operating in two reception classes in a Newcastle community primary school in 1986/7 reveals that, out of the 458 books which they offered their fifty-eight children in the first two terms, only eight contained a black character. And, whereas the most popular of the 458 books was taken for home-reading by the children thirty-seven times, only two of the books containing a black character were chosen more than three times (*Ten, Nine, Eight*, which was taken home twelve times, and *Whistle for Willie*, which was taken eight times). The seventeen books chosen twenty times or more [3] are not overtly racist as such but none of them contains a black character in either the text or the illustrations and, therefore, none of them reflected in any way the multiracial nature of the reception classes in which the children found themselves: 27½ per cent of the children were black.

Knight (1983) and Rice (1987) show a similar picture in their examination of best-selling reading schemes. Knight looked at three schemes in particular (*Ginn 360, Link Up* and *Storychest*) and found that, although she could recognise advances if she took a scheme like *Ladybird* as her starting point, all three were very disappointing: opportunities had been missed in Ginn's scheme; in *Link Up*, no attempt had been made to include minority-group British children in the stories in any positive way; and in *Storychest*, the publishers had made no attempt to recognize the multicultural nature of the audience. Rice found much the same picture when he examined the ten reading schemes most widely used in Sheffield schools. For example, whites were portrayed in 231 stories, animals in 157 stories and blacks in only fifty-two stories; *1, 2, 3 and Away* and the *Griffin and Dragon/Pirate* series presented no black roles at all. Out of the 440 stories in all ten schemes, Rice (1987) found only five 'making any attempt at all to deal with the contemporary black experience of Britain and, of these, three seemed bound by the assimilationist ideal of black people relinquishing their own culture in favour of the white British' (p. 95). He found overt racism (a story about caricature 'savages' and a limerick about a cannibal eating his niece) in *Ginn 360* and had to conclude:

> My overwhelming and lasting impression after examining the ten schemes is that black people are quite simply under-represented... and that when black characters do appear it is in a way that too frequently reinforces stereotypical views and attitudes about black people (p. 97).

The above examples are not isolated: the general picture of society presented to young children in popular picture-books and in best-selling reading-scheme materials is one which is white-dominated and in which the black experience is ignored and denied. It is true that some publishers and authors are attempting to change this picture and I deal with their attempts in **Sparks** below.

Sexism

The picture in the area of gender appears to be slightly rosier than that in the area of race. It is easier to find well-written and well-illustrated anti-sexist books than it is to find such books which are anti-racist (see **Sparks** below); but, as Stinton (1979) wrote of the *Mr Men* series, there are still many books which 'are written almost entirely from a male viewpoint, that of a club armchair, where women are a half-forgotten species' (p. 125). Engel (1981) examined recent award-winning picture-books and found that, 'rich as [they] might be with artistic and literary qualities, [they are] still lacking the vital ingredients for sex-role equality or even for a reflection of reality' (p. 652). And, of the seventeen books chosen most frequently by the Newcastle children mentioned above, only four [4] feature a girl or woman in a main role and only two of those roles could be said to present a positive image: Mrs Plug in *Mrs Plug the Plumber* shows initiative and courage (but she is the one called upon to change the little Plugs' nappies at the end of the book) and Alex's mother in *Alex's Bed* demonstrates that she needs no man to 'help' with carpentry. Seventy-two of the 458 books (i.e. a mere 13 per cent) showed a girl, woman or female animal [5] in a main role but only seven of them (1½ per cent of the total) showed that character in a positively independent light. And even if one takes male and female characters overall within picture-books, an imbalance is still there: Ford (1985) examined eighty-five books recommended by Bennett (1983) and found that 'males outnumber females by almost two to one in all appearances: they have more starring roles; they make more appearances as background characters; and they are mentioned in stories far more frequently than females' (p. 48). Indeed, according to this last factor, the situation has deteriorated since the 1950s, when 47 per cent of all characters in story-book text were female (Czaplinski, 1976); in the Bennett sample, only 35 per cent of the characters in the text were female (Ford, 1985).

Nor are reading schemes free from gender bias of this kind. Bordelon saw some improvement in some areas since the early 1970s but concluded that 'the nature of feminine activities has not changed substantially, and...textbooks and teaching materials imply that independence, initiative, strength, and ambition are exclusively male traits' (1985, p. 794). In the *Oxford Reading Tree*, for example, the main girl character, Biff, shows initiative and purpose but the adult characters in the stories are highly stereotypical. In Longman's *Reading World*, there are some stories in which an attempt is made to escape stereotyping (for example, *The Grumble* depicts a girl as the main character and contains women as a baker, a window-cleaner, a paper-girl and a mail-deliverer). However, the main impression the reader has is that, by the use of very bland anthropomorphized animals, the publisher is ignoring the real world altogether; and the teacher's handbook gives no indication that the issue of gender bias has been considered at all.

Politics

The British ruling class, like Plato, has never been unmindful of the powerful effect which education and, as part of that education, children's books will have upon the formation of children's ideological attitudes. As Leeson writes of the drive to provide 'good fiction' for adolescent readers in the 1870s:

> the impulse behind the campaign was to win acceptance for two gigantic acts of acquisition, which set the seal on the new order in Britain and the world in mid-nineteenth century: the Empire abroad and the public school network, which provided its cadre force, at home (1985, p. 91).

It is not surprising to find Kenneth Baker, a Conservative Party Secretary of State for Education and Science, suggesting that his imposed state curriculum should contain lists of books which children should have read by particular ages, for example, *Animal Farm* by the age of 11 and *David Copperfield* by the age of 15. Such prescription goes hand in hand with proscription. For example, the National Socialist Teachers Association in Nazi Germany, with the slogan 'Das Buch – Unsere Waffe' (The book is our weapon), prescribed ('Picture books shall *conserve* the timeless values of our folk ethics; they shall *guard* the traditional heritage of our forefathers; and they shall *fight* for the organic world view of the Führer' – quoted in Kamenetsky, 1984, p. 153); and they proscribed: they removed from schools all books which contradicted the Nordic-Germanic attitude, which had the 'wrong' attitude to Jews, which presented cooperation between races, which depicted international brotherhood across race, or which were written by Jews or dissenters (e.g. Jack London), for 'in children's literature the Nazis perceived one of their most important tools for re-educating children in the spirit of National Socialism' (ibid. p. xiii).

There is no need, however, to be so overt about the acceptable content of a children's book. An examination of contemporary popular picture-books or of reading-scheme materials reveals quite clearly that, encircling the all-white, male-dominated world adumbrated above, is a neat, well-ordered, middle-class universe. In Carrington and Denscombe's analysis of the *Thomas the Tank-Engine* series, for example, is revealed an ideology which shares many of the principles of the New Right:

> in common with Thatcherism, Awdry's stories emphasise the importance of individual responsibility, discipline, order, and respect for authority. The series also celebrates the work ethic, enterprise, utilitarianism, patriotism, and meritocratic values (1987, p. 48).

Nor is this an isolated example: Shannon (1986) examined thirty of the most popular American young children's books and found that he could not classify a single one as being 'collectivist' in tone; twenty-nine of the thirty were 'individualist', showing 'a clear tendency to espouse the self as the focus for activity, rather than co-operative endeavour or concern for living in harmony with others'. And even non-sexist or non-racist books, such as *I Want to See the Moon* or *Nandy's Bedtime*, depict cosy, comfortably-off households where children are well-supplied with toys, where there are no problems of space or food or clothing, and where the characters are shielded from homelessness, poverty and want. Sutherland calls this 'the politics of assent':

> it does not advocate in any direct sense, but simply *affirms* ideologies generally prevalent in the society . . . it is an author's passive, unquestioning acceptance and internalisation of an established ideology, which is then transmitted in the author's writing in an unconscious manner (1985, p. 151).

The ideology also seems acceptable and uncontroversial to the ordinary reader, and it is so powerful that only those authors who consciously decide to challenge it receive labels such as 'political' or 'controversial', which in its marginalization of such authors itself once more reaffirms the force of the dominant ideology:

The printed word...becomes a necessary vehicle for reinforcing, among others, the prevailing conception that the
dominating group has an almost divine responsibility to lead
the dominated in order to ensure their welfare, protect them
against their own inferior nature, and ensure a proper division
of labour and an adequate distribution of the material benefits
generated by the exploited (Falcon, 1980, p. 5).

So What?

If it is accepted that the brief case outlined above is true and that
young children's books have the effect of reasserting ruling-class
ideology and confirming the racist and sexist attitudes which the
readers already exhibit when they come to school (see Alhibai, 1987),
one might say that such a situation is only to be expected and that,
anyway, books, when set alongside language, family socialization or
other sources of information such as television, are a tiny part of such
attitudinal baggage. I disagree.

It is well-established (e.g. Spender, 1980; Smith, 1984) that
language plays a vital role in the formation of a person's world-view; I
would claim that, within language, storying plays a role which
solidifies and reinforces that world-view. Just as there is no human
society which lacks a highly developed and complex language to
explain and shape the world, so there would appear to be no society
which lacks story as an element of such explanation and shaping.
Among many other functions, story is used as myth to reveal
fundamental truths, as legend to construct an historical base to
society, as fable to assert a morality, as folk-tale to comment upon
human foibles, or as gossip to cement social relationships. At first,
and still in many societies, stories are oral; in literate societies they are
frozen into print, divorced from the teller and thus appear to project
impersonal and durable values. Anybody who has watched a class of
energetic 4-year-olds concentratedly project themselves into whole-
hearted involvement with, say, *Funnybones*, or any parent who has
had to cope with nightmares after their infant child has encountered
an apparently innocuous tale like *Beauty and the Beast*, can hardly
doubt the power of story to control and move. Stories have saved a
child from mental stagnation (Butler, 1979), have helped children to
deal with inner conflict (Bettelheim, 1978) or have themselves created
such conflict (Coard, 1971), and have provoked the serious attention

of stable modern states such as the Soviet Union (O'Dell, 1978) or the United States of America (Zimet, 1976).

Through stories, children receive a confirmation or a denial of their own social and personal identity. The white, middle-class boy has constant re-affirmation of both as he listens to stories at home and is inducted into the reading process at school, whether it be through more stories or through a structured reading scheme; and if he lives in an all-white suburb and goes to an all-white school, he need not even be aware that he is a member of a multi-racial society in which not everyone has a car, owns a house, is able to sleep in a warm, dry bedroom of their own and is always assured of plenty to eat. The black, working-class girl, however, is denied such positive images to enable her to know that she is welcomed or even accepted by the society into which she has been born; on the contrary, the books which her school is likely to give her contain the underlying message that she does not exist, either socially or personally. This denial of her existence has educational consequences as well; for,

> if readers, whether members of minority groups, or females, or from a background which is not suburban middle-class, find no positive images to relate to in the literature which they are offered as children, they are more likely to become alienated from books and thus from education generally (Hoffman, 1976, p. 119).

Wells (1986) has shown that hearing stories read aloud at home is one of two strong underpinning factors related to later educational 'success'[6]; I would submit that, if the black working-class girl can find nothing of herself in her narrative diet, she is denied even the chance of such an outcome.

Sparks

The picture which has been presented is a gloomy one. However, it is one which has been painted before and which has had its effect upon re-orienting practice: if one searches, sparks of light can be found in the general gloom.

Let us look first at the global situation. *The Butter Battle Book*, for example, is recommended by Rosemary Stones as 'a brilliant anti-nuclear fable that will help young readers to understand the moral issues that face the world'. *The Hiroshima Story* deals with the same subject-matter less allegorically and, in both illustrations and text, much more directly: a little girl sees the ghastly effects of nuclear warfare at first hand and the explicit moral is pronounced by her mother: '"Our suffering was no accident. Without your will to prevent it, it could happen again"'. Another direct tale of warfare ('conventional' in this instance) is found in *Rose Blanche*, a story of a German girl who helps some children in a Nazi concentration camp but who herself is shot in the confusion surrounding its liberation; then, on the site of the camp where she died,

> the cold retreated, fresh grasses advanced across the land. There were explosions of colour. Trees put on their bright new uniforms and paraded in the sun. Birds took up their positions and sang their simple message. Spring had triumphed.

The Malvinas war has also received attention: in *The Tin-Pot Foreign General and the Old Iron Woman*, a quarrel between the two vain protagonists leads to war. 'Some men were shot. Some men were drowned. Some men were burned alive. Some men were blown to bits. Some men were only half blown to bits and came home with parts of their bodies missing.' And after the war, 'the poor shepherds on the sad little island went on counting their sheep and eating them'.

Some books deal with the theme of conflict but in a less specific and direct way. The moral of *Two Monsters*, for example, is that conflict might not start at all if we paused to consider each other's point of view. *The Story of Ferdinand*, written in 1937 at the time of the fascist rebellion in Spain, has what might be considered by some to be the rather optimistic moral that a fight cannot occur if one side refuses to play its part: the young bull Ferdinand will not fight or butt his horns about like the other bulls, so when he is chosen by accident to be the star attraction at the bull-fight in Madrid, he sits in the middle of the bull ring and, ignoring the toreadors, smells the scent of the flowers in the spectators' hair.

> He wouldn't fight and be fierce no matter what they did. He just sat and smelled. And the Banderilleros were angry and the Picadores were angrier and the Matador was so angry he cried because he couldn't show off with his cape and sword. So they had to take Ferdinand home.

Another global theme which has been considered is that of conservation. Perhaps the best-known example of a story which deals with the issue is *Dinosaurs and All That Rubbish*. A man's all-consuming (literally) ambition to reach the stars destroys Earth, but when he has gone, the dinosaurs, roused from their millenia of sleep, restore the planet to beauty and freshness. On his return, the man at first does not recognize where he is, but when a dinosaur persuades him that he has indeed landed on the very planet which his own greed had destroyed, he asks for a bit of it back. The dinosaur rejects the concept of sole ownership: "'[The planet] is all yours, but it is also all mine. Remember that. This time the earth belongs to everyone, not parts of it to certain people but all of it to everyone, to be enjoyed and cared for'". Another plea for conservation, if somewhat gruesome, is to be found in *The Grizzly Revenge*, in which a cruel ruler and his crazy lady are destroyed by the very creatures to whose destruction they had devoted their lives. More positively, perhaps, *Father Gander Nursery Rhymes* (sub-titled *Traditional Nursery Rhymes updated for the 1980s*) offers new verses to old rhymes; added to *Twinkle, Twinkle, Little Star*, for example, we read:

> If the sky stays pure and clean,
> We will see your twinkle bright.
> But smoke, exhaust, and acid rain
> All will cloud your flickering light.
> Twinkle, twinkle, little star,
> I'd like to keep you as you are.

Issues of class can be dealt with implicitly, as in *A Walk in the Park*, or more explicitly, as in *Allumette*. In the former, Mr Smith and his little girl, Smudge, leave their inner-city two-up/two-down terraced house to take their mongrel, Albert, for a walk in the park; they meet Mrs Smythe and her son, Charles, who have left their detached (with garage) suburban house to take their pedigree labrador, Victoria, for a walk in the same park. The dogs and the children play with each other, but each of the two adults leaves for home without even acknowledging the other's presence. In *Allumette*, a match-girl's wretched conditions are about to lead to her death, when she is able to shame the rich into alleviating poverty by contributing to a fund which will ensure that there is always enough money to help those stricken by 'famine, fire, floods and war'; the solution to Allumette's problems is merely a palliative in face of the misery caused by capitalism, but that misery is at least explicitly recognized. Berg also has an explicit recognition of class in the *Nipper* series, which 'are written in the belief that every child needs to be able to look at a book or hear a story and feel "That's me!"' (Berg, 1972).

In the area of race, the sparks are few. There are some early picture-books, such as *Holes and Peeks* or *Ten, Nine, Eight* or *Nandy's*

Bedtime, which offer a positive image for a young black girl to fasten on to, and *Brown Bear, Brown Bear, What do You See?* glances at racial diversity, but these are insignificant in number compared with the plethora of other picture-books which ignore black children altogether. The *Jafta* series offers children an insight into life in South Africa, as does a book such as *Not so Fast, Songololo*; *Oh Kojo, How Could You!* has a Ghanaian background; and *Dig Away Two-Hole Tim* is set in Guyana; otherwise, we have to rely mainly upon small publishers like the Peckham Publishing Project, which produces such books as *Our Kids*, a photographic account of life in the inner city. There are also some superbly-produced picture-books of non-eurocentric myths which can be used to widen children's horizons beyond the merely anglo/eurocentric, myths such as *What Made Tiddalik Laugh* (Australian), *How the Birds Changed their Feathers* (Arawak, Guyana), *Once there were No Pandas* (Chinese). *Who will be the Sun?* (Kutenai, North America), *Hot Hippo* (Kikuyu, East Africa), *How Night Came* (Tupi, the Amazon) or *Tortoise's Dream* (Bantu). Such books are a useful complement to other myths like those of Adam and Eve or Prometheus.

Gender issues have received much more positive attention. If one is looking for positive characters for a girl to identify with, one can turn to *Ruby, the Red Knight* or *The Paperbag Princess*, both of whose main characters defeat the villains (a giant, a dragon and a wizard in the former and a fiery dragon in the latter), by using their wits rather than by violence. *Sunshine* and *Maisie Middleton* deal with girls in more ordinary circumstances who demonstrate an effective degree of independent initiative in a normal situation. *He Bear, She Bear* tries to combat sex-stereotyping: motherhood and fatherhood may be sex-determined, but not whether somebody will be a nurse, fire-fighter, doctor or train-driver.

> We'll jump and dig and build and fly...
> There's *nothing* that we cannot try.
> We can do all these things, you see,
> Whether we are he *OR* she.
> So *many things* to be and do,
> He Bear, She Bear, me...and you.

Alex's Bed and *I Want to See the Moon* give examples of one-parent families, a woman and her son in the former and a man and his son in the latter. *Father Gander Nursery Rhymes*, already mentioned above for its stance on environmental issues, 'tries to let little girls and little boys feel equally important' (Larche, 1986, p. 7); for example:

Jack be nimble, Jack be quick,
Jack jump over the candlestick!
Jill be nimble, jump it too;
If Jack can do it, so can you!

And there are some amusing re-workings of fairy-story themes; for example, in *All the King's Horses* the princess decides not to marry the woodcutter, and the paperbag princess tells Prince Ronald, "'You look like a real prince, but you are a toad." They didn't get married after all'.

In the Classroom

As has been suggested above, the teacher of young children does not have readily available a good selection of well-illustrated, well-told stories for young children which in the all-white school will effectively demonstrate the oddity of the pupils' situation and give them an empathetic insight into the lives of their black fellow-citizens; in the racially diverse class will offer a variety of positive images, with at least one of which any child of any race can identify; and in all classrooms will be a counterbalance to the otherwise dominant world-view, 'male-dominated, able-bodied, monocultural...filled with sexism, anger, violence, environmental and nutritional ignorance and insensitivity to the human condition' (Larche, 1986, p. 7).

However, such a shortage of positive stories does not mean that the classroom teacher is unable to use literature to encourage humane, collaborative and caring attitudes. That there exist some books which are suitable for such aims is demonstrated in the previous section; they, and others like them, should be added to the class's stock or borrowed from the local library or teachers' centre. If a reason needs to be offered beyond the obvious one that all children need to be assured of their own self-worth through what they read, it can be pointed out to those who disburse the school's capitation grant that evidence demonstrates that to offer a child a text within which they are able to find *themself* enables them more effectively to learn to read and maintains them as a reader more securely (see Klein, 1985; Campbell and Wirtenberg, 1980). Other additions to the children's reading can be made by the children themselves, either as a personal book (*My Name is Yasmin*) or as a class book (*The Day We Went to the Park*); the illustrations can be drawn or painted or photographic[7]. Other children in the school can write illustrated stories for their younger peers, which will be of benefit not only to the latter but also to the former, as they wrestle over the problems of authorship and collaboratively discuss questions of a story's moral or its underlying values. Stories, especially 'real-life' stories, can be exchanged between schools: between an urban school and a rural school, between a suburban school and an inner-city school, between a British school and one overseas. Or the teacher themself can write a story for their children, as did Penfold (1985).

The teacher also needs to keep in touch with new publications. Would the school subscribe to Letterbox Library or *Dragon's Teeth* or *Multicultural Teaching* or *Spare Rib*? Would it join the National Association for the Teaching of English, which has a section concerned with the development of language and literacy in young children? Local librarians and those in charge of children's books in teachers' centres are another useful source of information, help and guidance.

I have not advocated that books other than those which are positively anti-sexist, anti-racist and anti-capitalist should be thrown out of the classroom, if only because the children would be left with very little to read. Like Jeffcoate (1982) or Stones and Mann (1980), I would wish to extend the range of literature available to children, not restrict it. Books whose values do not accord with the ethos of the classroom should not be burnt or censored but should be used for a positive purpose, for 'such research evidence as there is... suggests that it is the discussion, not just the reading, of particular books that influences whether they have beneficial personal and social effects' (Jeffcoate, 1982, p. 28). Then children may come to the same kind of conscious realization about the dominant ideology as did the children in Minns's class, who corresponded with the editor of *The Sun* about his concept of sexism (Minns, 1985), or Jitinder, who knew that publishers would never publish a book about an Indian boy (Penfold, 1985). If children are to change the world, they first have to know it.

Notes

1. If the noun which I use is non-gender-specific, I use the pronoun 'they' to refer to it. I find the use of 'he' in such circumstances objectionable, reinforcing as it does the male world, and 'she/he' or '(s)he' clumsy. The use of 'they' in such a way in English grammar has a long history (as in 'Anybody who arrives late will not get their dinner') and if anybody should object on the grounds that 'they' is

plural and therefore cannot refer to a singular noun, one merely has to say to them, 'You are ignorant of English grammar', which, the addressee being singular and 'you' being plural, provides its own refutation.

2. In a letter to Geoffrey Trease, W. E. Johns, the author of the *Biggles* series, stated why he wrote for children:

> I teach sportsmanship according to the British idea...I teach that decent behaviour wins in the end as a natural order of things. I teach the spirit of team-work, loyalty to the Crown, the Empire, and to rightful authority (Quoted in Dixon, 1977b).

3. The five most popular books were *Over in the Meadow* (a song book) (37 borrowings), *I Want to See the Moon*, *Funnybones* (35 each), *The Snowman* (30) and *Burglar Bill* (28).

4. *Mrs Plug the Plumber*, *Meg on the Moon*, *Lazy Mary* and *Alex's Bed*.

5. Male anthropomorphized animals outnumber the females even more than boys outnumber girls. Even in otherwise positive books such as *Moose*, in which a very significant point could have been made by casting the moose as female, Michael Foreman has in fact made it male.

6. The first factor which Wells lists (op. cit.) is that of real interactive conversation: if a child is treated by their caregiver as an equal participant in conversations about meaningful subjects, they are likely to 'do well' in school.

7. In a multiracial reception class in Newcastle, children are taken to their own homes and a photographic record, with text, is made of the visit.

Children's Books Mentioned

Alex's Bed (1980) Mary Dickinson, pictures by Charlotte Firmin, London, Deutsch.

All the King's Horses (1976) Michael Foreman, London, Hamish Hamilton.

Allumette (1975) Tomi Ungerer, London, Methuen.

Animal Farm (1945) George Orwell, London, Secker and Warburg.

Beano Book 1988(1987) London, D. C. Thomson.

Beauty and the Beast by de Beaumont, in *The Giant All-Colour Book of Fairy Tales* (1971) retold by Jane Carruth, London, Hamlyn.

Biggles W.E. Johns.

Brown Bear, Brown Bear, What do You See? (1984) Bill Martin Jr, pictures by Eric Carle, London, Hamish Hamilton.

Burglar Bill (1977) Janet and Allan Ahlberg, London, Heinemann.

Butter Battle Book, The (1984) Dr Seuss, London, Collins.

David Copperfield (1849-50) Charles Dickens.

Dig Away Two-Hole Tim (1981) John Agard, illustrated by Jennifer Northway, London, The Bodley Head.

Dinosaurs and All That Rubbish (1972) Michael Foreman, London, Hamish Hamilton.

Father Gander Nursery Rhymes: Traditional Nursery Rhymes Updated for the 1980s (1986) Doug Larche, illustrated by Carolyn M. Blattel, Watford, Exley.

Funnybones (1980) Janet and Allan Ahlberg, London, Heinemann.

Grizzly Revenge, The (1983) Ruth Brown, London, Andersen Press.

Grumble, The (1987) Wendy Body, London, Longman.

He Bear, She Bear (1975) Stan and Jan Berenstain, London, Collins.

Hiroshima Story, The (1983) Toshi Maruki, story in English by Judith Elkin, London, A. and C. Black.

Holes and Peeks (1984) Ann Jonas, London, Julia Macrae Books.

Hot Hippo (1986) Mwenye Hadithi, illustrated by Adrienne Kennaway, London, Hodder and Stoughton.

How Night Came: a Folk Tale from the Amazon (1986) Joanna Troughton, London, Blackie.

How the Birds Changed their Feathers, 2nd ed. (1986) Joanna Troughton, London, Blackie.

I Want to See the Moon (1984) Louis Baum, illustrated by Niki Daly, London, The Bodley Head.

Lazy Mary (1982) June Meiser and Joy Cowley, London, Arnold Wheaton.

Little Black Doll, The (1965) Enid Blyton, Manchester, World Distributors.

Little Black Sambo (1898) Helen Bannerman.

Maisie Middleton (1977) Nita Sowter, London, A. and C. Black.

Meg on the Moon (1976) Helen Nicoll and Jan Pienkowski, London, Puffin.

Moose (1971) Michael Foreman, London, Hamish Hamilton.

Mrs Plug the Plumber (1980) Allan Ahlberg, pictures by Joe Wright, London, Penguin.

Nandy's Bedtime (1982) Errol Lloyd, London, The Bodley Head.

Not so Fast, Songololo (1985) Niki Daly, London, Gollancz.

Oh Kojo, How Could You! (1985) Verna Aardema, pictures by Marc Brown, London, Hamish Hamilton.

Once there were No Pandas: a Chinese Legend (1985) Margaret Greaves, illustrated by Beverley Gooding, London, Methuen.

Our Kids (1985) London, Peckham Publishing Project, 13 Peckham High Street.

Over in the Meadow (1986) O.A. Wadsworth, London, Viking Kestrel.

Paperbag Princess, The (1982) Robert N. Munsch, illustrated by Michael Martchenko, London, Scholastic.

Rose Blanche (1985), Roberto Innocenti, text by Ian McEwan, London, Jonathan Cape.

Ruby the Red Knight (1983) Amy Aitken, New York, Bradbury Press.

Snowman, The (1978) Raymond Briggs, London, Hamish Hamilton.

Story of Ferdinand, The (1937) Munro Leaf, illustrated by Robert Lawson, London, Hamish Hamilton.

Sunshine (1981) Jan Ormerod, London, Penguin.
Ten, Nine, Eight (1983) Molly Bang, London, Julia Macrae Books.
Tin-Pot General, The, and the Old Iron Woman (1984) Raymond Briggs, London, Hamish Hamilton.
Tortoise's Dream (1980) Joanna Troughton, London, Blackie.
Two Monsters (1985) David McKee, London, Andersen Press.
Walk in the Park, A (1977) Anthony Browne, London, Hamish Hamilton.
What Made Tiddalik Laugh, 2nd ed. (1986) Joanna Troughton, London, Blackie.
Whistle for Willie (1966) Ezra Keats, London, The Bodley Head.
Who will be the Sun? (1985) Joanna Troughton, London, Blackie.

Schemes and Series

Griffin and Dragon/Pirate, Leeds, Arnold.
Jafta, Cambridge, Dinosaur.
Ladybird Key Words Reading Scheme, Loughborough, Wills and Hepworth.
Link Up, Edinburgh, Holmes McDougall.
Mr Men, London, Thurman.
Nippers, London, Macmillan.
1, 2, 3 and Away, St Albans, Granada.
Reading 360: the Ginn Reading Programme, Aylesbury, Ginn.
Storychest, London, Arnold Wheaton.
Thomas the Tank-Engine, London, Kaye and Ward.

Sources of Information

Dragons Teeth, 7 Denby Road, London, W11 2SJ.
Letterbox Library, 8 Bradbury Street, London, N16 8JN.
Multicultural Teaching: to Combat Racism in School and Community, Trentham Books Ltd, 30 Wenger Crescent, Trentham, Stoke-on-Trent, ST4 8LE.
National Association for the Teaching of English, 49 Broomgrove Road, Sheffield, S10 2NA.
Spare Rib, 27 Clerkenwell Close, London, EC1R 0AT.

Other References

ALHIBAI, Y. (1987) 'The child racists', *New Society*, 82, 4 December, pp. 13–15.
BENNETT, J. (1983) *Learning to Read with Picture Books*, London, Thimble Press.
BETTELHEIM, B. (1978) *The Uses of Enchantment: the Meaning and Importance of Fairy Tales*, London, Penguin.

BORDELON, K.W. (1985) 'Sexism in reading materials', *The Reading Teacher*, 38, 8, pp. 792–7.

BUTLER, D. (1979) *Cushla and her Books*, London, Hodder and Stoughton.

CAMPBELL, P.B. and WIRTENBERG, J. (1980) 'How books influence children: what the research shows', *International Books for Children Bulletin*, 11, 6, pp. 3–6.

CARRINGTON, B. and DENSCOMBE, M. (1987) 'Doubting Thomas: reading between the lines', *Children's Literature in Education*, 18, 1, pp. 45–53.

COARD, B. (1971) *How the West Indian Child is Made Educationally Subnormal in the British School System: the Scandal of the Black Child in Schools in Britain*, London, New Beacon Books.

CZAPLINSKI, S. (1976) 'Sexism in award-winning picture-books', in CHILDREN'S RIGHTS WORKSHOP (Eds) *Sexism in Children's Books: Facts, Figures and Guidelines*, London, Writers and Readers Publishing Co-operative, pp. 31–7.

DIXON, B. (1977a) *Catching them Young 1: Sex, Race and Class in Children's Fiction*, London, Pluto Press.

DIXON, B. (1977b) *Catching them Young 2: Political Ideas in Children's Fiction*, London, Pluto Press.

ENGEL, R.E. (1981) 'Is unequal treatment of females diminishing in children's picture books?' *The Reading Teacher*, 34, 6, pp. 647–52.

FALCON, L.N. (1980) 'The oppressive function of values, concepts and images in children's books', in PREISWERK, R. (Ed.) *The Slant of the Pen: Racism in Children's Books*, Geneva, World Council of Churches, pp. 3–6.

FORD, K. (1985) *What are little girls made of?: a study of sexism and sex-stereotyping in children's books*, unpublished B.Ed. dissertation, Polytechnic of Newcastle upon Tyne.

HOFFMAN, M. (1976) 'The political content of children's reading', in ZIMET, S.G. *Print and Prejudice*, London, Hodder and Stoughton, pp. 105–21.

JEFFCOATE, R. (1982) 'Social values in children's books', in HOFFMAN, M. *et al.* (Eds) *Children, Language and Literature*, London, Open University Press, pp. 24–31.

KAMENETSKY, C. (1984) *Children's Literature in Hitler's Germany*, Athens, Ohio, Ohio UP.

KLEIN, G. (1985) *Reading into Racism: Bias in Children's Literature and Learning Materials*, London, Routledge and Kegan Paul.

KNIGHT, C. (1983) 'The evaluation of reading schemes for use in the multicultural classroom', *Multicultural Teaching*, II, 1, pp. 33–5.

KUYA, D. (1980) 'Racism in children's books in Britain', in PREISWERK, R. (Ed.) *The Slant of the Pen: Racism in Children's Books*, Geneva, World Council of Churches, pp. 26–45.

LARCHE, D. (1986) *Father Gander Nursery Rhymes: Traditional Nursery Rhymes Updated for the 1980s*, Watford, Exley.

LEESON, R. (1985) *Reading and Righting*, London, Collins.

LLOYD, E. (1984) '*Little Black Sambo*', *Dragons Teeth*, 20, p. 4.

MINNS, H. (1985) 'Girls don't get holes in their clothes: sex-typing in the primary school', in HODGEON, J. *et al.* (Language and gender working party) *Alice in Genderland: Reflections on Language, Power and Control*, Sheffield, National Association for the Teaching of English, pp. 21–8.

O'DELL, F.A. (1978) *Socialisation through Children's Literature: the Soviet Example*, London, Cambridge University Press.

PENFOLD, M. (1985) 'Paradoxes for teachers', *Dragons Teeth*, 22, pp. 6–7.

PLATO (1941) *The Republic of Plato*, translated with introduction and notes by F. M. Cornford, London, Oxford University Press.

RICE, I. (1987) 'Racism and reading schemes: 1986, the current situation', *Reading*, 21, 2, pp. 92–98.

SHANNON, P. (1986) 'Hidden within the pages: a study of social perspective in young children's books', *The Reading Teacher*, 39, 7, pp. 656–63.

SMITH, P. (1984) *Language, the Sexes and Society*, Oxford, Blackwell.

SPENDER, D. (1980) *Man Made Language*, London, Routledge and Kegan Paul.

STINTON, J. (1979) *Racism and Sexism in Children's Books*, London, Writers and Readers Publishing Co-operative.

STONES, R. and MANN, A. (1980) 'Censorship or selection?', *Children's Books Bulletin*, 3, pp. 2–3.

SUTHERLAND, R.D. (1985) 'Hidden persuaders: political ideologies in literature for children', *Children's Literature in Education*, 16, 3, pp. 143–57.

WELLS, G. (1986) *The Meaning Makers: Children Learning Language and Using Language to Learn*, London, Hodder and Stoughton.

ZIMET, S.G. (1976) *Print and Prejudice*, London, Hodder and Stoughton.

Chapter 9

Studying the World of Work: An Inevitable Controversy[1]

Alistair Ross

Is the world of work a controversial element in the primary school curriculum? I want to suggest in this chapter that there are two levels at which it might be considered to be so. Firstly, at what I shall call level one, are the arguments that the very inclusion of an industrial dimension within the primary school curriculum is in itself controversial. Secondly, at level two, the actual content of the industrial-based materials and ideas themselves may be controversial. This chapter will consider both arguments.

At level one, several possible reasons for regarding the inclusion of industry as controversial might be advanced. These range from suspicions about who is suggesting such an inclusion and concerns about their possible motives, worries about possible bias in the subject matter and its effect on young children, to a feeling that employment and the wider world are an area too distant from the concerns of the young child, and that they should somehow be protected from the potential ugliness of the real world.

This chapter will examine these arguments in turn. Who are the competing bodies suggesting that primary school children investigate the socio-economic world about them? Why are they doing this? Turning then to level two, the chapter considers whether such investigations in themselves are controversial? Is this an appropriate area of study for the young child?

But the argument presented here will go beyond this. It will suggest – back to level one – that primary teachers are now being *required* to include an industrial or world-of-work dimension within their curriculum. At the same time – on level two – they are also being required to approach it in a way that highlights the controversial aspects of our economic life. The chapter will give some examples of ways in which this might be done, some of which highlight the way our society is based on economic classes. I will suggest that whatever the reasoning behind the Government's attempts to insist that this area be included in the curriculum, and whatever the intentions of the various Education Acts to curtail political issues in the classroom, the practical effects of current policy oblige primary school teachers to explore critically with their children the foundations of our capitalist society.

Who is Advocating Industry Education in Primary Schools?

The links between the nature of schooling and future vocation have been explicit for centuries. The first English schools in the sixth century were designed to train priests and monks. Vocational schools in the eighteenth century served the armed services, commerce and engineering (Williams, 1961), and, as Jamieson (1986) points out, the nineteenth century public school curriculum, based on the classics, was justified as appropriate intellectual training for administrators, statesmen and colonial officials. The extension of popular education was justified on similar pragmatic grounds: James Kay-Shuttleworth wrote in 1867

> Many of our principal manufacturers have arrived at a conviction that a superior education is necessary to enable our artisans to acquire such knowledge as may enable them to continue a successful competition with foreign rivals (quoted in Maclure, 1986, p. 107).

While the industrial/vocational emphasis may have faltered (or never got under way) after this, (Wiener, 1981), 'vocational chic', as Kushner (1985) has described contemporary initiatives such as the Technical and Vocational Educational Initiative (TVEI), is hardly a modern phenomena.

The present debate dates from James Callaghan's speech at Ruskin College in October 1976. Callaghan's argument has been summarized by Watts (1983) as follows:

> industry [was] complaining that new recruits from school lacked the basic skills required for some jobs, and was further troubled to discover that the best trained students from university and polytechnic had no intention of joining industry (p. 67).

As unemployment increased further, politicians reiterated that there was a causal link between the presumed lack of industrial and technical elements in education and youth unemployment. Margaret Thatcher introduced the TVEI scheme to the House of Commons as providing 'a relevant curriculum for a changing world of work' (*The Times*, 1982). David Young, then Chairman of the Manpower Services Commission and charged with the introduction of TVEI, made the connection even more explicit in a letter to LEA Directors of Education in January 1983: 'The objective of TVEI is to widen and enrich the curriculum in a way that will help young people prepare for the world of work' (MSC, 1983).

Primary teachers have not been excluded from these exhortations to make their teaching relevant to the wider world of work, industry and enterprise. The White Paper *Better Schools* (DES, 1985) suggested that

> the content of the primary curriculum should, in substance, make it possible for the primary phase to... give pupils some insights into the adult world, including how people earn their living (para 61).

In 1986 Industry Year was launched, not merely directed at 'encouraging a better understanding of industry, its essential role, and its service to the community', but also specifically targeting primary and secondary schools as 'the most important area in which a long-term change in attitudes can be achieved' (Industry Year, 1985). An analysis of the disparate and competing diagnoses and prescriptions put forward by Industry Year belongs elsewhere: suffice it to note that many of the purported ills of British industry were laid at the doors of the 'anti-industrial attitudes' of schools (Industry Year, 1986; Wiener, 1981). There are other proponents of industry education, both in primary and secondary education, and some of their arguments will be presented below. The main thrust, however, has clearly come from these political sources.

Before examining the motives of politicians in advocating a vocational-led industrial focus within the curriculum, it may help to examine some of the possible structural relationships between industrial organization and schooling. It has been argued by writers such as Bowles and Gintis (1976) that it is the prime function of schools to produce a stratified and docile work force, with each strata provided with the sufficient skills necessary for their particular economic role. Proponents of this case would hold that the expansion of primary (or elementary) education was essentially undertaken for economic reasons, rather than arising (as is popularly supposed) from the democratic imperative that was expressed by Robert Lowe on the passing of the Reform Bill in 1867: 'I believe that it will be absolutely necessary that you should prevail on our future masters to learn their letters' (quoted in Maclure, 1986, p. 71).

Far from being won by workers over the opposition of capitalists and other entrenched interests, schools were imposed upon the workers (Katz, M, 1968). From their study of American education, Bowles and Gintis (1976) conclude:

> The expansion of mass education and the evolution of its structural forms was sparked by demographic changes associated with the industrialisation and urbanisation of economic and social activity. The main impetus for educational change was not, however, the occupational skills demanded by the increasingly complex and growing industrial sector... Rather, schools were promoted first and foremost as agents for social control of an increasingly culturally heterogeneous and poverty-stricken urban population in an increasingly unstable and threatening economic and political system (pp. 230–1).

Bowles and Gintis were analyzing the development of American schooling, and an exact comparison with the evolution of British primary schooling is not possible. Yet since their argument accords the capitalist organization of labour as the prime mover in the establishment of the educational system, it should therefore inform an analysis of the relationship between British schools and industry. According to their thesis, schools have a variety of functions. They:

> foster legitimate inequality through the ostensibly meritocratic manner by which they reward and promote students...

> create and reinforce patterns of social class, racial and sexual identification among students which allow them to relate 'properly' to their eventual standing in the hierarchy of authority and status in the production process.

> foster types of personal development compatible with the relationships of dominance and subordination in the economic sphere...

> create surpluses of skilled labour sufficiently extensive to render effective the prime weapon of the employer in disciplining labour – the power to hire and fire (Bowles and Gintis, 1976, p. 11).

Such an analysis runs against the tradition of education expressed, for example, by Holt (1983), who points to:

> the distinction between liberal education – education for freedom, for tackling problems as yet unknown – and

schooling as training, for instrumental tasks as they are currently perceived (p. 84).

Others have challenged the thesis on the grounds of its inappropriateness to the British experience. This chapter will show that there are at least some examples of primary education where the children are challenging the existing economic and social order within the existing curriculum.

Politicians, from both major parties, have been advocating a greater awareness of industry amongst educationalsits for some years. Callaghan's Ruskin speech led, *inter alia*, to the establishment of the Schools Council Industry Project (SCIP), which led efforts to introduce greater interplay and exchange between industry and schools.

This was followed by the TVEI scheme on secondary education in the early 1980s – 'one of the most massive injections of resources to foster change' (Whitty, 1985, p. 118) – which was imposed on the assumption that the products of schools were unemployable, and that this either accounted for, or was one of the main causes, of high unemployment. This deficit model of education is based on assumptions similar to that of Bowles and Gintis: that schools exist to produce workers. Notwithstanding that Paul Willis's study (1977) suggests that schools in working-class areas were already doing this quite effectively, the ideology of all the recent attempts to focus the curriculum in an industrial/technological/vocational direction has been that schools are failing their pupils. This may be through deficiencies in the processes of schooling, or in the content of the curriculum, or in the personal qualities of the pupil (Kushner, 1985). Fiddy's analysis of the 'recurring theme [in the TVEI thrust] is that a lack of jobs is to do with a lack of skills and/or attitudes, and a lack of skills is to do with schooling' (Fiddy, 1986, p. 87), and he goes on to argue that teachers must 'make it clear that generic or transferable skills, training in occupational families, or a broad-based traditional education will not provide jobs. The argument is not against vocational education *per se*. But the objection is to the implication that the acquisition of skills will, by itself, open doors to employment' (Fiddy, 1986, p. 94).

Similar and parallel moves have taken place in primary education. SCIP began working with primary schools in 1982, and now has a flourishing network. The TVEI initiative was not directed at primary schools, but the planners of Industry Year 1986 specifically targeted primary education. The chairman, Sir Geoffrey Chandler, claimed that children were first being given antipathetic attitudes to industry in their primary schools, and that if the more able children were properly motivated at that age they would be more likely to become interested in industry as a career in later life. Sir Geoffrey was perhaps considering industry in the narrow sense of privately-owned manufacturing industry, but his point seems clear: his view of industry education is that it is instrumental in sorting and directing the more able towards employment in industry.

There are a number of arguments about such a model of education. The real world beyond school is itself contentious, perhaps particularly when considering questions of work and unemployment. Naturally, work is an important part of modern society, and therefore, naturally, education must accommodate 'the world of work' in the curriculum. Industry education initiatives from sources that are suspect to teachers may well contain the capacity to be subverted from the teaching *of* work to teaching *about* it. As yet, however, no place has been given for teaching about unemployment and the lack of work, or about the distribution of the fruits of enterprise, or about the social organization of workplaces. I am suggesting here that we should attempt to educate children into a truly critical appreciation of our economic organizations, and that, as I will argue below, teachers have now been given (albeit unwittingly) the opportunity to make this a formal and overt part of the curriculum so that it need not be left to subversive activity.

Is this a Controversial Area?

Three major groups of reasons why 'the world of work' might be disputed as a legitimate area for the primary school curriculum, at level one, were identified at the beginning of this paper. As has been seen, some of the proposers of the idea seem to have overt and simplistic instrumental motives, and if their premises were accepted by teachers they would find themselves in a situation in which they were bound to fail. There are, however, other (and in my view more compelling) reasons for exploring work and employment with primary-aged children. These revolve around level two, the controversial nature of the subject matter itself, and the appropriateness of such subject matter as a suitable vehicle for developing critical skills and attitudes with primary-aged children.

Wellington (1986) has offered a useful set of conditions that help define an issue as controversial within the curriculum. A controversial issue must:

involve value judgements, so that the issue cannot be settled by facts, evidence or experiment alone

be considered to be important by an appreciable number of people. (Wellington, 1986, p. 3).

The authors of the White Paper *Better Schools* (DES, 1985), many of the advocates of Industry Year, and indeed the authors of the current (1988) Education Act clearly do not see that any value-judgments are involved when children investigate their industrial surroundings. However, primary children clearly do discover issues about which to argue, as the following series of eight vignettes from classrooms illustrates (Ross, 1983, p. 17):

Fourth year juniors discussed with a supervisor the tasks of the managers and directors in a small factory they had visited:

Patrick:	Why do the directors get more money than the workers?
Superv'r:	I don't know, I'll have to ask them when I get back!
Teacher:	What are you trying to say, Patrick?
Patrick:	All the directors might work in the office, and so on, they might send out orders and answer telephones all day, but they don't work on a bench, on machines and that, so I don't think that none of the directors should get no more money than the workers.
Nick:	Do you think that the directors should get more money than the workers?
Superv'r:	Well of course they got to. 'Cos they're the top, and they've got to have everything under control...
Sula:	Going back to Nick's point, when he said that workers should get more money than directors. Well, I don't think that's right. Directors should get most 'cos they're organising it, and they're you know like – responsible for running the factory, so they should get just a *little bit* more than the workers.

Fourth year juniors visited a local bank on three occasions, and built up a picture of how the bank accountant inteviewed people seeking a loan. One child wrote:

He judged people on how they presented themselves, and whether they were trustworthy or not. I would not like to be an interviewer like the bank accountant for it would be difficult to make a decision. If I misjudged a customer, I would be shaking.

In a role-play that followed, another child interrogated a would-be borrower on a proposed enterprise – on wages, machinery, workforce and retail outlets – before she leaned forward and asked 'Tell me, just what sort of collateral do you have to back this loan?' (Bentley, 1984, pp. 77–8).

First year juniors: the class visited a post office sorting office, interviewed the staff to discover the different tasks involved, and then devised their own simulation activity in school. A problem arose when some sorters did not know in which regional pigeon hole a particular letter should be placed, and simply disposed of it in the nearest convenient pigeon hole. The problems that this caused led to a vigorous discussion about the differences between cooperation at work and being inter-dependent at work. Given the concrete experience of sharing tasks and having to cope with other people's mistakes at work allowed them to engage in a quite sophisticated discussion (Ross, 1985, pp. 59–61).

Fourth year juniors set up their own mini-company making sweets: each child was interviewed by the class management team to fill the posts available. But when the two 'group accountants' demonstrated that they were not keeping a firm grip on the finances the whole company met to discuss their performance. Andrew had been generally lax and uninterested; Emma had shouldered the burden of both and made a mistake. Both were given an official warning by the class. Some time later, when a parent-helper had come in to be told what ingredients needed to be bought, it was found that the books didn't balance. The class discussion that followed split into three groups: one to dismiss Andrew, one to dismiss both Andrew and Emma, and an undecided group. Some members of the first two groups then threatened strike action if Emma was disciplined for Andrew's laziness. Eventually, after much discussion, Andrew was offered a different and less responsible post, and Emma was reinstated (Shea, 1986, pp. 59-61).

Infants organising a cafe-restaurant in class used 'the knowledge that they had from their families' first-hand experience of working in the food and restaurant trade... The amazing thing was the children's spontaneity in discussing things between themselves, who was going to cook, serve and eat the food. Many of the children had a clear cut idea of the hierarchy within the restaurant trade and several children wanted to take on the managerial role of being the "Guvnor". Eventually they agreed to take turns and share the job' (Clover and Hutchings, 1986, pp. 36–7).

Top infants discussed how much the greengrocer they had talked to should pay for his stock and how he should price his goods. Most thought that he should charge the same for his fruit that he had paid himself. A few believed he ought to resell goods at *less* than he had originally paid, since the goods were now clearly second-hand (Hutchings, 1987a, p. 3).

Third year juniors tour the workshops of a light engineering company. Some of their written observations picked out the different gender roles in the factory:

> Of the people who actually work in the workshops making things, none of these people are women. I asked the technical director about this. First I asked 'Do you know of any women who have worked in the workshops?' He said 'No.' Then I asked 'If a man and a ladie [*sic*] came for an interview who would you take?' He said: 'It depends who was best for the job.' But I personally think he'd take the man because of the situation its been all these years.
> I asked [Frank, a polisher] if he would like women to work with him now. He came out with a clear answer and said that he thinks women should not work with him because they would get dirtie and complaine about it.

Other children were struck by the number of pin-ups around some work benches. 'What would your wife say if she could see those?' demanded one girl. Other children were struck by the divisions between staff and workers, with separate doors and different provision of lavatories (Ross, 1988, p. 5).

Top infants set up their own business to make and sell biscuits, and needed to raise sufficient capital to buy their materials. They eventually bought 10p shares in the company, limiting the issue to one share per child and one per parent. In this instance, the share capital was simply returned when the venture was over: other primary schools that have organised mini-enterprises with share capital have also paid dividends; a few have even allowed trading in shares (Grant, 1987, pp. 160–1).

Here children are raising issues that require argument, discussion and consideration of values. These examples refer respectively to hierarchy and differential rewards; the ownership of industry and the raising of capital; cooperation and interdependence; discipline at the workplace; power and authority; profit and pricing; gender roles in the workplace and issues of class and status; and the distribution of profits. Some of these concepts are concerned with the capitalistic mode of production, its organisation and whether or not it is equitable. Others relate to the questions of inter-personal relationships at work and the organization of different functions between groups of workers. These are not easy questions, but they are ones that these children apparently found little difficulty discussing. It might be noted that in nearly all these cases the children tended to advocate ideas based more on notions of inherent 'fairness' than on the actual practice they had observed. They had in most cases observed industry, discussed it with the people involved and then challenged some of the premises that had been offered to them.

There is, then, evidence, classroom based and other (e.g., Tajfel *et al.*, 1970; Campbell and Lawton, 1970), that primary-aged children are prepared to raise important *moral* questions of fairness about their social world, and to do so in a way that may be perceived either as idealistic or naive. The questions raised concern the ways in which work is organized, how it is rewarded and how it is controlled. A sizeable proportion of the adult population also sees these as contentious areas. Many adults may accept these systems as the way our society is organized, but to children they can become important and legitimate issues of debate. *Pace* Wellington's definition, industry education in the primary school does revolve around a number of issues of opinion, and these issues are regarded as important by many adults – *and by the children* – as major questions about economic society.

Is it Appropriate for Young Children?

As the examples above may indicate, investigating 'the world of work' is certainly within the capabilities of primary school children. There are two issues that concern its appropriateness for the primary school: in terms of the content matter itself, and in terms of whether it is a suitable controversial issue.

Primary schools have always encouraged children in some ways to use the environment around them as a focus for some learning. Using first-hand material has increasingly involved children in the study of the locality: as the basis for close observational drawing, for the study of biological and physical phenomena, as a medium to begin to organize the spatial concerns of the geographer, and as a suitable starting point for the exploration of the past.

The social environment is a crucial dimension of the child's surroundings, and one in which important concepts that help organize social understanding must be developed. Some of these have been mentioned above: others might be conflict, social control, change, continuity and tradition. These can only be built up by children repeatedly encountering, discussing and generalizing from specific examples and instances of these concepts. Indeed, there are only three types of societal studies in which children will encounter such concepts: the study of societies in the past, the study of societies in other contemporary cultures, and the examination of the society around them. Without wishing at this point to debate the relative priorities of history, anthropology and sociology in schools, one might simply assert that primary-aged children should encounter examples of all three throughout their primary schooling, and that there is both a certain logic and a body of case studies that suggest that the child's studies of his or her own society should be an essential initial reference point.

Within our society, it is clear that the organization of work is one of the essential dimensions that must be included in any offering we make to children. They are clearly interested in work: it (or the lack of it) surrounds their families and their conversation from an early age; people at work are part of their everyday experience (from callers at the house, people at work on the streets and in shops, to people at work in schools); and problems concerning work are part of children's media diet. It is not possible, even if it were desirable, to shield children from the dominant role that our society ascribes to work. Paradoxically, while work is, in one sense, all around them, and they are aware of much of it, in another sense there is often a mystique that shrouds adult work from children.

This is not to argue that we need to teach children *for* work, or even *about* work. What is being suggested is not a form of vocational training for the primary school, or even the beginning of supplying information about careers. Nor should it be thrusting at children the benefits of enterprise (free or otherwise), or hagiographies of the great entrepreneurs of our society (such as, for example, Cyril Lord, John Bentley, Richard Murdoch, Robert Maxwell, Lord Kagan, Ernest Saunders and Gerald Benson?). Education *through* industry uses the workplace to put children into vivid contact with the realities of competition, conflict and cooperation (Blyth, 1984).

What of the argument that all controversial matters should be kept out of the primary classroom? The recent advice of one local education authority on this is unequivocal:

> It is neither desirable nor possible to exclude controversial issues from the classroom... It must be recognised that the curriculum can never be totally value free: even the selection or omission of issues involves value judgements (ILEA, 1987, p. 9).

Dearden (1981) and Stenhouse (1970) both argue for the inclusion of controversial issues in the curriculum on grounds of content. 'Matters of widespread and enduring significance which if neglected are likely to leave gaps in a child's education'. (Stenhouse, 1970, p. 11). But Stradling *et al.* (1984) also present a justification on the grounds of skills and processes: children examining a controversy acquire essential skills of searching for and evaluating evidence, questioning of sources, probing for bias and presenting considered viewpoints.

Future Implications of a Primary Schools Industrial Dimension: Level One

Teachers have been exhorted to make their teaching relevant to the wider world of work, industry and enterprise. The passage in *Better Schools* (DES, 1985) which refers to giving primary children 'insights into the adult world, including how people earn their living' has already been quoted. The series of consultation papers that led to the Education Reform Act also made references to what the Government clearly see as a continuing gap between school and 'the real world'.

Before this, the DES discussion paper *Teacher Training and Preparation for Working Life* (DES, 1982) urged all initial teacher education institutions to ensure that teachers understood the economic foundations of society, and the role of industry and commerce in wealth creation. This was followed by DES circular 3/84 on the accreditation of teacher education courses which established a set of criteria that all initial teacher education courses were required to follow. One criterion was that students should be able to make their pupils 'aware of the economic and other foundations of a free society' (DES, 1984, annexe para 12). This rather curious form of words (in themselves pregnant with unspoken value-judgments) has been interpreted by many initial teacher education institutions by including some kind of critical industrial awareness element within courses.

The National Curriculum document repeatedly refers to employment as an end-product of education. For example, it states that Government 'policies for the school curriculum [which] will... equip them for the challenges of employment in tomorrow's world.' (DES, 1987a, para 4). Emphasis has been added to this quotation: clearly schools have not been seen as hitherto providing sufficient. Again, schools must provide 'a curriculum which equips them with the knowledge, skills and understanding that they need for adult life and employment' (DES, 1987a, para. 7); and '...the various elements of the national curriculum bring out their relevance... and their practical applications and continuing value to adult and working life' (DES, 1987a, para. 8, iii). Such a curriculum is responsive to employers in more than simply its content: '...employers and the local community should know what a school's assessment and examination results indicate about performance and how they compare.' (DES, 1987a, para. 36, iii).

The consultation paper, *The Organisation of Education in Inner London*, refers to the need for 'the education service to become more responsive to the requirements of parents and employers' (DES, 1987b, para. 1). This part of our agenda seems set.

How Controversial Issues must be Handled: The Law and Good Practice at Level Two

There has been some considerable debate over the past fifteen years about how teachers should tackle controversial issues in the classroom. This initially came from the discussions of the Humanities Curriculum Project (HCP), a Schools Council undertaking led by the late Lawrence Stenhouse. On the issue of controversy as such, Stenhouse was clear: 'Given a dispute in society about the truth of a matter, the teacher might wish to teach the dispute rather than the truth as he knows it' (Stenhouse, 1975, p. 93). The HCP put forward the proposal that the teacher should act within this as a neutral-chairperson, allowing children to debate and discuss, ensuring that the evidence from all sides was available, but never expressing an opinion.

This position has prompted much discussion (see the chapter by Singh in this volume). There ought, it is argued, to be some form of balance:

> Balanced learning implies a situation in which pupils have access to a range of evidence, information and views... It is essential... that teachers ensure that in a series of lessons pupils encounter a range of views. This principle should apply in all contexts in which pupils encounter controversial issues (ILEA, 1987, p. 11).

Wellington, arguing from the specific example of the nuclear issue in schools, points out that:

> several viewpoints, some of them extremely important, [may be] never expressed at all... Is the teacher then under an obligation to present these viewpoints?... Such an attempt... may be necessary in maintaining balance in a discussion... Which is of overriding importance: balance or neutrality? (Wellington, 1986, p. 152).

With children of primary age, the experience of several teachers who have worked in these areas suggests that some less neutral stance is necessary, to ensure, by playing devil's advocate if necessary, that a range of viewpoints is available and given space for debate. It *is* possible, by chairing, to let minority views be aired, and if necessary airing them oneself as examples of alternative views, at least to dilute the view that holds that 'the antagonistic structure of society rigs the rules of the game. Those who stand against the established system are *a priori* at a disadvantage, which is not removed by the toleration of their ideas, speeches and newspapers' (Marcuse, 1976, p. 308).

The 1986 Education (No. 2) Act has changed the situation somewhat. The Act, firstly, forbids partisan political activities in junior (though not infant) schools:

> The local education authority... and the governing body and the headteacher shall forbid the pursuit of partisan political

activities by...junior pupils; and the promotion of partisan political views in the teaching of any subject in the school (DES, 1986, section 44).

Secondly, it provides that the same authorities shall 'secure that where political issues are brought to the attention of pupils...they are offered a balanced presentation of opposing views' (section 45). Thus if any controversial issue that is raised in school can be described as political, then the school *must* offer a full range of views on this. Although these clauses have not yet been tested in the courts, it was reported that the DES had advised that section 45 might be interpreted as meaning that if the pro-nuclear Ministry of Defence film *Protect and Survive* film were shown in school, it would *have* to be countered by some alternative viewpoint, such as that of CND.

As we have seen, teaching about the world of work is inherently likely to raise a series of issues about the distribution of the resources of the economy: of ownership of the means of production, of the distribution of profits and of power. These are inherently political questions, and, therefore, children will need to be treated to a range of viewpoints.

Children, Class and Capitalism

I am not suggesting that children will need to be exposed to the views of the main political parties on industry and employment (although these may, in some particular circumstances, be useful – for example, for children observing a major industrial dispute in their community and neighbourhood). The 'opposing views' which the legislation requires be given 'a balanced presentation' are not necessarily the opposing views of party politics.

There are different views about how business enterprises should be financed. Should the capital be raised by borrowing from institutions, by borrowing from private individuals, or by borrowing from the workers themselves? Primary children engaged in mini-enterprises have used all three possibilities, though none seem yet to have tackled more than one system, or made any comparison. How do they achieve the information to make decisions? Sometimes from adults other than teachers in the classroom – bankers and small-scale entrepreneurs explaining how they operate. There's a natural tendency for children to adopt similar methods. For example, after a range of classes had been involved in making case studies of different industries, I asked children: 'How could a person with an idea for making something get the money to start a factory?' Children under about 9 made comments such as 'Save up for it'. Some were more unusual – 'Rob a bank', or even 'Marry a rich woman'. The two parallel classes of 11–year–olds, however, gave different responses. Of the class that had investigated a local bank, 52 per cent suggested raising a loan from the bank (often mentioning that some form of security would be needed and the necessity of paying interest); only 26 per cent suggested issuing shares. The parallel class had launched their own magazine, and had raised the capital for this by allowing each member of the class to buy three 10p shares. 42 per cent suggested that a share issue could raise the capital, while only 8 per cent mentioned bank borrowing. The share-issuing class had a strict rule that shares could not be traded (in fact, it was more akin to a worker's cooperative than a private company). Another class who issued shares did allow trading, and one child sold her share to a visiting lecturer – to whom she later wrote to tell that, the company being wound up at the end of the year, shares were being redeemed at less than the price he had paid.

There are differences of opinion over how firms should operate. Should they be directed by those who provide the capital? Or by those who provide the labour? Or by some combination? Many children seem better able to perceive the ultimate functions of an enterprise: it is to produce goods or a service that is needed by the community, not simply (as many adults aver) to make a profit. When we describe industry and commerce (and the public services for that matter) providing the *wealth* of the community, we are referring to their products, not their profits. Frank discussion of these issues by children, involving adults from a trade union background as well as from managerial positions, can produce powerful reflections and insights.

The marshalling of such a range of opinions is beyond the capacities of the school alone. It is necessary – as well as being highly desirable – to involve the local economic community in this form of work in schools. Every primary school, by virtue of its enrolment, is surrounded by people who either are working or who wish to work. The most minimal level is that there are local shops and a DHSS office: there are often factories, offices, farms, hospitals, stations and warehouses. People from these establishments are very often willing to talk with young children, and where possible to let children visit their workplaces. The more locally a school tries, the greater the sense of shared community and the more likely a sympathetic response.

There are three broad ways that children can begin to explore a 'work' dimension with a local industry. Firstly, they can make a case study of a local workplace: visits to the workplace where workers, managers and trade unionists discuss what they do and how they interrelate provide data for classroom discussion and analysis. Workers can return to the school to see what children have done. Secondly, a group of children can plan and carry out their own mini-enterprise, raising capital, planning how to organize their production, making and marketing their goods, and distributing any profits (or losses). Thirdly, a class can simulate some work activity, taking on roles that introduce them to the decisions and problems that are found in a workplace.

Imaginatively treated, a close study of industrial themes with primary-aged children is able to sensitize children to a series of important issues. Bowles and Gintis (1976, p. 11) have alleged that:

> education helps defuse and depoliticize the potentially explosive class relations of the production process, and thus serves to perpetuate the social, political and economic conditions through which a proportion of the product of labour is expropriated in the form of profits.

If the scrutiny of children is turned on the production processes and the relationships within them, it is possible that this will no longer be true.

Note

1. This chapter is based on a seminar paper discussed at the Primary Schools and Industry Centre of the Polytechnic of North London in November 1987. I am grateful for the comments of my colleagues there; the responsibility for the final draft remains mine.

References

BENTLEY, J. (1984) 'Fourth year juniors studying work in a branch of a local bank', *The Social Science Teacher*, 13, 3, pp. 77–8.

BLYTH, A. (1984) 'Industry Education: Studies from the North West' in JAMIESON, I. (Ed.) *We Make Kettles; Studying Industry in the Primary School*, Longmans for the Schools Council, pp. 82–100.

BOWLES, S. and GINTIS, H. (1976) *Schooling in Capitalist America: Educational Reform and the Contradictions of Economic Life*, London, Routledge and Kegan Paul.

CAMPBELL, R.J. and LAWTON, D. (1970) 'How children see society', *New Society*, 19 November, pp. 237–40.

CLOVER, J. and HUTCHINGS, H. (1986) 'The variety of the urban environment: an infant school's experience', *Primary Teaching Studies*, 1, 3, pp. 29–37.

DEARDEN, R. (1981) 'Controversial Issues and the Curriculum', *Journal of Curriculum Studies*, 13, 1, pp. 37–44.

DEPARTMENT OF EDUCATION AND SCIENCE (1982) *Teacher Training and Preparation for Working Life*, London, HMSO.

DEPARTMENT OF EDUCATION AND SCIENCE (1984) *The Accreditation of Initial Teacher Education Courses* (Circular 3/84), London, HMSO.

DEPARTMENT OF EDUCATION AND SCIENCE (1985) *Better Schools*, Cmnd 9469, London, HMSO.

DEPARTMENT OF EDUCATION AND SCIENCE (1986) *Education (No. 2) Act 1986*, London, HMSO.

DEPARTMENT OF EDUCATION AND SCIENCE and WELSH OFFICE (1987a) *The National Curriculum 5–16: A Consultation Document*, July, 1987, DES.

DEPARTMENT OF EDUCATION AND SCIENCE (1987b) *Consultation Paper: The Organisation of Education in Inner London*, 11 September 1987, London, HMSO.

FIDDY, R. (1986) 'Education for employment and unemployment: is this the age of the trained?' in WELLINGTON, J. (Ed.) *Controversial issues in the curriculum*, Oxford, Blackwell, pp. 83–98.

GRANT, S. (1987) 'From "some kind of business" to "a life system"', *Primary Teaching Studies*, 2, 2, pp. 155–64.

HOLT, M. (1983) 'Vocationalism: the new threat to universal education', *Forum*, 25, 3, pp. 84–6.

HUTCHINGS, M. (1987a) *Report on Teacher Fellowship 1986–87* (mimeo), Primary Schools and Industry Centre, Polytechnic of North London.

HUTCHINGS, M. and ROSS, A. (1987b) *The Primary Schools and Industry Kit*, Polytechnic of North London.

INDUSTRY YEAR (1985) *Industry Year 1986*, (pub. May 1985), London, Royal Society of Arts.

INDUSTRY YEAR (1986) *Industry Year is Working: Sir Geoffrey Chandler reports at half-way stage*, Press Release, 22 July.

INNER LONDON EDUCATION AUTHORITY (nd, 1986) *The teaching of controversial issues in schools: Advice from the Inspectorate*, London, ILEA.

JAMIESON, I. (1986) 'The case for linking schools and industry', *Secondary Education Journal*, 16, 1, pp. 5–7.

KATZ, M. (1968) *The Irony of Early School Reform*, Harvard University Press.

KUSHNER, S. (1985) 'Vocational Chic: A Historical and Curriculum Context to the Field of Transition in England', in FIDDY, R. (Ed.) *Youth, Unemployment and Training: A Collection of National Perspectives*, Lewes, Falmer Press.

MACLURE, J. S. (1986) 5th ed. *Education Documents, England and Wales: 1816 to the present*, London, Methuen.

MANPOWER SERVICES COMMISSION (1983) *TVEI Operating Manual*, London, HMSO.

MARCUSE, H. (1975) 'Repressive Tolerance', in CONNERTON, P. (Ed.) *Critical Sociology*, Harmondsworth, Penguin.

ROSS, A. (1983) 'The Bottle Stopper Factory: Talking all together', *The English Magazine*, 11, pp. 14–18.

ROSS, A. (1985) 'Modelling the world of work: active learning about industry in the primary school', *Primary Teaching Studies*, 1, 1, pp. 55–63.

ROSS, A. (1988) *Case Study: Gender roles in a light engineering factory: Third year juniors investigate*, Primary Schools and Industry Centre/PNL Press.

ROSS, A. and SMITH, D. (1985) *Schools and Industry 5–13 – Looking at the World of Work: Questions Teachers Ask*, Schools Curriculum Industry Partnership (SCIP).

SHEA, A. (1986) 'Chasing Rainbows: Children having a say', *Primary Teaching Studies*, 2, 1, pp. 53–61.

STENHOUSE, L. (1970) *The Humanities Curriculum Project: An Introduction*, London, Heinemann.

STENHOUSE, L. (1975) *An introduction to curriculum research and development*, London, Heinemann.

STRADLING, R., NOCTOR, M. and BAINES, B. (1984) *Teaching Controversial Issues*, London, Arnold.

TAJFEL, H., NEMETH, C., JAHODA, G., CAMPBELL, J. and JOHNSTON, N. (1970) 'The development of children's preference for their own country: a cross-national study', *International Journal of Psychology*, 5, pp. 245–53.

THE TIMES (1982) 13 November.

WATTS, A.G. (1983) *Education, Unemployment and the Future of Work*, Milton Keynes, Open University Press.

WELLINGTON, J.J. (Ed.) (1986) *Controversial Issues in the Curriculum*, Oxford, Blackwell.

WHITTY, G. (1985) *Sociology and School Knowledge: Curriculum Theory, Research and Politics*, London, Methuen.

WIENER, M.J. (1981) *English Culture and the Decline of the Industrial Spirit, 1850–1980*, Cambridge University Press.

WILLIAMS, R. (1961) *The Long Revolution*, London, Chatto & Windus.

WILLIS, P. (1977) *Learning to Labour: How working class kids get working class jobs*, Farnborough, Saxon House.

Chapter 10

Demolishing 'The House that Jack Built': Anti-sexist Initiatives in the Primary School

Christine Skelton

> Where primary education is universal and free, girls tend to do
> as well as boys and sometimes better' (Megarry, 1984, p.15).

The view that primary schooling does not discriminate against girls is
one held by many people including teachers. However, substantial
evidence is available which demonstrates that such a belief is
misconceived (Clarricoates, 1980; Hough, 1985; French and French,
1986). Gender discrimination is as prevalent in the primary school as
in secondary education yet operates at a subtler level. For example,
whilst it is a relatively easy task to identify the imbalance in numbers
of girls and boys opting for science subjects it is not so easy to assess
the influence gender stereotyped reading schemes has on girls' self-
confidence. As it stands, then, schooling effects girls' and boys' life
chances in two ways: firstly, *selection*, that is, by providing situations
in which children either succeed or fail, and this in turn effects what
job opportunities are available to males and females; secondly, the
type of schooling children receive influences their *learning* specifically
with regard to the ideas, values and confidence girls and boys develop
through their educational experiences (Yates, 1987). The intention
here is not to rehearse the arguments adequately represented elsewhere
(Whyte, 1983; Marland, 1983; Holly, 1985) illustrating how and
where gender discrimination occurs in primary schooling; rather it is
to indicate *why* gender stereotyping is regarded as a non-issue in
primary education and *what* action has been taken to redress the
gender inequalities which exist (Skelton, 1985). At the same time, it
should be noted that although the principles which underpin anti-
sexist and anti-racist education share many commonalities, the studies
referred to in this chapter have focused upon predominantly white, if
not all-white, school populations. It is clear that work has to be done

which examines the relationship between the effects of sexism on white girls and the so-called double oppression of sexism and racism experienced by black girls within primary education. As such information is not yet available then the suggestions given in this chapter may have to be modified or changed in the light of future research into this area.

So, what is it about primary education that has resulted in gender issues being given so little attention? Most primary teachers pay lip-service to the idea that girls and boys should be given equal educational opportunities, but only a minority of teachers are aware of the implications the use of this term has for girls' experiences of schooling. The concept of equal educational opportunities as applied to gender was given increasing prominence by policy-makers in the 1970s, and was defined in terms of equalizing school resources and educational benefits; the idea being that if girls and boys were provided with equal access to the current educational system any imbalances in examination achievement and subsequent career opportunities would be resolved. The problem of gender inequalities in education was seen simply as relating to male and female examination achievement. However, by 1980 the question was being asked whether girls had gained anything from this interpretation of equal opportunities as the strategies developed to resolve gender differences did not tackle fundamental aspects of girls' education (see Weiner, 1986). As Lyn Yates (1987) has pointed out, the question as to why girls' equal access to education has failed to make any significant advances in widening career choices and further studies may be related to the content of what girls learn and the attitudes they form about their capabilities. The argument has moved from one which assumed that equal access to education is sufficient to ensure equality between the sexes (Byrne, 1978) to one which emphasizes the process of schooling on girls' attitudes and expectations. This has meant an examination of the male-female power relations within educational institutions, specifically the structure, organization and content of present-day schooling (Mahony, 1985; Lees, 1986).

So, when any discussion of 'equal opportunities' takes place we need to be aware of where the emphasis is being placed; that is, on *access* or *outcome.* Gaby Weiner and Madeleine Arnot (1987) have neatly summarised the distinction between the approaches. When there is a concern for girls' access to education (known as an 'equal opportunities' or libertarian approach) the strategies adopted include providing a common core of subjects for all pupils, analyzing classroom texts and resources for stereotyping, and devising policy guidelines and courses promoting gender 'awareness'. If the concern is for the outcome of girls' schooling experiences then strategies are adopted which place girls and women at the centre of the classroom, so challenging the dominance of male experience (known as a radical or anti-sexist approach). At the same time, although adopting an equal opportunities approach to girls' education fails to recognize male power many teachers have introduced anti-sexist initiatives by using some of the equal opportunities strategies as a 'way-in'. To refer to Weiner (1986) again, the two approaches are not discrete, rather anti-sexist or:

> girl-centred education (is) not necessarily an alternative to egalitarian strategies but (is) a much more powerful dimension and extension to their work (p. 273).

There are indications that primary teachers, especially at infant level, attach much importance to the notion of individual children developing their own way and at their own pace (King, 1978; Alexander, 1984). So, when primary teachers state that gender inequalities are not a problem in their classroom because 'all children are treated the same' they are most likely to be referring to girls and boys having access to the same schooling rather than to measures which confront structural inequalities. To develop and implement anti-sexist initiatives requires an awareness of how and where gender discriminatory practices occur, together with an understanding of the principles of anti-sexism. By focusing upon two specific areas, namely school hierarchy and organizational practices, and teaching approaches and resources I will illustrate my own and others' attempts to develop anti-sexist education in primary schools.

School Hierarchy and Organizational Practices

By considering the staffing structure of a 'typical' primary school the differences in male/female teaching status can be easily identified. At the beginning of the 1980s I was employed as a teacher at 'Andover Wynn', a large primary school situated on a new housing estate. The teaching staff of twenty included four males who held the posts of headteacher, senior master and third and fourth year junior team leaders. This imbalance in both number of male teachers in primary education and positions of responsibility is a common feature of schools (Whyld, 1983). In addition, the sexual division of labour amongst the ancillary staff reinforced the children's awareness of male dominance. That is, there was a male caretaker in charge of an all-female cleaning staff. Now, quite clearly, when there is such an obvious sexual division both in function and seniority, a powerful message is being daily enacted for the pupils. The reasons for these differences and the implications they have for the careers of women teachers have been discussed elsewhere (Marland, 1983; Evetts, 1987). It is enough to say that from the moment they enter school children are exposed to role models which clearly delineate adult males as the rule-enforcers, decision-makers and 'controllers' whilst adult females 'look after' the younger children and carry out the instructions given by the predominantly male hierarchy.

Although schools can do little to alter the ratio of male to female members of staff, steps have been taken to redress the current sexual division of labour within primary schools. 'Equal Opportunity' local education authorities (LEAs) are aware of the need to encourage women not only to apply for promotion, but undertake management courses specifically designed to develop women's confidence. As yet these courses are few and far between, but it is not simply a matter of women teachers being seen to hold positions of authority within schools that is the sole concern. The appointment of more women to posts of responsibility is only useful if these women use their position to challenge the staff hierarchies of which they have become a part. At the same time, there is value in providing children with alternative role models, and schools aware of the influence of gender role models have recognized the need to restructure the teaching staff's areas of responsibility to reflect females in a more positive light. Consequently, female teachers may coordinate the 'high status' areas of the primary curriculum, such as maths and science, and supervise extra-curricular computer clubs rather than needlework/handicraft clubs. It is equally important to have male teachers working with the younger primary-age children but there is often a reluctance to do so. The men on the staff of Andover Wynn would be quite happy to take the odd storytime session, yet were horrified at any suggestion that they take a class of infants for a year.

Part of the hidden agenda of teacher socialization is that the teaching of younger children should be undertaken by females. Male teachers are often dissuaded from teaching younger children either actively, in that 'it wouldn't benefit chances of career promotion', or by more subtle insinuations that there is something suspicious about a man who wants to work with young children (Skelton, 1985). Teachers of nursery/infant children are seen by many people as being of lower status than teachers of junior age children. It is not uncommon for a teacher who has taught a reception class one year and a junior class the next to be asked if they have been 'promoted'. And how many times have teachers of younger children challenged the expression 'going down to the infants'? Supposedly, the idea that one goes 'down' to the infants has little to do with the actual location in the school of the nursery/infant departments but rather more to do with an all-too-common perception of the teaching of young children as being equivalent to child-minding. The aim of anti-sexist education is to raise the status of women's characteristics, skills and achievements, so, as a 'woman's job', teaching the nursery/infant age range has first and foremost to be valued for its own sake. Some of the problems associated with achieving this aim have been noted by Acker (1983) in her assessment of the underlying assumptions that exist about the influence of gender on teachers' careers. She notes how female teachers are often blamed by researchers for their subordinate position in schools, and their apparent lack of ambition is often attributed to their orientation towards the family rather than a career. Radical changes in attitudes have to occur towards 'infant' and 'junior' teaching as well as what are 'appropriate' age bands for males and females to teach. Peter Gordon's (1986) study of the way men teachers view themselves suggests that the first step is for a school staff to examine their own attitudes and expectations of the teaching role through discussion and in-service courses.

Developing an awareness of gender discriminatory practices and implementing anti-sexist strategies requires the involvement of all the members of a school, children as well as adults. A problem immediately arises when there is no firm understanding of, or genuine commitment to, gender equality. In 1982 the LEA I worked for designated itself an 'Equal Opportunities' employer. Up until this time there had been no mention of equal educational opportunities by the staff of Andover Wynn and the day to day organization and routines of the school reflected all the gender discriminatory practices found in primary schools (see Clarricoates, 1978; Delamont, 1980). The LEA asked each school to nominate one of its teaching staff as Equal Opportunities representative. In the initial stages there was a notable absence of organized in-service courses for either the nominated representatives or whole school staff. The only contact the representatives from each school had with each other was through an unofficial working party which was formed to establish a communication network. The working party of twenty teachers included only two members of staff from primary schools and, perhaps not surprisingly, resulted in the issues specific to primary education never reaching the agenda. Without a supportive network and appropriate guidance as to what primary schools could do to resolve gender discriminatory practices meant that only overt forms of discrimination were tackled. The staff of Andover Wynn, like so many other primary schools in the Authority, believed they had dealt with gender discrimination simply by amending the way in which registers were called and ceasing to 'line up' the children in rows of girls and boys.

Obviously these superficial measures could not make any real changes in girls' option choices at thirteen plus, nor were they going to encourage girls to develop greater self-confidence. This does not mean to say that these school practices should be allowed to pass, but there has to be a recognition of what children are learning when exposed to these taken-for-granted forms of organization. For example, children are selected as 'monitors' to facilitate the smoother running of school and classroom organization, but the question is: who is asked to do what jobs and what are the children learning about their role in the school? Some monitoring jobs are seen as more suitable for one gender than another: so girls wash up the art pots, look after infants during wet playtimes and take messages around the school (missing out on lesson time), whilst boys set out the PE apparatus and have responsibility for moving computer equipment and 'problem-shooting'. There are clear implications here for girls' and boys' perceptions of their importance to the functioning of the school which cannot be resolved merely by switching roles. Similarly, it is not uncommon for primary schools to have two playgrounds one for infants and one for juniors, although some schools designate the infant playground as available to junior girls (Whyte, 1983). Even where this 'official' gender separation does not occur, segregation still takes place with the boys dominating the space by kicking balls and running about, ensuring that girls are pushed to the periphery of the playground (Wolpe, 1977; Mahony, 1985).

Several primary schools (in the ILEA) have taken up the challenge of devising schemes which place value on girls' playtime activities and confront boys' displays of aggression. These ideas range from demarcating playground space, allocating various areas for specific functions: using the hall at lunchtime for quiet activities such as reading and board games, and using PE lessons to provide children with alternative playground activities placing the emphasis on collaborative rather than competitive games. Whatever approach has been adopted the aim has been towards creating an ethos and atmosphere where girls can walk and talk without intimidation, ensuring that girls are given space inside and outside the building. The importance of collaborative work in establishing anti-sexist principles in the primary classroom has been noted by Hilary Claire (1986). She records how children, when left to themselves, gravitate into single sex groups, from the reception class upwards. Approaches should be adopted whereby teachers deliberately encourage mixed sex collective groups, as this form of organization helps children to see the other sex as partners and not rivals, and provides opportunities for girls and boys to get to know each other in both a work and play context.

The principles of cooperation, democracy and egalitarianism which are central to anti-sexism can also form the basis of the learning experiences provided for children in the primary classroom. There is a steady increase in the literature on collaborative learning (Sharan, 1980; Yeomans, 1983; Biott, 1987), and it is the use of this approach and teaching resources which will be taken up and developed in the next section.

Teaching Approaches and Resources

> The concern of strategies for reform has been that what is taught, the way things are taught and the way schools are organized should draw on what women have done and do in society as well as from men, and should value what girls bring to schooling and the ways they want to learn (Yates, 1987, p.19).

By the time children reach secondary school it is too late to expect girls and boys to develop an interest in particular subjects when the skills required have not featured in the primary phase of a child's education. The question is, what happens in primary schools which enables children to maintain traditional stereotypical 'interests'. As Alexander's (1984) work has suggested, the ideology of child-centredness may act as a constraint upon the implementation of an equal opportunities policy in primary schools. In theory, child-centred approaches involve children learning through discovery and choosing the activities they undertake. However, the 'free choice' element does not result in equal experiences as children tend to 'choose' traditional stereotyped materials. Thomas (1986) observed the free play of nursery age children and noted how the girls frequently played in the home corner and were reluctant to use the large toys in the outside area, whilst the boys preferred to undertake activities using big bricks and constructional toys. She also discovered very little evidence of cross-sex play, either in the classroom or out of doors. Even when children are directed by the teacher towards specific activities, the experiences they receive are very different and stereotyped images continue. Hough (1983) gives the following example of what happened when a teacher directed children to the 'choosing equipment':

> ... different roles (were) played out in the play house, the girls being mum, baby, or big girl, the boys would be daddy, a dog, a monster or playing out an adventure game. When using the large blocks the girls would construct a house, or a spaceship to play house in, the boys would construct motorways and spaceships for adventures (1983, p. 3).

In addition girls and boys do not get equal shares in the teachers' time. Recent research by the Equal Opportunities Commission in Belfast (1987) has shown that the informal teaching studies found in most primary schools help boys to be more assertive at the expense of girls. The open and less direct methods of teaching acted in favour of the 'visible' children in the class who interacted more with the other children. They also gained more of the teacher's time and attention. The 'visible' children in each class proved to be predominantly boys. We know that boys and girls have different learning styles, with boys active, participatory and demanding whilst girls are more passive, less participatory and lacking in assertive skills (Whyte, 1983). In most classrooms, it is the teacher who does most of the talking and any discussion takes place through the teacher. For example, a common format for discussion in a classroom is for the teacher to choose a topic, ask a question and remind children of the rules (e.g. 'put your hand up', 'don't shout out the answers'). But, as French and French (1986) have shown, small groups of boys (rather than boys as a whole) tend to dominate the 'discussion' and circumvent these rules by interrupting and passing more comments. Furthermore, the study in question suggests that teachers often select boys to answer questions as a way of controlling them.

The idea, then, that primary classrooms provide equal educational experiences because, on the surface, teachers attempt to provide the same opportunities, is totally misconceived. On the one hand any whole-class teaching approach cannot cater for the differences in learning styles of girls and boys, although the evidence given above suggests that boys are more likely to be able to deal with this situation. On the other hand, Hough's (1983) study has shown that the influence of the media, parents and peer group on girls' and boys' gender stereotyping cannot be overcome simply by forcing children to undertake specific activities in the vague hope they will develop 'all-round' skills. My first attempts at remedying gender inequalities with a class of first year junior children were concentrated upon balancing the amount of time and attention given to girls and boys. Like many other feminist teachers, I discovered that, whilst it was a difficult enough task to convince male colleagues they have to relinquish their hold on practices which sustain and reinforce their dominant status, it was an even more complex task convincing primary age boys. As Spender (1982) realized, even when teachers make a determined effort to equalize their time, the actions of boys prevent it taking place. The types of request girls and boys make differ, with the boys demanding more of the teachers time. For example, girls would ask 'Is this work right?', and 'What should I do now?' whereas boys would ask 'Can you help me/show me what to do?' It rapidly became clear that the approach I was adopting, a mixture of whole-class teaching and group work (with children sharing resources but completing individual tasks), did not alter the ability of the boys to dominate the classroom proceedings.

Classrooms can be microcosms of the power/control systems of wider society and, whether knowingly or unknowingly, generally reflect a patriarchal authority structure. Any attempts to challenge this situation demand a shift in the power balance away from relying on authority figures, at the same time making this explicit to the children. In practice, this means replacing competitive or individual-istic modes of working, whereby a child only succeeds at the expense of others' failure, with collaborative forms of working. The intention here is not to argue a case for collaborative groups (see Brunger, 1986; and Carrington and Troyna's chapter on 'race'), but to point out the aims and one or two of the problems of using this approach for anti-sexist purposes. As experience proved to me, collaborative group work is not simply a matter of sitting a group of children together, giving them a task and telling them to get on with it. One of the aims of anti-sexist education is to help children to develop respect for themselves and others, and this may be achieved by creating situations in which girls and boys must work together in order to complete a task.

So, in practical terms, this means setting up situations in which children learn to listen to each other. But they often have difficulty in listening to each others' ideas and in assimilating or assessing them when their ideas interrupt their own train of thought (Tann, 1981). When the intention is for girls to learn to value themselves and boys to learn to value girls' experiences, then group composition is of fundamental importance. Unfortunately, there are no simple solutions. The research by Tann (1981) showed that when children are placed in mixed groups, boys tend to take risks, are more dynamic and 'low ability' boys respond well. In contrast, girls are more consensus orientated and avoid challenging each other – their main concern, even in all-girl groups, is to seek agreement and reduce tension, thereby failing to probe or challenge each other. I found that deciding upon groups likely to be able to work together depended to a great extent on simply knowing the children and keeping the size of the groups to three or four. Once the composition of the groups had been decided, exercises and activities were devised which encouraged children to listen to each other, talk, and eventually report back to other groups (Horton *et al.*, 1982; Biott, 1984; Claire, 1986, are a source of practical suggestions).

What needs to be stressed here is that, although it is not *necessary* for girls to participate in discussion in order to secure educational advancement, it is important for the social aspect of girls' development. That is, in the context of discussion, girls learn to see themselves as less significant than boys and, unless appropriate steps are taken by the teacher, assumptions regarding boys' confidence and girls' reticence are continued and reinforced. The results of failing to challenge these assumptions are that stereotyped attitudes are reinforced, and manifestations in behaviour become more evident as children move through the educational system. (Mahony, 1985; French and French, 1986).

Changing one's teaching approach from one which is based upon authoritarianism and competition to one which promotes democracy and cooperation is but one factor in developing a classroom environment underpinned by anti-sexist principles. The materials used in schools are often biased in that they show females in marginal roles or render them invisible. As such, text books, literature, posters, science kits and project packs tend to reinforce traditional gender stereotypes (see Lobban, 1975; Kelly, 1981; Northam, 1982, and Whitley's chapter). When I first began to use collaborative techniques with my class it seemed that the choice was either to refuse to use any of the resources in my classroom or to develop strategies which would allow the children to question their gender bias. As it is impossible, or at least very difficult, to 'manage' a class of twenty-five plus children without resources, I set about devising several courses of action so that the materials could be used in a more appropriate way. An initial step was to change all the packaging of science kits, project packs and toys (e.g., Lego, table-top games) with an apparent gender bias. I also managed to obtain some non-traditional posters from the

ILEA Resources Centre and the EOC, also realizing that the children's pre-conceived ideas about appropriate careers for men and women would not allow them to relate, for example, to illustrations of female carpenters. Julia Hodgeon's (1985) work in nursery schools showed that female teachers would become involved with activities in the home corner or table-top games, such as jigsaws or lotto, but they would stand back from the 'messier' or mechanical activities and offer only verbal encouragement. Now, in the same way that sitting a child in front of a computer does not provide them with programming skills, giving children non-traditional role models does not overcome prejudice and discrimination. However, positive 'real-life' models may go some way towards creating alternative perspectives for girls and boys. So, a policy was adopted whereby the female ancillary staff and female parents became actively involved with the children using the woodwork bench or tasks involving sand and water, and, whenever possible, male colleagues would be asked to take cookery sessions or bandage cut knees at playtimes. With regard to textbooks and literature, the children were asked to rewrite popular fairy tales, changing the gender of the main characters, and a great deal of time was spent compiling class books on women scientists, women in history and women's achievements in the local community.

Teachers who are committed to providing equal educational opportunities, whether a supporter of 'liberal' or 'radical' ideas, usually welcome suggestions as to how the lot of girls can be improved. If changes are required in their teaching approach then, generally, alternative teaching strategies will be adopted. However, attempts by individual teachers to underpin classroom life with anti-sexist principles are likely to fail as, unless there is an effort by the whole school, individual teachers and their classes become isolated. After struggling for two terms with a first year junior class, certain events took place which highlighted the 'gap' an anti-sexist curriculum had created between my class and the rest of the school. For example, on the occasions when the children had to go to another teacher there was great consternation as to whether they should 'line up' as boys and girls, because the games teacher liked the boys to do football and the girls netball, and the music teacher preferred to have girls and boys sitting on opposite sides of the classroom to 'harmonize'. In effect the children were having to come to terms with two different school expectations and as one girl said, 'Sometimes I wish we could be like the other classes outside the hut (our mobile classroom) but I like being just people in the classroom'. In a similar way, as I was the token equal opportunities representative, my attitudes singled me out from colleagues and, although there was never overt aggression towards the anti-sexist initiatives I practised, it was often the subject of staffroom jokes. This kind of reaction is not uncommon, as Ord and Quigley (1985) discovered when they attempted to introduce anti-sexist initiatives into their school:

> It is frightening how quickly we run into hostility or dismissive amusement when even quite small changes are suggested...it is well to be aware...that power is not given away, that there will be conflict and that we need to be prepared for it. Opposition takes various forms: aggressive personal attacks, the raised eyebrows of 'oh no, not this again', the stereotyping of one or two members of staff as 'the equal opportunities people' (p. 106).

The reasons for this hostility are concerned with a deep-seated reluctance to challenge dominant ideological assumptions (Arnot and Weiner, 1987). Teachers would appear to be generally unwilling to broach in discussion so-called 'controversial issues' such as sexism (Alexander, 1984; Harwood, 1985), and often hide behind the notion of childhood innocence as a justification for not tackling these issues. Anti-sexist education involves developing a policy of positive discrimination for girls and many teachers believe that this move would marginalize boys, thereby undermining the essence of child-centred education. As Kate Myers (1981) has pointed out: 'The fact that girls have not had their fair share of attention for some years now, does not seem to inspire the same feelings of guilt' (p. 28). Support networks for teachers committed to both equal opportunities and anti-sexist education are of fundamental importance, both to promote a feeling of optimism that change can come about and to present a united front in a climate which is becoming increasingly difficult even to keep these issues on the agenda

Conclusion

The extent to which any real change can be brought about in girls' educational experiences in the current political climate is highly debateable. The history of feminists' struggle to ensure girls and women get an equal share of the cake has succeeded in obtaining what Acker (1986) has called the 'vague support' of the Department of Education and Science (DES). Searching for a policy on gender in DES reports and publications is akin to looking for a needle in a haystack. In the past few years a committee of inquiry has been set up to investigate racial disadvantage in education (DES, 1985a) and special needs children (DES, 1978). Yet no similar empirical investigation has been undertaken in respect of gender inequalities in education since the HMI reported on curricular differences in 1975, nor has the DES considered gender as a priority for in-service funding. Recent influential reports such as *Better Schools* (DES, 1985b), Curriculum Matters 5-16 series, and *Quality in Schools: the Initial Training of Teachers* (DES, 1987), make little or no reference to the question of gender discrimination. Similarly, with the exception of a few DES regional in-service training courses on aspects of gender stereotyping in education and short courses on promoting equal opportunities in schools (Orr, 1985), there have been no attempts by the DES to develop a consistent interventionist programme. The DES has neatly side-stepped its responsibility for ensuring that the measures laid down in the Sex Discrimination Act (1975) are complied with by placing the onus on LEAs, with the DES itself occupying only an 'advisory' role. More importantly, the guidance given in Circular 2/76 (DES 1976) to LEAs suggested strongly that any interpretation of the Sex Discrimination Act should be related specifically to *curriculum* inequalities:

> 9...Responsibility for evaluating curriculum to provide equal access to experience, information and guidance rests with local education authorities, managers and governors, and, most important of all, the teachers. While the Secretary of State will not hesitate to use his powers to stop any particular act of discrimination, he does not control the curriculum and it is important for teachers, with the support of local authorities, to take a hard look at the organization of the curriculum and to consider whether the materials and techniques they use, and the guidance they give, especially in the early years, inhibit free choice later. (p.5).

The results of this have been that, whilst many LEAs have Equal Opportunity policy statements, they remain at the level of being nothing more than pieces of paper sitting in advisors' filing cabinets and headteachers' desk drawers. These policy statements enable LEAs to be able to be seen to facilitate change without actually implementing change.

Also, however worthless these policies are when there is no intention to implement them, it should be realized that many equal opportunity statements fail to recognize that girls experience a specific form of oppression. As it stands, policies of equal opportunities have attempted to resolve current inequalities by trying to 'educate' girls, different cultural groups, working-class and handicapped pupils to aspire to, and achieve, in the same way as a white, middle-class, able-bodied male. Girls do not 'underachieve' at school, yet still lose out because of the discriminatory structure of school life. As Yates (1987, p. 10) has said:

> Saying that school and society does not sufficiently take account of girls and women might be a better way of seeing the problem than saying that girls lack things or are 'dis-advantaged'.

Academic success is obviously important today when there is greater competition for fewer jobs, and, increasingly, those jobs which are available demand technological skills, traditionally a male sphere. Equally as important is what we are teaching and how we are teaching. There is a clear need for teachers to reflect upon the structural constraints placed on the approaches they use in the classroom. Too often it is a case of 'Do as I say, not as I do'. Teachers may put up Equal Opportunities Commission posters on the wall or tell children they have to respect themselves and each other, but because of the pressures placed upon them, recourse is made to authoritarian, undemocratic techniques which only serve to reinforce the power/control systems operating in the wider society. At the same time, the possibility that 'real change' will occur in a political climate which celebrates and instigates policies on teacher appraisal, account-ability, a national curriculum, and testing, is, to say the least, a remote one.

References

ACKER, S. (1983) 'Women and teaching: a semi-detached sociology of a semi-profession', in WALKER, S. and BARTON, L. (Eds) *Gender, Class and Education*, Lewes, Falmer Press, pp. 123–40.

ACKER, S. (1986) 'What feminists want from education', in HARTNETT, A. and NAISH, M. (Eds) *Education and Society Today*, Lewes, Falmer Press, pp. 63–76.

ALEXANDER, R. (1984) *Primary Teaching*, Eastbourne, Holt, Rinehart and Winston.

ARNOT, M. and WEINER, G. (Eds) (1987) *Gender and the Politics of Schooling*, London, Hutchinson.

BIOTT, C. (1984) *Getting on without the teacher*, Sunderland Polytechnic/ Schools Council.

BIOTT, C. (1987) 'Co-operative group work: pupils' and teachers' membership and participation', *Curriculum*, 8, 2, pp. 5–14.

BRUNGER, A. (1986) *Collaborative Learning — Theory and Practice*, unpublished DAES dissertation, School of Education, University of Newcastle upon Tyne.

BYRNE, E. (1978) *Women and Education*, London, Tavistock.

CLAIRE, H. (1986) 'Collaborative work as an anti-sexist process', *Primary Matters*, ILEA, Centre for Learning Resources, pp. 43–5.

CLARRICOATES, K. (1978) 'Dinosaurs in the classroom — a re-examination of some aspects of the "hidden curriculum" in primary schools', *Women's Studies International Quarterly*, 1, 4, pp. 353–64.

CLARRICOATES, K. (1980) 'The importance of being Ernest, Emma, Tom, Jane: the perception and categorisation of gender conformity and gender deviation in primary schools', in DEEM, R. (Ed.) *Schooling for Women's Work*, London, Routledge and Kegan Paul, pp. 26–41.

DELAMONT, S. (1980) *Sex Roles and the School*, London, Methuen.

DEPARTMENT OF EDUCATION AND SCIENCE, (1976) *Sex Discrimination Act* (Circular 2/76), London, HMSO.

DEPARTMENT OF EDUCATION AND SCIENCE, (1978), *Special Education Needs. Report of the Committee of Inquiry into the Education of Handicapped Children and Young People*, Cmnd 7212, London, HMSO.

DEPARTMENT OF EDUCATION AND SCIENCE, (1985a) *Education for All. Report of the Committee of Inquiry into the Education of Children from Ethnic Minority Groups*, Cmnd 9453, London, HMSO.

DEPARTMENT OF EDUCATION AND SCIENCE, (1985b) *Better Schools*, Cmnd 9469, London, HMSO.

DEPARTMENT OF EDUCATION AND SCIENCE, (1987) *Quality in Schools: the Initial Training of Teachers*, London, HMSO.

EQUAL OPPORTUNITIES COMMISSION, (1987) *Gender Differentiation in Infant Classes*, Belfast, Equal Opportunities Commission.

EVETTS, J. (1987) 'Becoming career ambitious: the career strategies of married women who became primary headteachers in the 1960s and 1970s', *Educational Review*, 39, 1, pp. 15–29.

FRENCH, J. and FRENCH, P. (1986) *Gender Imbalances in Infant School Classroom Interaction*, (Final report to the EOC), Manchester, Equal Opportunities Commission.

GORDON, P. (1986) 'Examining our own attitudes — a male perspective', *Primary Matters*, ILEA, Centre for Learning Resources, pp. 14–16.

HARWOOD, D. (1985) 'We need political not Political education for 5–13 year olds', *Education 3–13*, 13,1, pp. 12–17.

HODGEON, J. (1985) *A Woman's World: Report on a Project in Cleveland Nurseries on Sex Differentiation in the Early Years*, Cleveland Education Committee.

HOLLY, L. (1985) 'Mary, Jane and Virginia Woolf: ten-year-old girls talking', in WEINER, G. (Ed.) *Just a Bunch of Girls*, Milton Keynes, Open University Press, pp. 51–62.

HORTON, N., TURNER, S. and WHITTON, S. (1982) *Anti-Sexist Teaching Strategies in the Primary School*, London, Centre for Urban Educational Studies.

HOUGH, J. (1983) *Deprivation of Necessary Skills*, Manchester, Equal Opportunities Commission.

HOUGH, J. (1985) 'Developing individuals rather than boys and girls', *School Organization*, 5, 1, pp. 17–25.

KELLY, E. (1981) 'Socialisation in Patriarchal Society', in KELLY, A. (Ed.) *The Missing Half*, Manchester, Manchester University Press.

KING, R. (1978) *All Things Bright and Beautiful*, Chichester, John Wiley.

LEES, S. (1986) *Losing Out*, London, Hutchinson.

LOBBAN, G. (1975) 'Sex roles in reading schemes', *Educational Review*, 27, 3, pp. 202–10.

MAHONY, P. (1985) *Schools for the Boys?*, London, Hutchinson.

MARLAND, M. (Ed.) (1983) *Sex Differentiation and Schooling*, London, Heinemann.

MEGARRY, J. (1984) 'Sex, gender and education', in ACKER, S. *et al.* (Eds) *World Yearbook of Education 1984: Women and Education*, London, Kogan Page, pp. 14–28.

MYERS, K. (1981) 'Beware of the backlash', *School Organization*, 5,1, pp. 27–40.

NORTHAM, J. (1982) 'Girls and boys in primary maths books', *Education 3–13*, 10, 1, pp. 11–14.

ORD, F. and QUIGLEY, J. (1985) 'Anti-sexism as good educational practice: what can feminists realistically achieve?', in WEINER, G. (Ed.) *Just a Bunch of Girls*, Milton Keynes, Open University Press, pp. 104–19.

ORR, P. (1985) 'Sex bias in schools: national perspectives', in WHYTE, J. *et al.* (Eds) *Girl Friendly Schooling*, London, Methuen, pp. 7–23.

SHARAN, S. (1980) 'Co-operative learning in small groups: recent methods and effects on achievement, attitudes and ethnic relations', *Review of Educational Research*, 5,2,pp. 241–71.

SKELTON, C. (1985) *Gender Issues in a PGCE Teacher Training Programme*, unpublished MA thesis, Education Department, York University.

SPENDER, D. (1982) *Invisible Women*, London, Writers and Readers.

TANN, S. (1981) 'Grouping and groupwork', in SIMON, B. and WILLCOCKS, J. (Eds) *Research and Practice in the Primary Classroom*, London, Routledge and Kegan Paul, pp. 43–54.

THOMAS, G. (1986) '"Hallo, Miss Scatterbrain. Hallo, Mr. Strong": assessing nursery attitudes and behaviour', in BROWNE, N. and FRANCE, P. (Eds) *Untying the Apron Strings*, Milton Keynes, Open University Press, pp. 104–20.

WEINER, G. (1986) 'Feminist education and equal opportunities: unity or discord?', *British Journal of Sociology of Education*, 7, 3, pp. 265–74.

WHYLD, J. (Ed.) (1983) *Sexism in the Secondary Curriculum*, London, Harper and Row.

WHYTE, J. (1983) *Beyond the Wendy House: sex role stereotyping in primary schools*, York, Longman for Schools Council.

WOLPE, A. (1977) *Some Processes in Sexist Education*, London, Women's Research and Resources Centre.

YATES, L. (1987) *Girls and Democratic Schooling*, Sydney, New South Wales Education Department and Curriculum Development Centre.

YEOMANS, A. (1983) 'Collaborative group work in primary and secondary schools', *Durham and Newcastle Review*, 10,51, pp. 99–105.

Chapter 11

Peace and Conflict

Dave Hicks

Educating for Peace

Much has been said and written about the role of education for peace in our schools, most of it misinformed and little of it reflecting the real interests or needs of teachers. This chapter will, therefore, begin by setting out an educational rationale for studying issues of peace and conflict, on scales from the personal to the global, and go on to note some of the discrepancies between the claims of critics and actual classroom practice. Examples will be given of both the content and process of education for peace by reference to one curriculum project, *World Studies 8–13*. In particular, examples will be given of classroom activities which enable students to explore issues of conflict and images of peace. The chapter concludes with a checklist of questions for teachers to use if they are interested in education for peace.

The term 'education for peace' has been used for nearly a decade now by educators and others in this country, and a lot longer by many in other countries. In the United Kingdom it can be seen as part of a long tradition of education for international understanding (Heater, 1986) and it should be seen in conjunction with a range of other educational initiatives, all of which seek, in different ways, to offer a curriculum more relevant to the needs of both children and society today. Such fields include personal and social education, world studies, development education, political education, and both anti-sexist and anti-racist education. Whilst each field may have its distinct origins and concerns they often overlap in practice. Taken together they have much to offer in the creation of a socially relevant education for the 1990s.

The interest amongst teachers in education for peace began for various reasons. Specifically, during the last decade, teachers in many different countries have looked variously at the state of the planet, of their country, education, or of their pupils and been disturbed by what they have seen. In particular they have been concerned about increasing levels of both direct violence between people, as in the case of assault, riot or war, and the equally damaging structural violence which may be built into oppressive social, political or economic systems. Noting the crucial importance of both peace and conflict in this latter part of the twentieth century, they have asked themselves what the implications might be for teaching and learning in school. Education for peace, both in this country and elsewhere, thus began as a grassroots concern amongst teachers in response to what they, and many others, saw as an increasingly violent world, a violence epitomized initially by the arms race and the threat of nuclear war.

It is worth noting, in passing, that the World Directory of Peace Research Institutions published by UNESCO lists some 300 bodies involved in some way with peace and conflict research. Peace research as a distinct field of enquiry emerged in the early 1960s and there is, of course, a School of Peace Studies at Bradford University. Although teachers with an interest in education for peace generally have little to do with peace researchers in universities it is useful to recall this parallel academic backdrop of concern.

Assumptions and Definitions

Burns (1983) has suggested that three broad assumptions generally underlie education for peace and they are as follows:

i) war and violent conflict are not conducive to human well-being;

ii) neither are they necessarily the result of inevitable aspects of human nature;

iii) peace, i.e., alternative ways of being, organising and behaving, can be learnt.

One of the central concerns of education for peace has been to widen the debate about the nature of human aggression. Thus, whilst it is currently popular to consider human aggression as an innate characteristic, exemplified by the work of researchers such as Lorenz (in fact once a prominent Nazi), much research has also been carried out which refutes such ideas (Montagu, 1976) and focuses instead on the learnt nature of both aggression and non-aggression.

The overall aim of education for peace is thus to develop the skills, attitudes and knowledge which are needed to resolve conflict peacefully in order to work towards a more just and less violent world (Hicks, 1986). More specifically, education for peace aims to:

i)   explore *concepts of peace* both as a state of being and as an active process;

ii) enquire into the *obstacles to peace* and the causes of peacelessness, both in and between, individuals, groups, institutions and societies;

iii) *resolve conflicts* in ways that will contribute to a more just and less violent world;

iv) study ways of constructing a range of *alternative futures*, in particular ways of achieving a more just and sustainable world society.

Specific objectives for education for peace must, of course, be consonant with the above aims, and these have been elaborated on elsewhere in more detail (Hicks, 1988). Thus, for example, under *knowledge* objectives one might expect to look at issues to do with conflict, peace, war, nuclear matters, justice, power, gender, race, ecology and futures. Such issues are, of course, seldom found together in one place on the timetable. They may be part of topic or project work or part of, say, Humanities, Geography, History, English or Religious Education. Education for peace, it should be made quite clear, is seldom seen as a separate subject but more often as a dimension across the whole curriculum.

Thus, appropriate objectives must also include *skills* such as critical thinking, cooperation, empathy, assertiveness, conflict resolution and political literacy, together with *attitudes* such as self-respect, respect for others, ecological concern, open-mindedness, vision and a commitment to justice. These attitudes and skills do not belong, quite properly, to one particular part of the curriculum. Education for peace is thus seen as an approach to teaching and learning as well as having its substantive content. In particular, attention is paid to the need for congruence between medium and message, so there is considerable stress on participatory and experiential styles of learning. Such approaches are well illustrated in both *A Guide to Student-Centred Learning* (Brandes and Ginnis, 1986) and in Brian Wren's *Education for Justice* (1986).

Whilst such concerns necessarily involve the exploration, on a variety of scales, of a range of issues to do with violence, conflict and peace – some of which will inevitably be deemed controversial – it is also important to recall the legitimation for such concerns. The educational rationale for education for peace, thus, has a three-fold basis, relating to a) the aims of education; b) the nature of childhood socialization; and c) educational ideologies.

Amongst the broad aims of education set out in *The Curriculum From 5–16* (1985) we have been reminded of the following:

- to help pupils to develop lively, enquiring minds, the ability to question and argue rationally and to apply themselves to tasks...
- to instil respect for religious and moral values, and tolerance of other races, religions and ways of life;
- to help pupils understand the world in which they live, and the interdependence of individuals, groups and nations.

Education for peace quite specifically attempts to respond to, and elaborate on, broad aims such as these.

Childhood socialization plays an important role in young people's perception of the world in which they live. Thus, not only are racist and sexist beliefs acquired at quite an early age, so are attitudes to violence, war and peace. Children would seem to have fairly well-defined ideas about war and peace by the age of 7 or 8. Whilst younger children can often see no justification for war whatsoever, the majority of 15-year-olds believe war is morally valid to punish an aggressor. Their concepts of peace, it seems, however, are much less clear than those of war (Heater, 1980). Recent research from various countries (Chivian, *et al.* 1985), including Britain (Davies, 1987), also indicates that many primary-aged children are worried about the threat of nuclear war and that such fears increase in adolescence. Education for peace specifically attempts to respond in a positive way to issues such as these.

Finally it should be noted that education for peace has its roots in, and tries to combine, two broad educational traditions: the person-centred and the reconstructionist. Thus, there is a particular focus on personal worth and personal growth but, at the same time, an emphasis on the need for educators to engage in social, political and economic debate and for classrooms to be seen as potential areas for change. It is important to note that some peace researchers and activists would, on the other hand, see schools as the epitome of structural violence and, therefore, unlikely places for the initiation of any really meaningful social change.

Interest in education for peace grew rapidly in the early and mid-eighties amongst teachers, educators and parents. Support came from teachers' groups, teacher unions and a variety of voluntary agencies, as well as from members of HMI (Slater, 1984). Several LEAs, such as Nottinghamshire, Avon, Manchester, Sheffield and Birmingham, have produced their own guidelines on education for peace and some have also appointed advisory teachers.

Countering Critics

Most criticism of education for peace has been extremely ill-informed and seems to bear little relationship to what most teachers have been, and are, actually doing in schools. Attacks have come from the political Right, often via the media, in ways which have deliberately sought to confuse rather than clarify the issues (Cox and Scruton, 1984). Whilst detailed refutations of these attacks have come from Aspin (1986) and White (1988), it is useful to highlight some of the main criticisms that have been made. Six points will be briefly dealt with here.

Firstly, critics argue, peace studies (as they prefer to call it) is not a proper subject and should therefore not be included on the timetable. As indicated above, however, few teachers are proposing a new subject called 'peace studies' but rather asking what teaching and learning could go on *within* existing subjects to help children understand issues to do with peace and conflict.

Secondly, it is argued, peace studies is really a cloak for teaching about unilateral nuclear disarmament. This is only *one* of the issues, however, that teachers may explore and, quite clearly, if disarmament is discussed it should include a variety of perspectives. It has been argued by White (1984) that most teachers seem to be *avoiding* the nuclear issue rather than confronting it in the classroom.

Thirdly, it has been argued that peace studies is really just training in good manners, something that has always been part of good education. But education for peace has to be about *more* than this, in particular it stresses the need for all students to develop a positive self-concept; to learn about ways of resolving conflicts less violently; to develop skills of cooperation and empathy, critical judgment and political literacy.

Fourthly, peace studies has been seen as a tool for the deliberate indoctrination of pupils, not least through the use of biased resources. Since one of the aims of education for peace is to develop children's critical judgment, so that propaganda in *any* form may be more readily identified, this seems an unwarranted criticism. It is, of course, based on a view of education which excludes the study of any contemporary issues from the classroom.

Fifthly, it is argued that peace studies pays a lot of attention to conflicts in the capitalist world but no attention to the evils of communism, which are much more substantial. Clearly, as children get older, they need to be aware of the world's major political systems, their origins, assumptions and achievements. They need to study, as objectively as possible, life in both capitalist and communist countries and weigh up some of the advantages and disadvantages of each to the inhabitants themselves.

Lastly, it has been suggested that it is dangerous to study issues of peace and conflict with younger children, due to their inability to grasp complex ideas. However, schools merely intervene in an on-going educational process, wherein parents, peer group and media, constantly teach children about such issues, whether on a local or a global scale. Reports from the teachers involved with the *World Studies 8–13* Project also indicate that children are very interested in, and in their own terms can be quite knowledgeable about, events in the wider world.

It is worth noting that one public opinion survey in Australia (McNair Anderson, 1985) found widespread support amongst members of the public for teaching about issues of peace and conflict. The survey did not, however, refer to the term 'peace education'. What we can perhaps learn from this is, that whilst critics may indeed have tarnished the label, which for some now results in a knee-jerk response, they have not affected public realization of the need for these issues to be part of good education.

World Studies 8–13

World Studies 8–13 began life as a Schools Council Project in 1980 and is now operating in nearly half the LEAs in England and Wales. The overall aim of world studies may be defined as: 'to develop the knowledge, attitudes and skills which students need in order to live responsibly in a multicultural society and an interdependent world'. The project is a good example of education for peace in action because it deals with both substantive issues and uses a person-centred methodology. Its success with teachers arises out of a judicious blend of these elements which together provide both practical classroom materials and offer a participatory and challenging model of in-service. This stress on active learning via a wide range of stimulating classroom activities is best illustrated in the Teacher's Handbook (Fisher and Hicks, 1985), and the Workbook (Hicks and Steiner, forthcoming), both of which highlight the nature of local-global links and their immediate impact on our daily lives and the lives of others. Activities in the Handbook focus on four themes. These are: conflict and cooperation; local-global links; images of the world; and alternative futures. Whilst this is the only national curriculum project with such a focus there are many other initiatives that have a concern for global perspectives in the curriculum. Thus the Centre for Global Education (Pike and Selby, 1987), Development Education Centres such as those in Manchester, Birmingham and Leeds, as well as numerous multicultural support services also constantly stress the need for issues of justice and inequality to be set in a global context.

Tables 1 and 2 set out briefly the Project's classroom objectives and these provide one ready guide to the concerns of world studies. They are followed by examples of classroom activities which illustrate some of the approaches being used by teachers, in this case particularly to raise questions about conflict and peace.

Table 11.1: Objectives for world studies: A summary

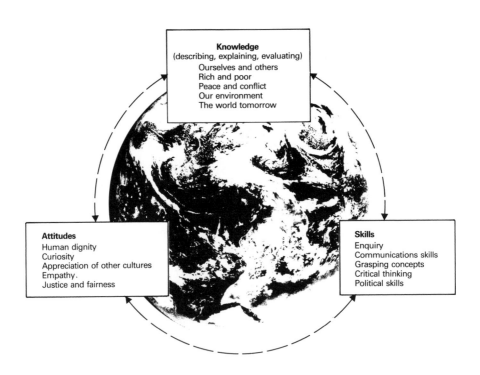

Knowledge
(describing, explaining, evaluating)
Ourselves and others
Rich and poor
Peace and conflict
Our environment
The world tomorrow

Attitudes
Human dignity
Curiosity
Appreciation of other cultures
Empathy.
Justice and fairness

Skills
Enquiry
Communications skills
Grasping concepts
Critical thinking
Political skills

Table 11.2: Objectives for world studies

Knowledge

Ourselves and others
Pupils should know about their own society and culture and their place in it. They should also know about certain societies and cultures other than their own, including minority cultures within their own society. They should understand the nature of interdependence, and the economic and cultural influence — both helpful and harmful — of other people on their own way of life.

Rich and poor
Pupils should know about major inequalities of wealth and power in the world, both between and within other countries and in their own. They should understand why such inequalities persist and about efforts being made to reduce them.

Peace and conflict
Pupils should know about the main conflicts currently in the news and in the recent past, and about attempts to resolve such conflicts. They should also know about the ways of resolving conflicts in everyday life.

Our environment
Pupils should know about the basic geography, history and ecology of the earth. They should understand the interdependence of people and planet and should know about measures being taken to protect the environment both locally and globally.

The world tomorrow
Pupils should know how to investigate and reflect on a variety of possible futures: personal, local, national and for the world as a whole. They should also be aware of ways in which they may act to influence the future.

Attitudes

Human dignity
Pupils should have a sense of their own worth as individuals, and that of others, and of the worth of their own particular social, cultural and family background.

Empathy
Pupils should be willing to imagine the feelings and viewpoints of other people, particularly people in cultures and situations different from their own.

Table 11.2: contd

Attitudes

Curiosity
Pupils should be interested to find out more about issues related to living in a multicultural society and an interdependent world.

Appreciation of other cultures
Pupils should be ready to find aspects of other cultures of value to themselves and to learn from them.

Justice and fairness
Pupils should value genuinely democratic principles and processes at local, national and international levels and be ready to work for a more just world.

Skills

Enquiry
Pupils should be able to find out and record information about world issues from a variety of sources, including printed and audio-visual, and through interviews with people.

Communication skills
Pupils should be able to describe and explain their ideas about the world in a variety of ways: in writing, in discussion and in various art forms; and with a variety of other people, including members of other groups and cultures.

Grasping concepts
Pupils should be able to understand certain basic concepts relating to world society, to use these concepts to make generalisations and to support and test these.

Critical thinking
Pupils should be able to approach issues with an open and critical mind and to change their ideas as they learn more.

Political skills
Pupils should be developing the ability to influence decision making at local, national and international levels.

Some Classroom Activities

The examples of classroom activities given here are not taken directly from the Project Handbook, but rather from other sources which teachers involved in world studies have found useful. The activities should not, of course, be used in isolation but rather as part of appropriate schemes of work. For further elaboration readers should look to *World Studies 8–13: A Teacher's Handbook* and to the other texts mentioned below.

1. Looking at Conflict

There are a variety of resources available for teachers who wish to look at ways of developing the skills of conflict resolution (Lieberman and Hardie, 1981; De Bono, 1985), and increasingly these focus on classrooms (Judson, 1984; Kreidler, 1984; Masheder, 1986). The following activity is taken from Kreidler's *Creative Conflict Resolution* (1984).

Fight Form

This is one way of getting children to look carefully at any violent conflict which they may have been involved in. It is best used in a context where a no-fighting rule is operated in the classroom.

When the children involved have calmed down, do not ask for an explanation but give them a Fight Form to complete. When they have done this read them over with the participants, focusing not on how or why the conflict developed, but on what they have each said they will do in any future such situation. Ask if their proposed actions will solve the problem better than fighting did? One can also have the two children exchange papers and then discuss, maybe with the help of the class, their reactions to each other's accounts. Over a period of time a class can become quite skilled in helping participants explore the implications of their own fight forms.

Understanding Conflicts

It is also possible for children to begin to look at a range of conflict situations that they may come across, both in their own lives, in the local community and the wider world. A set of questions which can be used to elucidate some of the key elements in any conflict are set out below. Completing such a questionnaire can take as little or as much time as the teacher wishes. It offers one framework for children to use in making their own investigations from materials they have brought or provided by the teacher. These could be in the form of newspaper cuttings, photographs, videos, written accounts, maps,

Table 11.3 – Fight Form

Name ....

1. With whom did you fight? ....

2. What was the problem? ....

3. Why did you start fighting? (Give two reasons) ....

   ....

   ....

4. Why did the other person fight with you? ....

   ....

   ....

5. Did fighting solve the problem? ....

6. What are three things you might try instead if this happens again?

   a) ....

   b) ....

   c) ....

7. Is there anything you would like to say to the person you fought with?

   ....

---

tapes, interviews and so on. It could be used to look at a dispute in the local community, say about urban redevelopment, an issue in the national news such as the disposal of nuclear waste, or the morality of Britain's export of arms to 'third world' countries. Teachers do need to exercise some caution, however, about oversimplifying the parallels between international conflicts and personal conflicts (Bryans, 1987).

Table 11.4 – Conflict Questionnaire

---

1. Problems
   a) What do you think this problem is about?
   b) What do other people think it is about?
   c) What differences of opinion are there amongst people?
2. Background
   a) What parties are involved in this conflict?
   b) What has actually happened so far?
3. Values
   a) What do the different parties hope to gain?
   b) How many possible solutions can you think of?
4. Action
   a) What is the best possible solution and for whom?
   b) Who benefits and who loses as a result?
   c) What, if anything, can we do about this issue?

---

2. Looking at Peace

It is important to recall that looking at peace also requires that we look at the obstacles to peace and ways of beginning to overcome them. Educators for Social Responsibility (1982; 1983) have identified seven broad obstacles. These are the *fear* experienced in most conflict situations; the question of *aggression* and whether it is natural or learnt; the human capacity for *stereotyping* which creates false images; *prejudice*, whether based on race, gender, disability or other forms of categorization; the role of *ideology* in reinforcing people's world views; *propaganda* as a tool of ideology and prejudice; and the creation of dehumanizing images of *the enemy*. Detailed study of any and all of these areas is really a prerequisite for any exploration of the nature of peace itself! It is also pertinent to note the distinction made by some peace researchers between negative peace, i.e. peace as the absence of war and overt violence, and positive peace, i.e. the absence also of structural violence and the presence of a wide range of welfare indicators. Galtung (1976) thus broadly conceptualized the problems of peace as those to do with violence and war; inequality; injustice; environmental damage and alienation; and the presence of peace as requiring non-violence; economic welfare; social justice; ecological balance and participation.

Children particularly need to be given opportunities for exploring the nature of peace, both as a state and as an on-going process, whether relating to individuals, institutions, groups or nations. The struggle for peace and justice is a long and often arduous one and, thus, we need to have clear images of the alternative futures that we might hope to bring about. Resources for studying peace include Educators for Social Responsibility (1983); Fien and Gerber, (1987) and Hicks (1988). The following activity is taken from *Perspectives: A Teaching Guide to Concepts of Peace* (ESR, 1983).

Images of Peace

This activity challenges students to broaden their concepts of peace through imaginative explorations in response to a series of questions.

1. Begin by offering some warm-up questions to introduce and reinforce the idea that there is no one correct answer, and to get their imagination whetted: What colour is happiness? What kind of animal is cooperation? What form of water is anger?
2. When they have the idea, move on to questions about peace. The questions can be presented on a sheet to be filled in, answered in small groups working cooperatively, or brainstormed out loud with the whole class to experience together the diversity of responses.
3. The following questions can get you started: What colour is peace? What kind of weather is it? What animal? What size? What sound? What taste? What holiday? What form of transportation? What aspect of nature? What form of water? You may also encourage students to come up with their own questions about peace for the rest of the class to answer.
4. A bulletin board display or mural can be assembled with the various poetic associations to peace, each one illustrated by the students who wrote it, and all of them grouped under the title 'The Many Faces of Peace'. Or, the examples can be made into a book and copies made for each student, the parents, and other members of the school community.

Children can, and should, move on from clarifications on a personal level to broader social considerations. Education for peace, therefore, raises questions about i) where we have come from; ii) where we are now; iii) where we want to get to; and iv) how we're going to get there. Certainly most peace educators would agree that we need to be envisaging quite radically different futures from today, as, for example, those proposed by Bahro (1986) or Capra (1983). Concretely, education for peace raises a number of critical and far-reaching questions for teachers and schools. The following checklist is one reminder of some of the key issues.

Table 11.5 – Education for Peace: Ten Questions to Ask

---

1. *Local/global*

Are issues of peace and conflict studied at a variety of scales ranging from both the personal and immediate to the global and long term? Are the rights of the planet considered as well as those of individuals and groups?

2. *Conflict analysis*

When studying a particular issue is the real nature of the conflict and its constitutent parts explored? Is it made clear what each party has to gain and lose and who has the power?

3. *Conflict resolution*

When studying a particular conflict is a range of possible solutions explored and due note taken of who would benefit in each case?

4. *Violence*

In considering the problems of violence are examples explored of both direct, personal and indirect structural violence? Are examples taken from children's experience as well as from further afield?

5. *Aggression*

Is it made clear that there is much debate about the nature of aggression: that it may be culturally learnt rather than biologically determined, that some societies are non-aggressive?

6. *Non-violence*

In looking at possible solutions to conflicts and approaches to life generally, are the benefits of less-violent and non-violent approaches stressed?

7. *Cooperative skills*

Are children encouraged and given the opportunity to acquire and develop cooperative skills via a range of small group activities and situations?

8. *Welfare and justice*

Is it made clear to children that any definition of peace must also embody a commitment to human welfare and justice?

Table 11.5 contd

---

9. *Preferred worlds*

Are children encouraged to visualize and plan both personal, local and global futures which embody their preferred worlds? Are they encouraged to develop the political skills needed to achieve their visions?

10. *Medium and message*

'There is no way to peace, peace is the way'. If the medium really is the message, is this reflected in appropriate, active teaching/learning methods, as well as in classroom climate and the way in which the school itself is run?

These activities give just a small flavour of what education for peace looks like in the classroom: an approach to education which stresses both socially relevant content and appropriate methodology. It is an approach which has much to contribute to anti-racist and anti-sexist education, and should perhaps look towards developing its own anti-militarist pedagogy (Reardon, 1986) as one of the critical concerns of the 1990s. As Harwood has commented: 'Peace education has achieved remarkable growth during the last decade (and) it has been successful in raising important human issues within the curriculum and in encouraging the introduction of active, experiential approaches to learning' (1987). Whatever the political climate, such initiatives must continue, for they need to become an integral part of children's experiences in both school and community if we are to achieve, in any form, the better worlds that we may dream of.

References

ASPIN, D. (1986) 'Peace studies in the curriculum of educational institutions: an argument against indoctrination', in WELLINGTON, J.J. (Ed.), *Controversial Issues in the Curriculum*, Oxford, Blackwell, pp. 119–48.
BAHRO, R. (1986) *Building the Green Movement*, London, GMP Publishers Ltd.
BRANDES, D. and GINNIS, P. (1986) *A Guide to Student-Centred Learning*, Oxford, Blackwell.
BRYANS, M. (1987) in 'Controversy over ESR curriculum: oversimplifying the complexities of war and peace in the classroom?' *Peace Education News*, Spring, Canadian Peace Educators' Network, Alberta.

BURNS ,R. (1983) *Education and the Arms Race*, Melbourne, Centre for Comparative and International Studies in Education, La Trobe University.

CAPRA, F. (1983) *The Turning Point: Science, Society and the Rising Culture*, London, Fontana.

CHIVIAN, E., SOLANTAUS, T. and VARTANYAN, M. (Eds) (1985) *Impact of the Threat of Nuclear War on Children and Adolescents*, International Physicians for the Prevention of Nuclear War.

COX, C. and SCRUTON, R. (1984) *Peace Studies: A Critical Survey*, London, Institute for Defence and Strategic Studies.

DAVIES, R. (1987) *Hopes and Fears: Children's Attitudes to Nuclear War*, Centre for Peace Studies, St. Martin's College, Lancaster.

DE BONO, E. (1985) *Conflicts: A Better Way to Resolve Them*, London, Harrap.

DEPARTMENT OF EDUCATION AND SCIENCE (1985) *The Curriculum from 5 to 16*, London, HMSO.

EDUCATORS FOR SOCIAL RESPONSIBILITY (1982) *Dialogue: A Guide to Teaching About Nuclear Issues*, Mass., Cambridge.

EDUCATORS FOR SOCIAL RESPONSIBILITY (1983) *Perspectives: A Teaching Guide to Concepts of Peace*, Mass., Cambridge.

FIEN, J. and GERBER, R. (Eds) (1987) *Teaching Geography For a Better World*, Edinburgh, Oliver and Boyd.

FISHER, S. and HICKS, D. (1985) *World Studies 8–13: A Teacher's Handbook*, Edinburgh, Oliver and Boyd.

GALTUNG, J. (1976) 'Peace education: problems and conflicts' in HAAVELSRUD M., (Ed.) *Education for Peace: Reflection and Action*, IPC Science and Technology Press, pp. 80–97.

HARWOOD, D. (1987) 'Peace education in schools: demise or development in the late-80s?' *Teaching Politics*, 16,2, pp. 147–67.

HEATER, D. (1980) *World Studies: Education for International Understanding in Britain*, London, Harrap.

HEATER, D. (1986) *Peace Through Education*, Lewes, Falmer Press.

HICKS, D. (1986) *Studying Peace: The Educational Rationale*, Centre for Peace Studies, St. Martin's College, Lancaster.

HICKS, D. (Ed.) (1988) *From Conflict to Justice: A Handbook on Peace Education*, London, Methuen.

HICKS, D. and STEINER, M. (Eds) (forthcoming) *A World Studies Workbook*, Edinburgh, Oliver and Boyd.

JUDSON, S. (Ed.) (1984) *Manual on Children and Nonviolence*, Philadelphia, New Society Publishers.

KREIDLER, W.J. (1984) *Creative Conflict Resolution*, Glenview, Illinois; Scott, Foresman and Co.

LIEBERMAN, M. and HARDIE, M. (1981) *Resolving Family and Other Conflicts*, Santa Cruz, Unity Press.

MASHEDER, M. (1986) *Let's Cooperate: Activities and Ideas for Parents and Teachers of Younger Children*, London, Peace Pledge Union.

McNAIR ANDERSON (1985) *Attitudes to Education*, Sydney, McNair Anderson Associates Pty. Ltd.

MONTAGU, A. (1976) *The Nature of Human Aggression*, Oxford University Press.

PIKE, G. and SELBY, D. (1987) *Global Teacher, Global Learner*, London, Hodder and Stoughton.

REARDON, B. (1986) *Sexism and the War System*, New York, Teachers College Press.

SLATER, J. (1984) 'An HMI perspective' in *Educating People for Peace*, London, National Council of Women of Great Britain, pp. 22–7.

WHITE, P. (1984) 'Facing the nuclear issue: a task for political education', in *Lessons Before Midnight: Educating for Reason in Nuclear Matters*, Bedford Way Papers No. 19, University of London Institute of Education, pp. 29–38.

WHITE, P. (1988) 'Countering the critics' in HICKS, D. (Ed.) *From Conflict to Justice: A Handbook on Peace Education*, London, Methuen.

WREN, B. (1986) *Education for Justice*, London, SCM Press.

Chapter 12

The Teaching of Sexuality

Sarah Gammage

Two areas of controversy will be aired in this chapter – sex education and morality. The amount of attention and heat generated by sex education varies. In the run up to the 1987 General Election, much attention was focused on it during the debate on the new Education Bill, and the decision to locate responsibility for sex education with governors and parents is part of a wider trend to restrict the power of local education authorities. At times it seemed possible that sex education might disappear from the school curriculum altogether. Yet, within schools, there has been a steady growth in interest in areas of the curriculum such as personal and social education, together with provision of materials and demand for training of teachers to undertake it. There has been the complication of the 'AIDS' factor and the fear, hysteria and gloomy speculation about its spread and impact. There has been some, hitherto almost unthinkably explicit, discussion about sexual behaviour, alongside what seemed a backlash against any kind of sex education at all. Although ridiculous, it is possible for school governors to decide to include AIDS education but reject sex education on the school curriculum. Morality is much less fashionable and obscure, and I will discuss it explicitly later.

The Lobby Against Sex Education

Views about sex education have been powerfully expressed. Peter Bruinvels (1986), the former Conservative MP for Leicester East, wrote that, 'It is essentially a private matter and the inherent right of each parent to instruct their child as they think fit' (p. 20). Riches (1986) of *Family and Youth Concern* links sex education 'to increasing numbers of teenage pregnancies, illegitimacy, promiscuity, disease and broken marriages' (p. 6). A booklet prepared by the Conservative Family Campaign (1986) states that the nature and content of sex education programmes in some schools has been 'allowed to fall into the hands of pressure groups with a vested interest in breaking down the structure of the family by promoting promiscuity' (p.2).

These statements are typical. They make assertions without supporting evidence. They make unsubstantiated claims about teachers' attitudes and influence, and causal links between rates of illegitimacy, divorce and sexually transmitted diseases and the state of marriage and family life. The statements tend to be generalized, oversimplified and emotive. They compound a number of arguments. They use idealized concepts of marriage and family life rather than concepts based on reality. They demonstrate ignorance about personal and social education programmes in schools. The suggestion seems to be that if we could put father back in charge as the breadwinner, with total responsibility for children's actions, many of the ills of society would be cured. It would be very impractical to turn back the clock even if such a state of affairs ever existed. Thankfully, these views are not those of the majority of parents although they are loudly and vociferously declaimed. They do, however, divert time and attention away from the important issues.

Parents and Sex Education

It is right and proper that parents should be deeply concerned about the kind of sex education their children are receiving at school. There is very recent information about parental attitudes in research by Allen (1987), based on interviews with representative samples of teenagers aged 14–16 years and their parents in three cities in England. Among the findings were that 96 per cent of parents and 95 per cent of teenagers thought schools should provide sex education to children and young people; 2 per cent of parents and 1 per cent of teenagers thought that sex education should be provided by neither school nor parents; and 2 per cent of parents and 4 per cent of teenagers thought that only parents should provide sex education (p. 197). These findings have not attracted much publicity, yet they are detailed and thorough. Parents clearly do want to know much more about sex education in schools, which is perfectly reasonable. This and a number of other issues to do with sex education is what we should be attending to.

It is absolutely essential to be clear about what is being argued at this point. No one is arguing that schools should have the monopoly on sex education, or that an essential right to communicate to children on important matters should, or even could be, removed from parents. Many parents cannot, will not, or simply do not educate their children explicitly about sex. In Allen (1987):

> 62 per cent of parents said they found it difficult to give Sex Education to their teenage children. The main reason given was embarrassment on the part of the parents, coupled with a lack of knowledge or the ability to find the right words to put it over (p. 203).

Many parents may be neither inadequate nor wilfully neglectful but naturally reserved about communicating on sexual matters to their children. This particular book addresses issues concerned with middle school children, usually aged from 8 years to 13 years old. The 8 to 10-year-old child may happily discuss the nuts and bolts of sexual anatomy and intercourse, with parents. Once children begin to develop sexually at puberty, embarrassment and reserve may characterize previously open conversations, and parents of teenagers may find it far more difficult to provide 'good' sex education.

Clare (1986), a well known psychiatrist, highlights the reserve, not only of parents but of children too, when it comes to sexual matters. He writes:

> My adolescent offspring, and I do not believe that they are in this regard a-typical, value their privacy. They do not want uninvited information to be thrust upon them. While they are not adults, they are not children either, and didactic, heart-to-heart exchanges are more the stuff of rather po-faced educational material than the real-life cut and thrust of parent-adolescent relationships (p. 21).

Random Learning

Children and young people are learning about sex whether adults deliberately and consciously intervene or not. Children learn all manner of desirable and undesirable attitudes from observing their parents. They receive much information from their peers who are enormously informative, but often very inaccurate, on sexual matters. There must be many people who owe a debt to the dirty joke for information about sex, unforthcoming from parents or school. Then there is the influence of the media. There is a mass of material from film, video, radio, television, newspapers, magazines and advertisements about sex, giving a confused and contradictory picture. One unfortunate and consistent message is about idealized body images and personality characteristics of males and females. There tends to be an emphasis on large busts and passivity for girls. Teenage 'agony aunts' describe the large proportion of letters they receive from teenage girls who are worried about their busts. The most unfortunate children of all learn from the bitter experience of being sexually abused by their own parents. In this context of random learning, teachers and parents face the same challenge. This is about their responsibility toward the young, the goals of education, the harmful influences of society and how to counteract them by providing sane, calm, reflective opportunities for young people to learn. School sex education programmes are vitally necessary to counteract what is frightening and untrue, to provide facts and dispel myths, to provide curious children with sound answers and to counteract the distorting images of males and females. There is a host of far more positive aims for sex education and these will be examined later.

Aims and Objectives for Sex Education

Twenty years after the so-called 'Swinging Sixties', teachers are still lacking in confidence about their role as sex educators. They are very vulnerable to the controversies that flare up from time to time and are often forced to justify their subject. Yet they have struggles enough inside their own schools to establish personal and social education as a valid subject on the core curriculum. In the hierarchy of knowledge, 'soft' areas like social education are way behind in the pecking order for time, space, and resources. Mathematics, science, English, history, geography and so on, take priority. There is increasing emphasis on teaching vocational skills needed for jobs rather than a wider, broader approach to educating of the whole person, for life. If the proposed core subjects do occupy over three quarters of the curriculum in future, sex education will have to compete even more with many other very worthwhile valuable areas, which are non-traditional subjects.

In this context it is especially important for teachers to be clear and purposeful in their aims and objectives. If schools do not achieve this clarity their programmes will be ragged, incoherent and even more vulnerable. Many schools undertake sex education as a 'knee-jerk' reaction to crises such as school girl pregnancies or unwanted activities behind the bicycle shed. Many schools run sex education programmes which they simultaneously disown. Outside experts or volunteers can easily be caught in this trap. Such lessons can be extremely uncomfortable because the visitor gets 'dumped' with all the anxieties and problems shelved by the school regarding sex. Consequently, sex education is not always done well.

It is interesting how the aims of sex education have changed over the decades and how they have reflected more, and now less, permissive cultural climates. I wonder how acceptable the following optimistic aims would be today? Schulz and Williams (1968) say: 'Sex Education should aim to indicate the immense possibilities for human fulfillment that sexuality offers' (p. 4). Harris (1971) says Sex Education is 'to help people to satisfy their sexual needs in the fullest possible sense' (p. 9). There are more recent 'down to earth' aims, such as that quoted by Rosser (1986):

> The aims of any programme of Sex Education should be to present the facts in an objective and balanced manner and to enable pupils to understand the values and other factors which influence attitudes and behaviour in our society, to form their own opinions and to make informed, reasoned and responsible choices (p. 13).

Aims can be formulated by asking questions such as how a successfully sexually educated person would think, behave and treat other people. One would need to extrapolate from this to society as a whole. Statutorily, it is now a matter for individual schools to decide on their own aims and objectives. Because of DES guidelines, general common sense, and the 'logic' of the subject, many schools will have very similar aims and similar programmes.

Within broad overall aims, specific age- and stage-related objectives can be formulated and are clearly articulated by Went (1986). For instance, in the 5- to 8-year-old band, children need to gain accurate information, to develop acceptable words to describe anatomy, to be able to ask and have answers to questions about how babies get in and get out. This age group identifies with babies rather than adults, and reproduction should be considered looking at animals and young of all kinds, at parental care, family life of all varieties, individual growth and development, personal relationships and caring for others. 9- to 13-year-olds must be prepared for pubertal changes and some children in the class will already be at this stage of physical development. Pupils need to increase their understanding of human reproduction and their awareness of the range of human sexuality. They need to begin to understand about contraception, sexually transmitted diseases, to increase their consideration of other people and to develop their social skills. Schools have to decide how much to plan and *structure* their approach to Sex Education, and how much to leave it to responding to tbe expressed interests of the pupils. The latter method I consider less reliable, in that children may not be able to articulate their needs clearly nor teachers able to listen, note and respond. It would be easy to neglect important areas. Went (1986) advocates a spiral curriculum with two strands — factual and normative. Both strands should increase in complexity as children get older and they become more aware of an increasingly complex world and need increasingly more complex information and skill to negotiate it. In order to ensure both strands are catered for, a planned rather than a random approach is desirable. There are too many difficulties about sex education that could tempt schools to avoid it altogether. Schools have a variety of sensitive factors to contend with: the differentially maturing pupil — on the one hand, the pre-pubertal boy who will probably not be facing major physical changes until 13, and on the other, the girl who starts menstruating at 9. Then there is the need to be sensitive to the differing views of parents, particularly those with ethnic or religious backgrounds which cause them to have many reservations about allowing their children to have any sex education at all. There will be concern about whether and how to tackle subjects such as homosexuality, which can be misunderstood and lead to damaging media attention. Finally, sexuality as a topic cannot and should not be 'matter of fact'. There will not usually be many teachers confident or skilled enough to undertake the teaching of it.

Flight into Facts

By and large it is reasonably straightforward to plan and elaborate a coherent and well thought out programme of sex education which succeeds in imparting good sound information to pupils. Yet I have noticed in schools and teachers a tendency to indulge in 'flight into facts'. Very good resources are available for teachers and pupils, and it is tempting to contain and confine sex education merely to giving the facts. Teaching 'about' or giving information is a role that teachers are trained for and familiar with. It is the 'teacher as expert' in a didactic role. Helping pupils to learn about sexuality and to become morally mature is not such familiar territory. Teachers are, and feel, out of their depth. Their role requires a change but they are not sure what the new role should be. In general, it is not part of basic, or in-service training for teachers. It requires distinguishing between teaching 'about' something and helping pupils make sense of experience. Teachers may become reasonably comfortable teaching about anatomy, reproduction, human sexual response, sexually transmitted diseases, contraception, different kinds of family institutions, courtship, marriage and family life. However, pupils need to understand and make sense of their own experiences of sexuality, of their own family life and relationships, and develop an increasingly mature appreciation of the moral considerations of expressing their own sexuality. Toomey (1986) interviewed pupils from her old school in Swansea:

> There is far too much emphasis on the biological process and not enough talk about the wider social issues... we need to be able to talk about the emotional effects of a sexual relationship and different sorts of relationship such as homosexuality (p. 7).

This clearly requires more from teachers than the ability to communicate information effectively. It challenges them to understand their own sexuality, to make sense of their own family life and to appreciate the moral dimension. Very often, teachers are extremely uncomfortable about their own sexuality, have never questioned or looked at their own relationships and would prefer to keep morality, in any explicit sense, out of it altogether. This can be dangerous, as illustrated by Savage (1967) in a cartoon which shows a school mistress addressing her eager pupils, who says:'The Board of Education requires me to give you some basic information on sex, reproduction and other disgusting filth'.Not all teachers should or need to undertake sex education any more than everyone should teach mathematics or foreign languages. People who do not think that sex is a good enjoyable activity had best leave sex education alone. Otherwise, it is a matter of learning. It can be illuminating to look at what part of that process might be.

Training for Teachers in Sex Education

Courses to train teachers to be better sex educators often begin with a 'choosing a language' exercise. Members are invited to 'brainstorm' words for vagina, penis and sexual intercourse. Not only does this 'warm' people up at the beginning of a course but it also reveals interesting reactions. It may be that it awakens the adolescent inside us, who goes from strength to strength producing more exotic, colloquial or shocking names. It may reveal a prude, who is actually deeply unhappy about aspects of his or her own sexuality and finds it very distasteful to hear and see explicit sexual words written up prominently. This exercise helps to innoculate adults against some of the words used by young people, which are intended to shock. Some words are just ones we are unfamiliar with but which are meaningful to pupils. We need to get over the stage of being 'shocked' by pupils and so do they. We also need to avoid patronising or rejecting pupils because they use different vocabulary. It can be very easy to 'distance' pupils by using very clinical terms. Any group needs to negotiate a vocabulary that is acceptable to that group at the outset. This is as true for middle school pupils as teachers or any other group of adults.

Other activities can help individuals to check out and confirm facts, for which there are many resources, both comprehensive and reliable. Multiple-choice questionnaires are useful and a good way to start a session. A guarantee of producing some hilarity is to say: 'Right, we all, of course, know the plumbing. May I have a volunteer to draw the male/female parts on the flip chart just to begin?' Try it yourself! You may be surprised. Myths and prejudices such as 'you won't get pregnant if you do it standing up' can be considered through the 'True/False' statements exercise. Even the informational or factual sessions will help reveal to participants many of their assumptions, prejudices, hang–ups, fears and miconceptions. We hold all kinds of unconscious views of sex which may be revealed to our pupils but not to us. It is best to discover and acknowledge them. Do we regard sex as a powerful, dark, dangerous urge to be suppressed? Do we regard it as something to indulge in frequently for health reasons? Do we enjoy it, dislike or fear it? These assumptions will shape and colour how we conduct lessons. There is a useful statement by the World Health Organisation which says that sexuality:

> motivates us to find love, contact, warmth and intimacy; it is
> expressed in the way we feel, move, touch, and are touched; it
> is about being sensual as well as sexual. Sexuality influences
> thoughts, feelings, actions and interactions and thereby our
> mental and physical health.

Our values about sex will strongly influence the 'what' and 'how' of teaching it. A statement such as the one above would provide a sound basis from which to develop teaching.

Teachers need to learn to respond to children when they ask questions at inappropriate moments or when they are very busy or preoccupied. Children may stop a teacher in the corridor, or at the end of a lesson, or ask on behalf of 'a friend'. One needs to give them swift, satisfactory answers. There is no short cut but to practise these with 'carousel' type exercises where short questions are fired at one, at minute intervals, by fellow members of the course. Children will not necessarily confine their questions to neat categories of fact, value or social context. On the contrary, they will tend to ask questions in which these elements are compounded. Here are some examples of questions asked by middle school pupils:

> Is 'making love' to a person the same as sexual intercourse?
> Is intercourse fun?
> Why do people giggle when you say masturbate?
> Is there any sure way to keep from getting pregnant?
> What makes people gay?
> How can I die of ignorance?

Probably the most difficult area for teachers is uncertainty about the constraints and boundaries of their own role. They may feel threatened because they think that their own sexuality is 'on the line', and fear that they will be too vulnerable and exposed to their pupils. In one sense they are, as I have already argued. If you find sex distasteful, as did the *playboy* character, it will communicate itself to pupils. Pupils may or may not be aware of it, although it will still influence them. This is very different from revealing personal details about one's sex life or allowing pupils to do so. Quite simply one should not. A direct question, such as one about the frequency of intercourse with one's partner, should be met quite firmly with a response about their respect for your privacy and your respect for theirs. Such clear boundaries need to be drawn for your own protection and that of the pupils. There is 'performance pressure' to be aware of. The need to demonstrate that you function very well or badly as a sexual being is *not* what your pupils need. Learning to be a good sex educator is not only a matter of becoming familiar with the facts and the techniques to convey them, or becoming comfortable talking sexually and accepting one's own sexuality. There is also a need to acknowledge the moral component.

The Teacher's Dilemma

It is a highly artificial and rather academic exercise to separate out morality and sexuality. Morality is part of all behaviour. In a conversation with two heads of middle schools, I asked them whether sex education in a moral context should include telling children what is right and wrong in sexual behaviour. After all, one could argue quite sensibly that clear messages are more easily learned than unclear ones, adults are highly influential over the young, and there are clearly forms of sexual activity that children would be far better not indulging in at an early age. More than that, sexual intercourse is illegal for girls and boys under 16 years of age. Head teachers are often aware that there are girls in middle schools who are sexually active. One would not want one's own daughter to be active in this way. One head teacher responded that whilst acknowledging one's own views of what sexual behaviour was right or wrong, one was not entitled to tell pupils how they should or should not behave in expressing their sexuality, any more than one was entitled to tell pupils how they should or should not vote. The other head teacher pointed out that in a good primary school, in every subject, the pupils were taught to weigh up, measure and judge the realities of any situation based on accurate information. He believed that it was for schools to inform widely about facts and consequences but not to take decisions away from children by telling them what to do, and that the same applies to decisions about sexual behaviour, that sex education should provide information and leave children to decide. This represents what good liberal education is about but I suspect that it would have many critics today. Let us look at how the arguments might proceed.

The critics might say that, if a child pushes another over in the playground the teacher would not, and should not, leave the child to weigh up, measure and judge for her/himself, but should intervene and tell the child it is wrong to behave in this way. Yet sexual behaviour is far more profound and deeply involving of human beings, and fundamental in its consequences. It is as primitive a force as violence. Why then would we, as responsible thoughtful people, back off from interventions in sexual behaviour, whereas we would intervene in the playground? Why would we intervene with the bully but not the sexually active 11-year-old?

One must intervene in the playground. It is necessary to prevent unacceptable, inconsiderate or violent behaviour displayed in front of one, because one has to deal expediently with immediate trouble and prevent further harm. Physical intervention and verbal reinforcements are required. Yet one can only use these methods when there is an opportunity to point to a lack of consideration for others and respect for persons, on the spot. We should teach children respect for persons in all their behaviour, especially in the expression of sexuality. By and large, when the sexual behaviour of pupils is concerned one is not on the spot and one cannot point out what should and should not be done. It would be a gross intrusion of privacy if one were in such a position and a very odd one to say the least. In the sphere of sexual behaviour, teaching of moral behaviour has to be indirect. In the playground intervention there is teaching about values that one would wish to be transferred to any situation, especially that involving sexuality. In the playground incident we are dealing *expediently* with violent or inconsiderate behaviour. It is clear that we are not forcing moral behaviour on the bullying child, merely preventing further harm. It would only be a moral decision of the child when, on their own, without the threat of authority or punishment hanging over their head, he or she actually resisted that behaviour from choice. In the area of sexuality it is exactly the same. Moral decisions have to be arrived at by the person him or herself.

Considering Morality

Morality and moral education are profoundly unfashionable and misunderstood areas. Yet it is tremendously dangerous to avoid the moral considerations of sexuality. Moreover, the 1986 Education Act (No 2) says that when sex education is given it must encourage pupils 'to have due regard to moral considerations and the value of family life' (p. 47). If we do not consider what morality is we might end up with considerations that would please the vociferous few referred to earlier in the chapter, but not the majority of parents or teachers, and which may have little to do with morality. Sexuality, like any behaviour, has always had moral consequences and these consequences are, for oneself and others, now potentially more drastic and more poignant. Though expediency rather than morality tends to prevail in society, questions of good and bad, right and wrong do override all other considerations, whether we pay any attention to them or not. Not only that, but we all do constantly moralize, mostly in a covert, hidden way. On the one hand, at the heart of everything are questions of right or wrong; on the other, most of us are highly unaware, unsophisticated and untrained in our moral thinking, let alone behaviour. There seem to be two identifiable positions as regards moral matters, both of which seem to me to be highly unsatisfactory. I would argue for a third position rejecting both of these.

One position is the 'moral control' or 'moralizing' position which has been well illustrated at the beginning of this chapter. Statements of what is right and wrong are often based on so-called traditional values more appropriate to previous idealized eras. There are either clear statements such as 'It is wrong to have sex outside marriage', or 'It is wrong to practise homosexuality', or very abstract and generalized prescriptions about the rightness of marriage and family life. Many ills of society, according to this view, are seen as caused by breaking moral rules. The solution to the problem is to get people to conform to 'the rules'. The task of education, it follows, is to inculcate these 'rules' firmly into young people. Then, not only will individuals be happier in stable, conventional families, but society too will be orderly and as it should be. There is quite a problem here for teachers. We know that one child in every eight lives in a one parent family and that one child in five could see his/her parents divorce before he/she reaches 16. Three households in ten are married couples with dependent children. Teachers cannot, and should not, teach children that the only acceptable form of family life is that of mother, father and children. This would be to deny that the experience of love, care and responsibility are possible without this configuration of people. It would also be gross insensitivity toward the backgrounds of pupils.

The other position is one I will call moral 'laissez-faire'. This treats everyone as having a right to have, and act upon, his/her own moral views. 'Moral' is what an individual judges to be right for him or herself. 'Right' is often the same as what you like. There can be as many moral views as there are people because each person has to choose what is right for them. The educator has to be a neutral-chairperson, who is a model of tolerance, conveying neither approval nor disapproval of anyone else's views. The 'laissez-faire' position has arisen, I believe, as a backlash against the moralizing or 'moral control' position, and is relativism taken to its more absurd logical conclusion. Both positions are unsatisfactory. There is a contradiction in the 'moral control' position because a moral decision cannot be moral unless it is made freely. There is a contradiction in the moral 'laizzez-faire' position because it requires an overriding, absolute moral value of tolerance which is often upheld with moral fervour. Worse, neither position helps young people, or anyone else for that matter, to make sense of an extremely complicated world where there is a great deal of choice and few clear guidelines. Moralizers often 'turn people off'. The young especially react to this approach. The 'laissez-faire' approach leaves the young confused and floundering

about. There is another position that I will call the 'moral acknow-
ledgement' position which accepts that feeling and reason must bear
upon moral choice and behaviour, that moral thinking is a developmental process and that we *can* learn to be mature or 'moral' in our
decision-making.

Moral Education

We need to begin by acknowledging that we all do judge and
moralize. We conceal these judgments but we do judge nevertheless.
We refrain from judging our friends because we like them. We refrain
from expressing our opinions too vociferously because we find it
distasteful and very unfashionable. We want to be seen as liberal and
tolerant. However, 'closet' moralizing is not helpful to us or young
people. It means that we maintain a veneer of sophistication or
tolerance which is misleading. Our moral opinions are actually not
being tested against those of other people. We are not engaging in the
kinds of dialogue which would expose our views to challenge. We are
not having to justify, examine or modify our judgments. We miss out
on the whole healthy process of developing our moral thinking. The
outcomes can be moral opinions that become extremely polarized.
The 'moralizer' adheres to rigid rules and cannot tolerate any
challenge in case they collapse. The 'laissez-faire' adherent refrains
from judgments, suppresses unease at unacceptable behaviour and
goes along with things 'against his better judgment'. The 'moralizing'
parent sets a rule about the time they expect their son to come in and
expects rigid conformity. The 'laissez-faire' parent sets no boundaries
and puts up with disruption. Young people remain confused in a
world where the consequences of sexual activity can be profound. Yet
choosing is a skill that one can improve on with .practice. Sexual
information-giving spills over easily into questions about values and
morals. Whilst the moralizers would have teachers instruct the young
in what they should and should not do, teachers of Sex Education
actually have a much more difficult, time-consuming process to
impart.

Content and Process

Having declared my position on moral education, there remains an
area of confusion about what one tries to teach pupils and how one

does this; a confusion about the values inherent in the *content* and the *process* by which they are conveyed. Earlier I commented on teachers needing to establish clear boundaries about how much they self disclose in order to protect pupils. Such issues about the right to privacy and restraints on self-disclosure are not to be confused with issues about creating an atmosphere in which pupils may learn effectively. This is to do with the *process* of learning rather than with the *content*. It is the difference between *permission-giving*, about speaking freely and openly, and *permissiveness* which allows or encourages children to do as they like. The Conservative Family Association members would no doubt dispute this point, but it is a critical one in the argument and is a fundamental element of a particular philosophy of learning.

One view of education sees it as a matter of filling empty vessels. The teacher is seen as an expert who has access to knowledge to transmit to pupils. A different view sees teachers and pupils engaged in an interactive process. The teacher's skill is to provide firm boundaries and plenty of opportunities for pupils to explore, relate new knowledge to what they know already, and judge for themselves. Teachers must respect the knowledge and experience of pupils because we are all equal as moral agents. In teaching about sexuality, teachers particularly need to respect pupils' needs and concerns. If teachers foreclose on topics for discussion, education in the fullest sense cannot take place.

Let us take the issue of homosexuality. Most boys apparently experience a 'homosexual' phase at puberty. This may mean a passing crush on another male or an actual physical encounter. Homosexuality is practised by a significant number of men. Many regard it as a factor undermining marriage and family life. Any boy experiencing the homosexual phase must experience considerable worry and confusion about his sexual orientation, being aware of society's attitudes. Most boys are not homosexual, but many may fear they are. Much anguish could be avoided if boys understood their experience. If homosexuality is excluded from classroom discussion, how can most boys come to understand their experience? Yet advocates of the 'moral control' position would argue that to allow such discussion would be to give permission to experiment and encourage homosexuality. They would see this as undermining marriage and family life. Yet it is not a sound pedagogical principle to believe that not to mention what is undesirable will eliminate it. It is by getting young people to talk openly, that attitudes and views can be examined. There is also a big moral issue about intolerance of other people's sexual orientation, which cannot be examined in detail here. Would one want one's own children to ridicule and persecute another who caused them no harm other than to indulge privately in different sexual practices? Put another way, do we want to use teaching methods which inculcate insensitivity to other people's views. Surely, it is better to explore differences of opinion and allow opportunities for views to be modified and opinions to be developed.

Core Moral Values

Sex education in a moral context involves putting into practice one of the basic moral values, respect for persons. Teachers have to teach pupils the process of making moral decisions. There is the Value Clarification method outlined by Simon, *et al.* (1972) where one learns to perform the seven stages of valuing through various exercises. The stages are: prizing and cherishing beliefs; publicly affirming them; choosing freely; choosing from alternatives; choosing after consideration of consequences; acting; acting with a pattern, consistency and repetition. Pupils have to learn to listen to others, to respond to their views, to explain what they mean, to look at situations from another's point of view, to universalize or generalize from a particular statement. The teacher is not a neutral-chairperson. He/she has his/her own moral opinions, but refrains from imposing them on young people whom they are helping to develop as moral thinkers. The teacher will need to act as the devil's advocate at times, to present the pupils with moral dilemmas where values will have to be put in order of priority. All that I have described applies to all aspects of life including sexuality. Moral education should not be left to chance as it tends to be. Most groups of people agree that there are four core moral ideas: respect for persons, justice and fairness, truthfulness and keeping promises and contracts. It seems strange that these core values are rarely *explicitly* affirmed in school.

As the influence of religion and the church declines we must bank up the moral reserves of our young people from direct sources. Lawrence Kholberg died in 1987. His name will mean nothing to most people. But his work on the stages by which people develop and mature in their moral thinking could well be a standard text for all educators. In the end I am glad that the Education Act (no. 2) 1986 requires that Sex Education be 'given in such a manner as to encourage those pupils to have due regard to moral considerations'. Education should aim to educate morally and sex education can show the way.

References

ALLEN, I. (1987) *Education in Sex and Personal Relationships,* London, Policy Studies Institute.
BRUINVELS, P. (1986) Letter, *The Guardian* 16 September.
CLARE, A. (1986) 'Sex and the confused parent', *The Listener,* 2 October p. 21
CONSERVATIVE FAMILY CAMPAIGN (1986) *Sex Education and Your Child,* London, Conservative Family Campaign.
DEPARTMENT OF EDUCATION AND SCIENCE (1986) *Education Act (No.2),* London, HMSO.
HARRIS, A. (1971) 'What does "Sex education" mean?' *Journal of Moral Education,* 1,1 pp. 7–11.
RICHES, V. (1986) in CLOUGH, P. 'Putting love into sex education', *The Times,* 4 June.
ROSSER, J. (1986) in RODWELL, L. 'Love and the facts of life', *The Times,* 3 October.
SAVAGE, B. (1967) 'Cartoon', *Playboy,* February, p. 29.
SCHULZ, E.D. and WILLIAMS, S.R. (1968) *Family Life and Sex Education,* New York, Harcourt, Brace and Co.
SIMON, S.B., HOWE, L.W. and KIRSCHENBAUM, H. (1972) *Values Clarification,* London, Dodd, Mead and Company.
TOOMEY, C. (1986) 'Tell us all the facts of life in class, say children', *The Sunday Times,* 19 October, p.7.
WENT, D. (1986) *Sex Education,* London, Bell and Hyman.

Chapter 13

Combating Racism through Political Education

Bruce Carrington and Barry Troyna

Introduction

Teachers can be adept at ignoring racial conflict between their pupils, utilising a variety of techniques to put the blame elsewhere. With the 'original sin' technique, racial name-calling can be safely ignored, as 'They naturally tease each other about everything... Children are so cruel'. Conversely, some maintain their pupils' innocence: 'It's all love and peace... obviously my own opinions are coloured by the way I was brought up and I feel it's the same with the kiddies in the playground, both parties'.

Many teachers are reluctant to discuss anything to do with race in their classrooms. On one inservice course, a group of infants teachers were shocked by another who had done so: 'You know she had really discussed the colour of skin!'. They were clearly amazed by her temerity: 'You've got to tread very carefully' (Dunn, 1986, p.188).

As Dunn's vignettes based upon his experience as an evaluator of inservice provision in multicultural and anti-racist education suggest, many teachers, especially of younger children, may look upon 'race' as a taboo subject and deny (or underestimate) the influence of racist attitudes and behaviour on pupils in primary schools. In this chapter, we stress the need for all primary schools – irrespective of their location or ethnic composition – to play an active role in combating racism. In order to dispel some of the myths and misconceptions about children's propensities for racism, and thus demonstrate that there is a *need* for anti-racist education (ARE) in the primary school, we begin by briefly appraising the evidence on the onset and development of individual racism (see Short's chapter for further discussion). To allay the unease surrounding the *implementation* of the initiative in this sector we engage directly with the criticisms that ARE is: (1) a form of proselytization or indoctrination; (2) divisive in its effects; and (3) anathema to 'good' education. Having identified the salient characteristics of ARE, we then attempt to enunciate a set of principles which might underpin the organizational, curricular and pedagogical strategies of *all* primary schools. We show that ARE – together with other initiatives predicated upon an unequivocal commitment to social justice, equality, human rights and participatory democracy – seeks to equip young people with the range of skills and dispositions needed to become decent, fairminded, responsible and informed citizens. We illustrate our arguments by referring to a range of case studies of ARE in the primary school.

'It's all Love and Peace'

Although there may be a tendency for primary teachers to regard younger children as 'colour blind' and free from the malign influences of racism and prejudice, there is considerable evidence to show that such perceptions have no basis in reality. By three, children are not only capable of making distinctions on the basis of 'race' but many also express a preference for members of their own group and exhibit feelings of hostility towards other groups (Davey 1983; Milner 1983; Ken Thomas 1984). Furthermore, as Jeffcoate's (1979) research in a Bradford nursery school has suggested, whereas young children often voice pejorative views about Blacks, they generally confine such remarks to the peer group. Because the presence of an adult authority figure, such as a teacher, has the effect of inhibiting this type of behaviour, he argues that such children may already be aware of the taboo status of 'race'. It is not surprising (given the early onset of individual racism), that in addition to incidents involving racist name-calling, jokes and mimicry and forms of physical abuse and harassment, teachers in junior schools may find themselves in a situation where they have to confront neo-fascist organizations attempting to distribute literature or gain recruits among their pupils (Francis 1984; Nixon 1985).

As Lord Swann and his colleagues noted, manifestations of racism and prejudice are not restricted to schools in ethnically-mixed areas (DES 1985). For example, Mould's (1987) work in Tyne and Wear has indicated that such attitudes are rife among young people attending 'all-white' (or predominantly white) schools. As an LEA advisory teacher, Mould was concerned that many senior staff seemed to believe that there was no racial prejudice in their schools, no incidents of racial abuse and no feelings of white superiority. In an attempt to 'clarify the situation' (and thus obviate resistance to her LEA's newly-introduced policy in multicultural education), she invited about two hundred young people (9-year-olds, 13-year-olds and sixth formers) to produce some '"cold" writing on the topic of "black people"'. Teachers were asked not to discuss this work with the pupils; it was undertaken anonymously. Mould's analysis of the scripts revealed that:

> approximately 75 per cent of these children held negative attitudes about black people and, of those one-third held strongly hostile attitudes. Almost all children talked of Britain as a white society, and almost all those who advocated acceptance and access to equality of opportunity did so from a paternalistic point of view (1987, p.51).

Whereas little has been written about racism in mainly-white areas, a recent study of gender differences in leisure opportunities and behaviour among young South Asians in the North of England has suggested that racism acts as a major restraint upon their lifestyles (Carrington *et al.* 1987). More than three-quarters of the 114 persons (aged between 11 and their early 20s) interviewed during this research were able to recount various *direct* experience of racism, ranging from violence through to verbal abuse.

Despite the accelerated growth of racist harassment within and beyond the metropolitan centres of the UK, the murder of a Bangladeshi pupil in the playground (sic) of a Manchester Secondary School, and the prevalence of racist views amongst 'the Thatcher generation' of school-leavers (Williams 1986), ARE continues to excite opposition (Alibhai, 1988). In the media, for instance, it is characterized as one of the 'loony tunes' of the Left, a depiction which draws its credibility largely from the media's distorted, even fraudulent accounts, of the promotion of ARE in some LEAs and schools (Beckett, 1987; Parekh, 1986). Routinely it is assigned demoniac properties, lampooned as an irrelevant fad and assailed for being inimical to both academic standards and the pastoral goals of education. It is, in the words of one forthright critic, 'political, confrontational, accusatory and guilt-inducing in its approach' (Lynch, 1987, p. x). In the words of another, this time a primary school teacher attending an INSET course on multicultural education: 'I think the way it's being done is getting at people like myself. It really gets me against it. It's far too strong – it comes over as being very left wing' (cited in Robertson, 1987, p.39). Significantly, these critiques centre less on the substantive nature or underlying principles of ARE, more on the manner in which it is advocated and the strategies used for its dissemination. In this sense, the criticisms disparage ARE as indoctrination, as the term is defined by John White (1970). According to this view, indoctrinators are identified primarily by their concern to instill 'certain substantive beliefs *in such a way* that they will not later be questioned or changed' (cited in Wringe, 1984: p.35 emphasis added). Now, if the conception of ARE as indoctrination is to be sustained then we would need to adduce empirical support for the following and related propositions. First, that the *methods* of ARE are at variance with the development of open-mindedness and rational autonomy. Second, that these methods are generative of beliefs, values and knowledge which are impervious to change. Let's look at each of these claims in turn. Of course, ARE is a diffuse concept which is amenable to a wide range of definitions and interpretations. Along with Hall (1980), Barb Thomas (1984) and Troyna and Williams (1986), however, we are firmly committed to a view of ARE as a constituent of a more broadly conceived programme of political education (Troyna and Carrington,1989). And in this context we would provide the opportunity for pupils:

> to take a critical stance towards political information; be open-minded and show respect for evidence; act in an empathetic manner; extend their appreciation of how power is exercised (and by whom); and explore fundamental questions relating to social justice and equality (Troyna and Carrington, 1989).

In our efforts to activate these ideas in schools and colleges (Short and Carrington, 1987; Troyna, 1988) we have been mindful of the need to develop pedagogical approaches which are not only congruent with, but exemplary of, ARE principles. That is to say, we eschew pedagogy which legitimates teacher exposition, didacticism and an asymmetrical relationship between teacher and pupils. The reason for this is clear; together with Young (1984) we see *this* pedagogical style – which continues to dominate primary school classrooms (cf. Biott, 1987; Galton, 1987) – as indoctrinational. As Young argues:

> It is difficult to avoid the conclusion that the dominant pattern of classroom communication is indoctrinational. In not one, but a multitude of ways, it is structured so as to exclude, repress and prevent exploration of questions concerning the validity of facts and simple generalizations which make-up the bulk of information transmitted in classrooms (1984, p.236).

The conception of ARE to which we and others (e.g., Brandt, 1986) subscribe and attempt to operationalize is fundamentally opposed to these indoctrinational practices. Thus, it celebrates negotiation rather than imposition; cooperation and collaboration in preference to competitive individualism; and it prescribes a democratized learning ethos in place of the established classroom setting, where learning is privatized and knowledge is owned and legitimated by the teacher. What is more, unless these pedagogical principles are enacted during the primary school phase, later attempts at developing children's capacity for critical and rational thinking are almost bound to fail. As Patricia White points out, by the onset of secondary school, children are set in their ways. Their political and social attitudes are well-established and not readily amenable to change (White, 1983, p. 11).

The typification of ARE strategies as indoctrinational is in our view misplaced. Rather than being illiberal and indoctrinational, either in effect or intent, ARE embraces pedagogical and organizational styles designed to challenge the pre-eminence of expository teaching and the knowledge transmission view of the curriculum.

In spite of these laudable goals, ARE continues to be interpreted as a divisive ideology. Criticism along these lines can assume these forms. On the one hand, there are those who maintain that a consideration of cultural and ethnic differences exacerbates tension and enhances the potential for prejudice, especially in multi-ethnic schools. Clearly this was the view of one primary school teacher who maintained that: 'It can be dangerous to delve too deeply. It can stir up trouble by highlighting cultural differences' (cited in Robertson, 1987, p. 39). Teachers who adhere to this view abrogate entirely responsibility for developing either multicultural or anti-racist perspectives in their schools. On the other hand, there are those teachers who reject ARE in favour of multicultural education. Here the (apparent) negative and confrontational properties of ARE are juxtaposed against multicultural education. With its emphasis on the acknowledgment of ethnic and cultural lifestyles and exotica, individual prejudice (rather than structural racism), consensus and harmony, multicultural education constitutes a more palatable, less threatening conception of educational reform (Milner, 1983). A recent survey of teachers' responses to their LEA's policy on multicultural education indicated both sets of views. Significantly, however, the vast majority of primary school teachers maintained that multicultural education – and the practices it espouses – did not depart in any radical sense from their established procedures (Troyna and Ball, 1987).

Once again, however, we witness the dismissal of ARE on grounds which resemble more closely caricatured portrayals of this educational ideology than its reality in the primary (and secondary) classroom. We have argued that ARE principles cannot be realized unless appropriate and compatible pedagogical styles are developed. We have seen that this calls for collaborative modes of learning. In this context, claims of divisiveness simply cannot be sustained. On the contrary, the research of Slavin (1983), and Sharan (1980) in the United States and, in this country, Yeomans (1983) and Salmon and Claire (1984), demonstrate the veracity of Edith King's claim that:

> In a school that has a single-minded concern with academic performance so that student is pitted against student in a competitive arena, very different lessons are being taught. Schools that are successful in developing prejudice reduction are ones in which minority and majority students come together as co-operating equals (1986, p. 334).

King's resumé of the research linking collaborative learning to improved ethnic relations within the school is important. Nonetheless, it should not be construed as a denial of the significance of academic achievement to ARE. Yet, one of the most potent strings in the bow of 'anti-anti-racists' is that the promotion of this educational ideology is achieved at the cost of high academic standards. Certainly, this was the argument of the Secretary of State for Education when he ordered HMI to carry out an inspection of Brent LEA's anti-racist/ multicultural education policy (Oldman, 1987). In 1987, of course, it also figured in the Prime Minister's speech to her party's annual conference, where she contrasted anti-racist mathematics – 'Whatever that means' – with the need to ensure that children are able to count and multiply (cited in Gow, 1987, p. 15). In response to Mrs Thatcher and her fellow travellers, we would point to the research evidence on collaborative group work. This shows that such an approach serves not only to enhance young people's social awareness, interpersonal and ethical skills, but does so without any apparent, adverse effect on their level of attainment. Indeed, under certain conditions levels of attainment may actually improve (Yeomans, 1983).

Similar claims can be made for 'peer tutoring' or 'cross-age tutoring', another pedagogical approach which supports our conception of ARE. Carol FitzGibbon has argued that this technique may:

> be one of the most effective interventions yet found for improving achievement, both for tutors and those tutored: tutors learn the work (i.e., subject matter) thoroughly because they have to teach it and tutees benefit from individual attention' (1983, p. 160).

What is more, this technique enhances 'friendly feelings', to use FitzGibbon's terms. As such, it represents an important contribution to the collaborative (rather than competitive) ethos of the classroom within which the goals of ARE might be realized.

By defining ARE more precisely and identifying some of the pedagogical and organizational strategies which stem logically from its underlying principles, we have shown that, as a conception of educational reform, it neither threatens academic standards nor degenerates into crude forms of proselytization or indoctrination. Indeed, the converse is true. ARE constitutes an emancipatory notion of educational change which embraces styles of teaching and classroom organization that have the potential to facilitate the cognitive, social and affective development of children. In this sense we would claim that ARE is entirely compatible with 'good' primary practice.

Anti-racist Education in the Primary School: Strategies for Change

In attempting to outline strategies for change which focus on the *process* of primary education, we are mindful of Bill Taylor's stricture that: 'the majority of Britain's population ...does not live in inner cities nor is it in regular contact with non-white people' (1984–5, p. 1). As we have indicated, such schools, despite teachers' frequent disclaimers to the contrary, do 'have a problem' so far as the issues of 'race' and racism are concerned. As we have already shown, when this 'problem' is addressed particular attention should be given to teaching styles and classroom interaction. We now consider the framing and implementation of anti-racist initiatives in the curriculum.

Racism and the Primary Curriculum

All schools should be offering their pupils as part of a 'good' education – the ability to accept a range of differing and possibly conflicting points of view and to argue rationally and independently about the principles which underlie these, free from pre-conceived prejudices or stereotypes, and to recognise and resist false arguments and propaganda – as in a sense 'political' skills. We believe that effective political education must help pupils to appreciate the contribution which they as individuals can make to the decision-making process at various levels. Effective political education should also lead youngsters to consider fundamental issues such as social justice and equality and this should in turn cause them to reflect on the origins and mechanisms of racism and prejudice at an individual level.

Some educationists have argued that school pupils are insufficiently mature and responsible to be able to comprehend politically sensitive issues such as racism and to cope with them in a balanced and rational manner. Even primary-age pupils however have views and opinions on various 'political' issues and are subject to a range of overt and covert political influences based on values and assumptions from their homes, their peers and the media (DES 1985, pp. 335–6).

While the Swann Committee endorses our view that every school should include teaching about racism within a wider programme of political education, it offers little concrete guidance as to how this recommendation might be implemented, or what measures might be taken to obviate teachers' or parents' resistance to the proposal.

A strong case can be made for dealing with questions relating to 'race' and racism in schools in a holistic manner. As Troyna (1987) has suggested, phenomena such as racial scapegoating and stereotyping cannot be effectively challenged unless young people are encouraged to examine alternative (and hopefully more plausible) explanations of, for example, urban decay or drug abuse. This, he contends, cannot be done if:

> ...the issues of 'race' and ethnic relations are considered in isolation; rather, they need to be seen and considered as pertinent aspects of the social structure along with, say, class and gender. This demands a more broadly based approach, the rejection of pre-packaged 'teaching about race relations' materials and the generation of key concepts around which teaching sessions might be based. The aim is to ensure that students not only recognise the specific nature of racial inequality but the nature of the inequalities they themselves experience and share with black people as girls, students, young people or as members of the working-class. It is an approach which identifies empathy with rather than sympathy for the oppression of black people as a goal. Further, it concedes that informed collective action constitutes the most

effective challenge to racism. The intention, then, is to replace divisions and scapegoating with alliances. Research into this mode of intervention might facilitate the development of models which build upon the principles of ARE (1987, p. 316).

An holistic approach may also be defended on the grounds that children might interpret *any* curricular initiative which focuses narrowly on the issues of 'race' and ethnic relations as a form of proselytization. Consequently, they would be more likely to resent such teaching and react to it with either indifference or outright hostility (Robertson 1986). The following case-studies incorporate ARE within a holistic perspective.

Short and Carrington's ethnographic study is an evaluation of an integrated project (*In Living Memory*) undertaken with 10- and 11-year-old children at 'Oldtown' Primary School. The school had an 'all-white' working-class catchment and was in a mining area with high levels of adult and youth unemployment. The project was primarily concerned with changes in popular culture and lifestyles (ie., fashion, music, leisure, housing, family organizations), and changes in employment patterns and opportunities since 1945. It began with the immediate experiences of the children and members of their family. Parents, grandparents and others were interviewed by the children about their employment histories and experiences of the world of work and perceptions of cultural change. These 'oral histories', together with such artefacts as family photographs, memorabilia and local archive materials, provided a starting-point for a study which extended beyond the local environment. It ultimately allowed an examination of post-war immigration to the UK and an analysis of aspects of racism. In planning this intervention, every effort was made to democratize the classroom and encourage frank and open discussion; collaborative group work was used extensively throughout the project.

Various techniques were employed to probe the children's understanding of 'race' and racism, counter racial stereotyping and scapegoating, and promote the development of empathy. For example, a discussion of recent historical changes in the demand for labour in the British economy not only permitted the issues of racism and immigration to arise spontaneously, but also provided a context in which populist misconceptions about Blacks as a cause of unemployment could be subjected to critical scrutiny. Furthermore, members of the class were asked to put themselves in the position of either Afro-Caribbean or Asian workers living in Britain during the 1950s. In this capacity, they were then asked to write to a relative or friend and describe their experiences in this country. The exercise not only enabled the teacher-researchers to assess the pupils' knowledge of racism in the labour market, housing and other spheres, but it placed the pupils (almost all of whom had no direct experience of other ethnic groups) in a situation where they might gain greater insights into the black experience in Britain. As well as inviting the children to compare their letters with black autobiographical accounts of the period, other stimuli were employed to develop empathy with Blacks. The aim was to show that British-born Afro-Caribbeans and Asians continue to face many of the difficulties which had earlier confronted their parents and grandparents. Among other things, the class was introduced to Bernard Ashley's novel *The Trouble with Donovan Croft* (1977). This was selected because of its realistic portrayal of life in a multiracial junior school, the sensitive way in which racial incidents are described, and the ease with which children of this age can identify with its central characters. In addition, the children were presented with the following scenario for discussion; both in small groups, and as a class (p. 228):

> You are playing in the street where you live when a pantechnicon draws up and unloads. Mr Taylor, a lorry driver from Birmingham, gets out. He says he's got a couple of 11-year-old children and he wants advice about this school. What will you tell him?

Almost as an afterthought, the researcher then added:

> Oh, by the way, the family is Black, from the West Indies, but the kids were born in England.

A number of interesting points emerged from the class discussion and the follow-up activity, a written exercise entitled 'The Taylor Twins' First Day at School'. During the class discussion more than half an hour elapsed before any reference was made to 'race'. However, when the issue was eventually raised, the children's remarks indicated that they had some understanding of the nature of individual racism and an awareness that not all whites behave in a racist manner:

> I wouldn't count on anyone liking your kids... They'll be Black and everyone else in the school's got a different colour skin and it won't mix with them. (John)

> I don't think it's fair how they get picked on because the

whites think they're different in all ways. But it's just the colour that's different, not the personality. (Samantha)

I think that sometimes the mums and dads are to blame because maybe the kids have been brought up not to speak to black children. (Patsy)

If I was playing with a Black person and a white person came up and called them names, I'd say what do you think you'd feel like if you moved away and had to go to a school where there was a lot of coloured children? You wouldn't like it. (Terry)

Some members of the class had internalized certain facets of racist discourse and perceived British-born blacks as alien, and regarded physical differences as necessarily implying cultural differences:

Well I think they would get skitted (have fun poked at them) even more when we're doing geography and talking about where *they came from* and they can answer all the questions. (John, emphasis added)

Some white people are too stuck up to play with them. They don't want to play with them just because they wear different clothes to us. (Carol)

I think the reason why white children won't play with them is... that they like different types of things. (Liz)
(1987, pp. 229–31).

Teachers implementing an anti-racist initiative in a setting such as 'Oldtown' (located more than 30 miles from any urban centre with a significant black population), are faced with a number of practical pedagogical difficulties which may assume greater prominence than, for example, in the all-white suburban school or multiracial urban school. In so-called 'non-contact areas', where children's first-hand experience of 'race' and ethnic relations tends to be more circumscribed, teachers often have no other option than to deal with such matters through the use of stimuli largely based upon secondary data (e.g., black autobiographical accounts, newspaper articles, photographs and census materials) or through fantasy (e.g., role play and fiction). Whilst these stimuli, in an enquiring and democratic classroom environment, may encourage pupils to reflect upon 'race' and other issues relating to social justice and equality (and thereby develop their political and moral autonomy and interpersonal skills), the following question nevertheless remains: to what extent is the success of anti-racist education dependent upon pupils having *direct* experience of other ethnic groups? Reciprocal visits between multiracial and all-white schools may provide the basis for this experience, as recent accounts of such exchanges between two secondary schools (Hatcher, 1986) and two primary schools (Lee, Lee and Pearson, 1987) have indicated.

Lee and her associates' ethnographic study evaluates an anti-racist intervention involving two upper junior classes and their teachers at Park School (a working class, multiracial inner-city school) and Riverside School (a socially mixed, all-white surburban school). The teachers believed that inter-school visits would provide the children with the opportunity to 'share and explore each other's social perspectives; particularly those relating to race' (1987, p. 209). In preparation for those exchange visits, the teachers embarked upon a parallel programme with their classes 'involving a considerable amount of work on stereotyping, name-calling, sex-roles and the general bias in the media'. As a follow-up to this work, the classes met and worked together on four occasions: Park School entertained Riverside to a Divali celebration and a puppet show and later hosted an urban nature trail. Riverside also hosted a trail and provided a number of collaborative, problem-solving activities involving children from both schools. There is always a danger with exchanges such as those described here, that they reinforce, rather than challenge, racial and other stereotypes (Bochner, 1982). Lee and her colleagues, however, appeared to surmount this difficulty by involving the children in activities which stressed cooperation and by making the visits an *integral* part of a wider programme of political education. They draw the following conclusion:

> It seems to us that to establish anti-racist education as a democratic process it must be underpinned by a progressive pedagogy...we tentatively suggest that progressive practice values cooperation and collaboration through talk rather than simply individual exploration and opens the way to critical enquiry (Lee, Lee and Pearson, 1987, p. 219).

These same principles underpinned the ARE initiative taken by Francis (1984) with fourth year juniors in a multiracial primary school in London. According to Francis, history, environmental studies, language work and drama provide the most suitable areas of the curriculum for examining 'race' and ethnic relations with children of this age. In common with Harwood (1985) and Ross (1984), he stresses that the point of departure for the teaching of controversial issues at primary level should be the children's own experience. To illustrate this point, he describes a project which began with a class discussion of racial incidents at his school, and then proceeded to examine related national and international issues, including media reporting of the New Cross Fire, and injustice and inequality under apartheid.

Working with younger children (aged between 7 and 10) in several multicultural schools, Burgess (1986) has shown how oral and written history, biographies and children's fiction can be used to examine both sexism and racism. Like Francis, she stresses the importance of 'starting with the children's experiences and building on them'. Together with others involved with the implementation of educational policies to promote social justice and equality, she is aware of the shortcomings of didactic forms of pedagogy:

> We also tend to define for children what kinds of experiences we as teachers are interested in, and this means that communication tends to be one way. Children will not ram down our throats things they have come to expect we don't want to hear. Our reluctance to give the children and parents a voice is the reason why so many teachers still persist in the notion that racism does not exist in school and that white children 'don't notice' racial differences, or black children 'don't care' about racial abuse (Burgess, 1986, p. 151).

Giving Parents a Voice

So far, we have identified a range of intra-school strategies in the development of ARE in primary education. It is our conviction that these need to be enshrined within a formal and public whole-school policy on ARE. That is to say, a policy which implicates all members of staff (teaching and administrative) in the construction and implementation of an approach which provides coherence and consistency to the children's experiences. Of course, the realization of this goal is not likely to be entirely free of professional resistance. As David Hargreaves has pointed out, the 'cult of individualism' and commitment to the maxim of 'live and let live' remains axiomatic in the professional culture of teaching (1980, p. 141). For this reason, amongst others, attempts to develop whole-school policies on anti-racism have often failed (Troyna, 1988). But despite the opposition likely to be encountered in this context the establishment of anti-racism as a procedural value in the school, around which consensus ought be formed, must be of pre-eminent concern. After all, the absence of a broad commitment to ARE is likely to presage a state of affairs in which a range of contradictory messages on the issue of anti-racism are conveyed to the children and their parents. This was the situation which Kate Myers found in a nursery school where the commitment to anti-sexist initiatives was half-hearted:

> A nursery teacher reported how she changed the 'Wendy House' to the 'Home Corner' and painstakingly encouraged the boys to use this area of the classroom. She was subsequently horrified to hear a classroom assistant tell two little boys who were playing with the dressing-up clothes that boys didn't do that sort of thing and wouldn't they prefer to play with the lego (1985, p. 30).

Naturally, the whole-school approach also has consequences for the nature of relationships amongst the staff, as David Milman's account of the development of a multicultural policy at Childeric primary school in London indicates (1984). To begin with, the process of policy-making allows for participatory decision-making, a stress on collegiality and the opportunity to express misgivings and anxieties in a non-competitive setting. Furthermore, it provides a basis for school-based INSET and for the identification of monitoring and appraisal strategies.

However important these strategies, it would be disingenuous of us to confine our discussion to intra-school initiatives. After all, whilst children might spend 15,000 hours in school, a further 70,000 are spent beyond the school gates (Heath and Clifford, 1980). This is not to suggest that schools can do little to change attitudes or ways in which inequalities are conceived and interpreted by children – although some teachers do jump to this conclusion (Yates, 1987). Rather, it is to advocate genuine collaboration between parents and staff in promoting ARE. The development of a whole-school policy on ARE might provide the opportunity for establishing a closer link between the home and the school which, in itself, is likely to enhance more effective teaching (Mortimore and Mortimore, 1984). It might also provide a suitable context for parents to elucidate their reservations and apprehensions about their children's educational experiences generally, and their education within the school in particular. If the research of Cullingford (1984) is to be believed, parental views on the principal aims of schooling are likely to be discrepant with those of teachers. The recent incidents in Dewsbury are, of course, an indication of how professional views on ARE might be at variance with those of some white parents (Alibhai, 1988). Against this background, it is imperative that parents are informed of, and integrated into, the process of change along ARE lines.

Different approaches to expedite the involvement of parents in this process will, of course, be adopted by different schools. Nonetheless, the following strategy, adopted by Jean Campbell at Langbourne Primary School in London, seems to us to provide useful guidance for others. She describes how parents and teachers collaborated as a working party which established the following objectives:

1) To provide a 'forum' for ideas and support for each other.
2) To plan the overall directions for introducing sex and race equality at our school.
3) To include parents in the planning procedures.
4) To provide an avenue for other parents to be kept informed on the school's progress on these issues (Campbell, 1986, p. 33).

It is likely that some teachers would construe this development as another feather in the cap of the 'deskilling' movement; that is, another attempt to ensure that the education service is consumer-led and denuded of 'professional expertise'. It is also likely that some teachers would point to the virulent racism of the local community and insist that it was impervious to change. The research of Frank Coffield and his colleagues in the North East of England would suggest that this is the reality facing a number of schools in that region at least (Coffield *et al.*, 1986). Unlike some proponents of multicultural education (e.g., DES, 1985; Lynch, 1987) we do not believe that racist views can be dislodged simply through dialogue and appeal to reason. Instead, we advocate community education as a process through which change along anti-racist lines could be effected. This recognises the role of the school within the local community but, at the same time, acknowledges that the education of the children must assume pre-eminence in the identification and pursuit of the school's objectives. In other words, it would be incumbent on teachers to emphasize the ways in which an education predicated on anti-racist, anti-sexist lines might be of benefit, not only to the individual children but also to the community in which they live. The active involvement of parents in the development of initiatives along these lines seems to us to be the most appropriate way forward.

References

ALIBHAI, Y. (1988) 'Tribal Dance', *New Statesman and Society*, 22 July, pp. 18–19.

ASHLEY, B. (1977) *The Trouble with Donovan Croft*, Harmondsworth, Penguin.

BECKETT, F. (1987) 'Loony Tunes', *The Times Educational Supplement*, 5 June, p. 25.

BIOTT, C. (1987) 'Co-operative group work: pupils' and teachers' membership and participation', *Curriculum*, 8, 2, pp. 5–14.

BOCHNER, S. (1982) 'The Social Psychology of Cross-Cultural Relations', in BOCHNER, S. (Ed.), *Cultures in Contact: Studies in Cross-Cultural Interaction*, London, Pergammon Press. pp. 5–44.

BRANDT, G. (1986) *The Realization of Antiracist Teaching*, Lewes, Falmer Press.

BURGESS, C. (1986) 'Tackling Racism and Sexism in the Classroom', in GUNDARA, J., JONES, C. and KIMBERLEY, K. (Eds), *Racism, Diversity and Education*, London, MacMillan. pp. 133–53.

CAMPBELL, J. (1986) 'Involving Parents in Equal Opportunities: One School's Attempt' in ILEA, *Primary Matters: Some Approaches to Equal Opportunities in Primary Schools*, London, ILEA. pp. 33–4.

CARRINGTON, B., CHIVERS, T.S. and WILLIAMS, T. (1987) 'Gender, Leisure and Sport: A Case-Study of Young People of South Asian Descent', *Leisure Studies*, 6, 3, pp. 265–79.

COFFIELD, F., BORRILL, C. and MARSHALL, S. (1986) *Growing up on the Margins*, Milton Keynes, Open University Press.

CULLINGFORD, C. (1984) 'The Battle for the Schools: Attitudes of Parents and Teachers Towards Education', *Educational Studies*. 10, 2, pp. 113–19.

DAVEY, A. (1983) *Learning to be Prejudiced*, London, Edward Arnold.

DEPARTMENT OF EDUCATION AND SCIENCE (1985) *Education for All* (Swann Report), Cmnd 9543, London, HMSO.

DUNN, D. (1986) 'In-Service Mis-education', in ARORA, R. and DUNCAN, C. (Eds) *Multicultural Education: Towards Good Practice*, London, Routledge and Kegan Paul. pp. 182–99.

FITZGIBBON, C. (1983) 'Peer-tutoring: a possible method for multi-cultural education', *New Community*, 11, 1/2, pp. 160–6.

FRANCIS, M. (1984) 'Anti-racist teaching in the primary school', in STRAKER-WELDS, M. (Ed.) *Education for a Multicultural Society: Case Studies in ILEA Schools*, London, Bell and Hyman. pp. 228–34.

GALTON, M. (1987) 'Change and Continuity in the Primary School: The Research Evidence', *Oxford Review of Education*, 13, 1, pp. 81–93.

GOW, D. (1987) 'The unknown quantity', *The Guardian*, 3 November, p. 15.

HALL, S. (1980) 'Teaching race', *Multiracial Education*, 9, 1, pp. 3–12.

HARGREAVES, D.H. (1980) 'The occupational culture of teachers' in WOODS, P. (Ed.), *Teacher Strategies*, London, Croom Helm. pp. 125–48.

HARWOOD, D. (1985) 'We need political not Political education for 5–13 year olds', *Education 3–13*, 13, 1, pp. 12–17.

HATCHER, R. (1986) 'Making sense of living in multicultural Birmingham', *Multicultural Education Review*, 6, Summer/Autumn, pp. 20, 21.

HEATH, A. and CLIFFORD, P. (1980) 'The seventy thousand hours that Rutter left out', *Oxford Review of Education*, 6, 1, pp. 3–19.

JEFFCOATE, R. (1979) *Positive Image: Towards a Multiracial Curriculum*, London, Writers and Readers Publishing Co-operative.

KING, E. (1986) 'Recent experimental strategies for prejudice reduction in American schools and classrooms', *Journal of Curriculum Studies*, 18, 3, pp. 331–8.

LEE, V., LEE, J. and PEARSON, M. (1987) 'Stories Children Tell', in POLLARD, A. (Ed.) *Children and their Primary Schools: a New Perspective*, Lewes, Falmer Press. pp. 207–19.

LYNCH, J. (1987) *Prejudice Reduction and the Schools*, London, Cassell.

MILMAN, D. (1984) 'Childeric School: Developing a multicultural policy', in STRAKER-WELDS, M. (Ed.) *Education for a Multicultural Society: Case Studies in ILEA Schools*, London, Bell and Hyman. pp. 34–42.

MILNER, D. (1983) *Children and Race: Ten Years On* London, Ward Lock.

MORTIMORE, P. and MORTIMORE, J. (1984) 'Parents and School', *Education*, October, pp. 1–4.

MOULD, W. (1987) 'The Swann Report: an LEA Response', in CHIVERS, T.S. (Ed.) *Race and Culture in Education*, Windsor, NFER-Nelson. pp. 44–60.

MYERS, K. (1985) 'Beware of the Backlash', *School Organization*, 5, 1, pp. 27–40.

NIXON, J. (1985) *A Teacher's Guide to Multicultural Education*, Oxford, Basil Blackwell.

OLDMAN, D. (1987) 'Plain speaking and pseudo-science: the 'New Right' attack on antiracism', in TROYNA, B. (Ed.), *Racial Inequality in Education*, London, Tavistock. pp. 29–43.

PAREKH, B. (1986) 'Prejudice and the Press', *New Society*, 7 November, p. 28.

ROBERTSON, W. (1986) 'Generating Change: approaches to teacher education at Sunderland Polytechnic', *Multicultural Teaching*, 4, 3, pp. 43–5.

ROBERTSON, W. (1987) *Towards Anti-racist Curriculum and Practice*, unpublished report: DES Course 1/86: Education for Cultural Diversity, Sunderland Polytechnic.

ROSS, A. (1984) 'Developing political concepts and skills in the primary school', *Educational Review*, 36, 2, pp. 131–9.

SALMON, P. and CLAIRE, H. (1984) *Classroom Collaboration*, London, Routledge and Kegan Paul.

SHARAN, S. (1980) 'Co-operative Learning in Small Groups: Recent Methods and Effects on Achievement, Attitudes, and Ethnic Relations', *Review of Educational Research*, 50, 2, pp. 241–71.

SHORT, G. and CARRINGTON, B. (1987) 'Towards an Antiracist Initiative in the All-White Primary School: a Case Study', in POLLARD, A. (Ed.) *Children and their Primary Schools: a New Perspective*, Lewes, Falmer. pp. 220–35.

SLAVIN, R. (1983) *Co-operative Learning*, London, Methuen.

TAYLOR, B. (1984–5) 'Multicultural Education in a Monocultural region', *New Community*, 12, pp. 1–8.

THOMAS, B. (1984) 'Principles of antiracist education', *Currents*, 2, 3, pp. 20–4.

THOMAS, K. (1984) 'Intercultural relations in classrooms', in CRAFT, M. (Ed.) *Education and Cultural Pluralism*, Lewes, Falmer Press. pp. 57–77.

TROYNA, B. (1987) 'Beyond Multiculturalism: towards the enactment of antiracist education in policy, provision and pedagogy', *Oxford Review of Education*, 13, 3, pp. 307–19.

TROYNA, B. (1988) 'The career of an antiracist education school policy: some observations on the mismanagement of change', in GREEN, T. and BALL, S. (Eds) *Progress and Inequality in Comprehensive Education: A Reconsideration for the 1980s*, London, Croom Helm.

TROYNA, B. and BALL, W. (1987) '"Views from the Chalk Face": School Responses to an LEA's policy on Multicultural Education', *Policy Paper 1*, Warwick, Centre for Research in Ethnic Relations, 2nd edn.

TROYNA, B. and CARRINGTON, B. (1989) '"Whose Side Are We On?" Ethical Dilemmas in Research on "Race" and Education', in BURGESS, R. (Ed.) *The Ethics of Educational Research*, Lewes, Falmer Press.

TROYNA, B. and WILLIAMS, J. (1986) *Racism, Education and the State: The Racialisation of Education Policy*, London, Croom Helm.

VASSEN, T. (1986) 'Curriculum considerations in the primary school', in GUNDARA, J. et al. (Ed.) *Racism Diversity and Education*, London, Hodder and Stoughton. pp. 121–32.

WHITE, J. (1970) 'Indoctrination: a reply to I.M.M. Gregory and R.G. Woods', *Proceedings of the Philosophy of Education Society of Great Britain*, 4, pp. 107–20.

WHITE, P. (1983) *Beyond Domination: An Essay in the Political Philosophy of Education*, London, Routledge and Kegan Paul.

WILLIAMS, M. (1986) 'The Thatcher Generation', *New Society*, 21 February pp. 312–15.

WRINGE, C. (1984) *Democracy, Schooling and Political Education*, London, Allen and Unwin.

YATES, L. (1987) *Girls and Democratic Schooling*, Unpublished report, Sydney, New South Wales Education Department and Curriculum Development Centre.

YEOMANS, A. (1983) 'Collaborative Group Work in Primary and Secondary Schools', *Durham and Newcastle Research Review*, 10, pp. 99–105.

YOUNG, R.E. (1984) 'Teaching equals indoctrination: the dominant epistemic practices of our schools', *British Journal of Educational Studies*, 22, 3, pp. 220–38.

Contributors

Hilary Burgess	Senior Lecturer in Primary Education, Westhill College, Birmingham.
Bruce Carrington	Lecturer in Education, University of Newcastle Upon Tyne.
Sarah Gammage	Education Officer at *Relate* (formerly the National Marriage Guidance Council).
David Hicks	Director of the Centre for Peace Studies, St. Martin's College, Lancaster.
Tony Jeffs	Senior Lecturer in Social Policy, Newcastle Upon Tyne Polytechnic.
Una McNicholl	Member of the Community Education Team, Gateshead Borough Council.
Andrew Pollard	Reader in Primary Education, Bristol Polytechnic.
Alistair Ross	Director of the Primary Schools and Industry Centre, Polytechnic of North London.
Geoffrey Short	Senior Lecturer in Education, Hatfield Polytechnic.
Basil Singh	Senior Lecturer in Education, Sunderland Polytechnic.
Christine Skelton	Lecturer in Primary Education, University of Newcastle Upon Tyne.
Barry Troyna	Lecturer in the Social Aspects of Education, University of Warwick.
Steve Whitley	Principal Lecturer in Primary Education, Sunderland Polytechnic.

Index

Children and Controversial Issues

children's understanding of (*contd*)
  gender 23–4
  nationality 15–6
  politics 18–20, 39, 72–3
  'race' 20–3, 206–7, 213–5
  sexuality 193–4
  social justice 146
  'world of work' 147–8, 151–2
  war and peace 175
Claire, H. 162, 165, 210
Clare, A. 191
Clayton A. 46
Clarricoates, K. 156, 160
Clifford, P. 218
Clover, J. 145
Chivian, E. 175
Coard, B. 125
Cockroft Report 79, 82
Coffield, F. 219
Cohen, B. 101–2
Cohen, L. 6, 38, 49
Cohen, S. 6, 57
collaborative learning 162, 185, 210–1
Connell, R.W. 6, 39
Conservative Family Campaign 189, 202
controversial issues
  nature of 2, 56–7, 98, 142–3, 150–1
  teaching approaches 3, 36–7, 66–9, 95–101, 143–6, 149–53, 181–6, 211–16
Council of Europe 61
Cox, C. 176
Crick, B. 36–7, 93, 100
CRO 107
Croll, P. 71, 78, 84–5, 88
Cullingford, C. 218
Curriculum 5–16 31, 77, 80–1
Czaplinski, S. 122

Damon, W. 14, 24
Darby, A. 108
Davey, A. 206
Davies, R. 175
Dawson, R.E. 39
Dearden, R. 33, 98, 148
Dearlove, J. 41
De Bono, E. 181
Delamont, S. 160

Denscombe, M. 124
Department of Education and Science 2, 31, 41, 58, 63–4, 80, 139, 143, 148–50, 160, 163, 168, 175, 206, 212, 219
Desforges, C. 12
developmentalism 12–13, 17–20, 39–74
Dewey, J. 50, 64
Dixon, B. 8, 19, 120
Donaldson, M. 17, 74, 88
Dray, J. 29
Dunlop, F. 32
Dunn, D. 205
Dunn, R. 5

Education Act, 1986 2, 30, 36–7, 54–5, 150, 199, 203
Education Act, 1988 1, 60
education for peace
  aims and objectives 173–4
Educators for Social Responsibility 183–4
Elliot, J. 65
Engel, R.E. 122
Entwhistle, H. 32
equal opportunities 157–8
Equal Opportunities Commission 163
Evetts, J. 159
Falcon, L.N. 125
Fiddy, R. 141
Fien, J. 184
Fisher, S. 184
FitzGibbon, C.T. 210
Flatham, R.E. 102
Fletcher, C. 49
Ford, K. 120, 122
Francis, M. 206, 216–7
Franklin, B. 39
French, J. 156, 163, 165
French, P. 156, 163, 165
Furth, H.G. 15

Galton, M. 71, 78, 84–5, 88, 208
Galtung, J. 183
Gardner, H. 25
Gaspar, I. 36
Gelman, R. 18
gender differentiation 47, 156–7